Introduction to Nonviolence

Also by Ramin Jahanbegloo

THE GANDHIAN MOMENT
DEMOCRACY IN IRAN

Introduction to Nonviolence

Ramin Jahanbegloo

First published 2014 by
PALGRAVE MACMILLAN

Palgrave Macmillan in the UK is an imprint of Macmillan Publishers Limited,
registered in England, company number 785998, of Houndmills, Basingstoke,
Hampshire RG21 6XS.

Palgrave Macmillan in the US is a division of St Martin's Press LLC,
175 Fifth Avenue, New York, NY 10010.

Palgrave Macmillan is the global academic imprint of the above companies
and has companies and representatives throughout the world.

Palgrave® and Macmillan® are registered trademarks in the United States,
the United Kingdom, Europe and other countries

ISBN 978-0-230-36129-4   hardback
ISBN 978-0-230-36130-0   paperback

This book is printed on paper suitable for recycling and made from fully
managed and sustained forest sources. Logging, pulping and manufacturing
processes are expected to conform to the environmental regulations of the
country of origin.

A catalogue record for this book is available from the British Library.

A catalog record for this book is available from the Library of Congress.

Printed in China

Contents

List of Profiles

Acknowledgments

I would like to express my gratitude to the many people who helped me through this book – to all those who provided support, offered comments, assisted in the editing, proofreading and design. Thanks to my publisher, Stephen Wenham at Palgrave Macmillan, who encouraged me to write this introduction to nonviolence. I would like to thank my research assistants, Ramin Gharavi and Nikola Apostolov Dimitrijevic, for helping me with putting together two chapters of this book. I would like to thank Richie Nojang Khatami for helping me in the process of editing. This work would not have been possible without the moral support of the Centre for Ethics and Department of Political Science, University of Toronto. Last and not least, thanks to Khojasteh Kia, my mother, without whom this book would never have seen the light of day.

RAMIN JAHANBEGLOO

To my nonviolent friend, Raj Rewal

Introduction

This introductory text presents an overview of the central philosophical approaches to nonviolence, and of nonviolent practice through history. It examines the understanding of nonviolence developed in key religious traditions and in contemporary philosophies. Each religious approach to nonviolence will be discussed in great depth through examples drawn from Hinduism, Jainism, Buddhism, Christianity and Islam. Key theorists of nonviolence, from Socrates and Tolstoy through to the contemporary scholar of pragmatic nonviolence, Gene Sharp, will also be examined – along with their critics. Our understanding of these different traditions and philosophies will then illuminate the practice of key political figures of peace-making, from Martin Luther King and Desmond Tutu to the Dalai Lama and Aung San Suu Kyi, and the techniques of recent nonviolent movements, such as the Green Movement in Iran and elements of the Arab Spring. Though discussed individually, the reader will find common elements in all of them, which gives the book a systematic approach to the general theme of nonviolence.

What is nonviolence?

It is first worth unpacking the nature of nonviolence – and violence. This book has for its point of departure the essential idea that nonviolence is a positive civilizational value in our world – that is to say, there are forms of nonviolence that are necessary for the continuity of our life on earth. Nonviolence is, therefore, a part of human history which should concern us all. The history of nonviolence surpasses the framework of the western world and is in line with the philosophical, political and religious structures of all human cultures. Nonviolence is not a new idea. It is as old as the history of human societies. Humanity has been hurt and humiliated by violence for centuries. Nevertheless, there have been privileged moments of history where human beings became aware of the effects of the violence that they inflicted on each

1

other, and on other living beings, and tried to find ethical and political means to oppose it. The answer to the question of nonviolence, therefore, goes hand in hand with the attempt to answer another question: what is violence and what causes it in human beings? A simple definition of violence is an action which involves harm or injury to another human being or living creature. Some would say that humans are violent like animals and as such violence is part of the animal nature of human beings. Others, like Konrad Lorenz, would say that violence breaks the limits of aggression, which is limited in animals. In other words, while aggressive instincts exist in animals, yet the tendency towards senseless violence reaches its peak in human beings. Violence is, thus, part of humanity's social construction and its historical destiny. Human beings seldom kill for food – or if threatened – but they do kill each other or any other species out of hatred, prejudice, politics, or, even, just for amusement. We need, therefore, to ask if violence is a perversion of the animal aggressiveness or an exercise of an uncontrolled force and power.

In her 1970 book *On Violence*, Hannah Arendt (see Profile I.1) establishes a crucial distinction between power, force and violence. According to Arendt (1970, p. 56): 'Power and violence are opposites; where the one rules absolutely, the other is absent. Violence appears where power is in jeopardy, but left to its own course it ends in power's disappearance.' For Arendt, the term 'violence' should never be used interchangeably with 'power' in the study of politics. Power springs up from human relations and acting in concert of a community. But, 'Violence,' she writes, 'can always destroy power. Out of the barrel of a gun grows the most effective command, resulting in the most instant and perfect obedience. What never can grow out of it is power' (p. 53). As such, power can never be created out of violence because power is historically legitimate, but violence, though justifiable, can never be legitimate. Power is legitimate because it helps people to get together, but violence 'does not depend on numbers or opinions, but on implements' (*ibid.*). Through her explanation of power and violence, Arendt concludes that:

> Neither violence nor power is a natural phenomenon, that is, a manifestation of the life process; they belong to the political realm of human affairs whose essentially human quality is guaranteed by man's faculty of action, the ability to begin something new. (p. 82)

Profile I.1 **Hannah Arendt**

Hannah Arendt (14 October 1906 to 4 December 1975) was a German-American political theorist. She was born in Hanover into a secular Jewish family. She grew up in Königsberg and Berlin. Inspired by theology and philosophy, Arendt decided to study theology at the University of Marburg, with Rudolf Bultmann. It was during her time at Marburg that Arendt was introduced to Heidegger's *Existenzphilosophie* and began her long relationship with Heidegger. Arendt also studied with Husserl and later became a student of the existentialist philosopher, Karl Jaspers, at the University of Heidelberg. It is under Jaspers that she wrote her dissertation in 1929 on 'St Augustine's Concept of Love'. In 1958 her book *Rahel Varnhagen: The Life of a Jewish Woman*, was published, and was a biography of a Jewish salon hostess in Berlin in the early 1800s who converted to Christianity. After the rise of Hitler in 1933, Arendt was arrested by the Gestapo for conducting research on anti-Semitic propaganda, but managed to escape and fled to Paris. In 1940, she married the German Marxist philosopher Heinrich Blücher and they both found safe passage to America. For the rest of her life, Arendt lived in New York, where she taught at the New School for Social Research. She published her masterpiece, *The Origins of Totalitarianism*, in 1951, which traced the ideological roots of Stalinism and Nazism. Her next three books on political theory were *The Human Condition* (1958); *Between Past and Future* (1961); and *On Revolution* (1968). In 1960, Arendt covered Eichmann's trial in Israel as a correspondent for *The New Yorker* and published it in 1963 under the title: *Eichmann in Jerusalem: A Report on the Banality of Evil*. Arendt's research on thoughtlessness and the sense of a shared world led to a series of lectures on judgment and thinking which were published later as a book: *The Life of the Mind* (1978). In 1975 Hannah Arendt was awarded the Sonning Prize for Contributions to European Civilization by the Danish government. She died the same year from a heart attack in her New York apartment. Her personal library was deposited at Bard College in 1976. In 2012 a German film entitled *Hannah Arendt* was released, directed by Margarethe von Trotta, with Barbara Sukowa in the role of Arendt.

The more violence is tamed in the political arena, the more people could be involved in the process of politics. This active presence of the people in the political community must be nonviolent, for violence reduces the legitimacy of a political community. Arendt's argument for nonviolence is based primarily in the pragmatic concern that it provides democratizing effects that can link people together and help them to act in concert. It is fair to say that Arendt's worry that the capacity for action is threatened by violence finds its echo in the statement that 'The practice of violence, like all action, changes the world, but the most probable change is to a more violent world' (p. 80). If, as Arendt says, violence is not natural or instinctual but artificial and instrumental, then violence belongs to the realm of human contingency and rational calculation. Thus, nonviolence also belongs to the political realm of human affairs and cannot be practised as a biological necessity. In addition, Arendt reminds us that resistance to violence must be counted as a political problem and not only as a moral issue. Arendt shows us that, if violence should be understood as a social and political act, it also has the capacity of demolishing our common social and political world.

Therefore, it is by saying 'no' to violence that mankind shapes its common political world. As such, the history of nonviolence presents itself to us as a refusal of historic violence. But denying history as violence not only refutes it, but also transcends it. By a radical contrast, nonviolence opposes violence in history while proposing its own history: one that assures respect for human dignity. To understand nonviolence, it is necessary, therefore, to go back to its history. To redraw the history of nonviolence, we need to rediscover and rearrange the narratives of exceptional figures who carried the destiny of humanity on their shoulders. Their actions spanned personal initiatives, movements of resistance and disobedience. But, one way or another, actions taken by these historical figures aimed to defend human dignity and to underline a moral vision of the world. It would be correct, therefore, to think of nonviolence not only as a purely ethical attitude, but also as a means of resistance to injustice. By these methods, the strategy of nonviolence expresses itself as a true force of resistance to tyranny and oppression. But to be effective, this resistance should be in line with the political and collective structures of civil society. This type of nonviolence, known as 'strategic or pragmatic nonviolence', took shape in history as a spontaneous response of an oppressed population to a social and political situation judged as intolerable. The twentieth century presents varied cases of nonviolent actions of this kind where nonviolent social actors attempted to withstand institutional violence by means of an insurrectional nonviolence. The struggle conducted by Nelson Mandela against the politics of apartheid and the fight of Václav Havel facing the communist system can be considered as emblematic of a strategic nonviolence. By recourse to the means of persuasion and noncooperation, this nonviolent form thus looks to transform the public space of the civil corporation. It is founded, and in some ways guarantees, a space of deliberation and of discussion where the members of the corporation can debate their problems. If one admits with Hannah Arendt (1958, p. 26) that 'to be political, to live in *polis*, meant that everything was decided through words and persuasion and not through force and violence', then strategic nonviolence appears to be an attempt to create, or to manage, democracy. Put in these terms, the drive to live together in a social-historically created political context substitutes the relations of domination and submission between humans for relations of dialogue and mutual exchange. As such, strategic nonviolence is a pragmatic form of nonviolent action. Because of its pragmatic nature and its manner of politicizing the public space it proposes to establish a relation of reciprocity between individuals; a relation that is based on respect of the dignity of the opponent. But to respect the opponent does not mean to convert her or him. Here we find the point of divergence between strategic nonviolence and a second type of nonviolence, 'principled nonviolence'. Principled nonviolence is a nonviolence of conscience, not of strategy. Built on an ethical or religious conviction, it is presented in the form of a categorical imperative which is addressed to the individual by a religious or philosophical doctrine: 'You shall not kill' or 'You shall love your neighbour.' It is not formulated as a strategy of resistance to a specific political context, but as a rule of life. Principled nonviolence, however, can take a strategic standpoint without abandoning its ethical and religious substance. Here, nonviolent engagement and religious belief go hand in hand. It is, thus, not surprising that two great names of principled nonviolence in the twentieth century were Mahatma Gandhi and Martin Luther King. The history of the twentieth century is full of social and political experiences that demonstrate that nonviolence resistance is an integral part of conflict transformation. More specifically, the past 50 years have witnessed an unprecedented flowering of nonviolent experiences around the globe. In many areas of the world, such as Latin America and Asia, where armed struggle was once seen as the only path to freedom, nonviolent campaigns are now considered as institutionalized methods of struggle for democratic invention and democratic governance. One of the important tasks that nonviolent movements have set for themselves is the successful provision of 'good governance'. For them, the real test of democracy is not only in the peaceful process of transition but also in nonviolent consolidation of democratic institutions. For the advocates of nonviolence around the world, democracy is not just an 'institutional arrangement for organizing the political society', but also a new attitude and approach towards the problem of power. As such, the true expression of nonviolence is not the conquest of power, but the development of the power of truth.

Nonviolent philosophy, however, is not a twentieth-century invention. The challenges and difficulties of democratic transformation and civil resistance have followed the examples of Buddha, Jesus, Tolstoy and others. For all these thinkers of nonviolence, the twin practices of self-discipline and disinterested service were necessary to control an unjust and inappropriate power. Gandhi (1931, p. 199) considered 'Democracy disciplined and enlightened [as] the finest thing in the world.' What he meant was that democratic governance is not a power over the society, but a power within it. In other words, if democracy equals self-rule and self-control of society, empowerment of civil society and collective ability to rule democratically are the essential constituents of democratic governance. Democracy and nonviolence, therefore, are inseparable. Where democracy is practised, people are honoured for what they are. This requires a transformation of human relations until none are violated because all participate in democratic power. To have power in a democracy means to take part in the decision-making that affects each individual's fate. It means self-institution and self-rule.

For many thinkers and practitioners of nonviolence the significance of nonviolence lies principally in a commitment that involves self-rule and self-discipline. Such a commitment must include a profound concern for truth and welfare of all in the society. Centuries before Mahatma Gandhi spoke about *swaraj* as self-rule and *satyagraha* as struggle for truth, Jainism, Buddhism and Hinduism had adopted the doctrine of non-harm in South Asia. The term 'nonviolence' is itself a modern translation of the Sanskrit word *ahimsa*, which Gandhi drew from the ancient texts of Hinduism. It comes from the root *hims*, a desiderative for the verb *han*, to harm or injure. Prefixed with a privative *a*, it is translated literally as the 'absence of the desire to injure'.

In the *Upanishads*, in the *Yoga Sutra* and in the *Baghavad Gita*, ahimsa is considered as 'the highest duty' adhered to anyone seeking perfection. A careful reading of the *Baghavad Gita*, which is the middle section of a great epic, Mahabharata, reveals that ahimsa is acknowledged as created by Krishna and attributed as a characteristic of those who are born 'to the divine lot'. The teachings of Krishna in the *Baghavad Gita* explicitly renounce harm and injury. In this way they became the inspiration for a life committed to nonviolence and self-rule. The centrality of ahimsa is also paramount in the tradition of Jaina that was founded around 800 BC by Parsva in South Asia and reformed 200 years later by Mahavira. Although Jainism remained a minority movement, its philosophical influence upon the wider life in the Indian subcontinent has been disproportionate. When one looks at Gandhi's life, one has to recognize that he was brought up in a religious atmosphere deeply influenced by Jainism. In Jainsim, ahimsa is practised as a vow in order to overcome the negative influence of karma. This means that acts of violence are avoided because they will result in an obstruction to a state of liberation at some future time. This has led the Jain community to consider nonviolence as a foundation for all its social activities. Gandhi's attitude towards Jainism can perhaps be treated in relation with the fact that for him, as for the Jains, truth includes nonviolence and nonviolence is the necessary and indispensable means for the discovery of truth. The other movement of thought and religious and social practice that deeply influenced Gandhi, and is considered today to be a specific Asian solution to the problems of democratic governance, is Buddhism. Breaking away from the ritualism of the Vedic religion, Gautama Buddha gave the world a great example of personal commitment to a nonviolent way of organizing social life. Buddhist teachings place a considerable emphasis upon the precept of 'non-injury' and have thus made their own contribution to the philosophy of nonviolence. Among the ideals that Buddhist monks are expected to exemplify, 'nonviolence' appears as a.principal value. Buddhist philosophy begins in the self and moves from there to affect the other. For Buddhism, the other will be served if the self is transformed. To experience 'nonviolence' in Buddhism is to be aware of this interconnectedness of life. Therefore, in Buddhism the solution to violence is individual rather than social. When nonviolence is defended in Buddhist terms, it is strongly based on the idea of 'suffering of the self'. Violence, therefore, is forbidden not only because it harms the other, but because it primarily harms the self.

Gandhi showed the world that the most revolutionary idea in human history is the truth of nonviolence. As Gandhi asserted, the idea is 'as old as the hills', going back to Mahavira, Buddha and Christ, developed by Leo Tolstoy and nonviolent practitioners of many lands. But it was Gandhi's experiment with truth in the first half of the twentieth century that proved that nonviolence could be used on a large scale to help to achieve democratic governance. For Gandhi, nonviolence entailed more than a renunciation of bombs and bullets; it was, above all, concerned with the idea of democracy as 'swaraj' or self-rule. Long before he emerged as leader of the nonviolent movement in India and was hailed as the Mahatma, Gandhi had embraced the idea of 'swaraj' in the later phase of his South African period. For Gandhi, the goal of 'swaraj' could not be obtained by simply replacing British domination with Indian domination; the problem was much deeper and more complex, involving a change in the very meaning and character of governance. Evidence for this can be found in many of Gandhi's (1960b, p. 212) writings – including what he wrote in his journal *Harijan* in February 1946: 'A nonviolent evolution is not a program of seizure of power. It is a program of transformation of relationships ending in a peaceful transfer of power.' In other words, for Gandhi, the liberation of India from alien rule was merely the first step towards a radical reconstruction of the social and political order in India and ultimately in all countries. As far as India was concerned, this involved a radically decentralized and non-pyramidical society in which each individual would be at the centre of an 'oceanic circle'.

As we can see, democratic decentralization was crucial to Gandhi's concept of nonviolent society. He portrayed his preferred political system as a *panchayat raj* or a republic of villages. Gandhi's political philosophy is therefore one that presupposes democratic governance. He has a theory, which combines a radically individualistic view of man with a communitarian view of society. According to Gandhi, decentralized decision-making ensures the well-being of all those who are affected by such decisions. The rationale of Gandhi's premise is derived from the democratic imperative that all those whose interests are affected by decisions ought to take part in the governance process. In other words, the spontaneous redistribution of power in the country naturally results in a vigorous drive towards autonomy in the villages and small political units. That is why, in his view, freedom of the individual had to be the hallmark of an independent country.

Gandhi maintained a proper balance between 'nonviolent resistance' and 'constructive work'. Gandhi's 'constructive programme' requires a collective capacity for building and maintaining a strong civil society. Strengthening civil society is a way to attain what Gandhi called *poorna swaraj* or complete independence by truthful and nonviolent means. This is to say that the promotion and consolidation of democratic governance and economic freedom are, for Gandhi, two sides of the same coin.

What Gandhi and other theorists and practitioners of nonviolence teach us is that sustaining and consolidating democratic governance and building a pluralist civil society is always a work-in-progress requiring constant attention and responsibility. As another famous Asian practitioner of nonviolence, His Holiness the Dalai Lama (1999, pp. 3–7), once said: 'While it is true that no system of government is perfect, democracy is the closest to our essential human nature and allows us the greatest opportunity to cultivate a sense of universal responsibility.' The process of democratic transition has not yet come to an end in the global century. We also have a long way to go in facing the challenges of consolidating and sustaining democracy around the world. Whether we like it or not, now we all effectively live in a global networked world, where tensions can be inflamed instantly through the transfer of information from one cultural context to another. This new situation raises the stakes in terms of how to find a balance between democracy and cultural diversity. The central question in this debate is as simple as it is difficult. What is more important for the advancement of democracy in the world – to ensure the freedom of expression of all citizens within the limits marked by law or to protect the collective interests of cultural and religious traditions? This challenge can provide an opportunity for a broad spectrum of activists and scholars to join together in a penetrating exploration of nonviolent alternatives to global violence in the present era. For Gandhi (1938a), 'belief in nonviolence is based on the assumption that human nature in its essence is one and therefore unfailingly responds to the advances of love'. As such, a Christian, a Muslim or a Jew following Gandhi's teaching would not feel estranged. Unfortunately, too much of the discussion of the current 'wave' of democratization in illiberal countries focuses almost solely on the presumed democratizing potential of political mechanisms with no reference to nonviolence. To achieve consolidated democratic governance, the necessary degree of autonomy of civil society must be embedded in the rule of law. A nonviolent civil society, with the capacity to generate and articulate ideas and values and to create associations and solidarities among the citizens, can help start a democratic transition and help consolidate and deepen democracy. Democratic governance, however, requires that habituation to the norms and procedures of democratic conflict-regulation be developed. A high degree of nonviolent practice is a key part of such a process. The force of the claim that democracy is a universal value for all kinds of societies and cultures lies ultimately in its constructive function in the consolidation of value and practice of nonviolence. This is where the debate of democratic governance belongs. It cannot be disposed of by assumed religious or political taboos imposed upon cultures and societies by their various pasts, which are generators of violence and hatred. More recently, the wave of demonstrations and protests across the Middle East and the Maghreb, known collectively as the Arab Spring, showed the world that movements in Tunisia and Egypt were, for the most part, exemplary campaigns of nonviolent protest and civil disobedience with the successful overthrow of the dictatorships. It may be difficult at this point to draw a conclusion that this dynamic of nonviolent resistance has created an essential paradigm change in the political culture of the Middle East and the Maghreb. But it goes without saying that nonviolent grass-roots movements in Iran, Tunisia, Egypt and Syria have opened up debates regarding prospects for nonviolent democratization in the twenty-first century.

Further reading

Galtung, J. (1965) 'On the Meaning of Nonviolence', *Journal of Peace Research*. A very useful article on nonviolence by a well-known figure in peace studies.

Kumar, M. (ed.) (1984) *Nonviolence: Contemporary Issues and Challenges*. An accessible and lively introduction to contemporary issues of nonviolence.

Steger M. B. and Lind N. S. (eds) (1999) *Violence and Its Alternatives: An Interdisciplinary Reader*. A rich collection which provides the reader with a deep insight into the process of taming violence.

Zinn, H. (ed.) (2002) *The Power of Nonviolence: Writings by Advocates of Peace*. An admirable collection of essays which examines several modes and dimensions of nonviolence.

Chapter 1

Nonviolence in Hinduism, Jainism and Buddhism

Nonviolence as a religious virtue is found in three of India's main religions: Hinduism, Jainism and Buddhism. From the very beginning, nonviolence was a dominant aspect of religious thought in Buddhism and Jainism, but it wasn't until Mahatma Gandhi's anticolonial struggles that the virtue of nonviolence in Hinduism was brought to the fore. All three religions find the root of their nonviolence in the ethic of ahimsa (non-injury or harmlessness).

In Hindu tradition and post-Vedic literature, the female term 'ahimsa' is portrayed as the wife of *dharma* (law). As such, it may be concluded that ahimsa should be understood as a natural law applicable to everyone. Dharma – in its Hindu context a spiritual goal – is not only essential for the ordering of human life, but also for the attainment of individual liberation (*moksa*) as spiritual freedom. As such, in the Hindu context, dharma is not something imposed from the outside, but must be fulfilled as an inner law of human beings in order for it to find expression on earth (Radhakrishnan 1939).

The best example of the dual importance of ahimsa and dharma is found in the *Bhagavad Gita*. The *Gita* shows that, in order to obtain spiritual freedom, a sense of duty and responsibility is required in the form of ahimsa. The classic comes from the *Mahabharata*, one of two significant epics from India. It is in the *Gita* that Lord Krishna refers to nonviolence as one of his qualities and explicitly advocates non-injury and nonviolence. In all, the *Gita* refers to ahimsa in four different places. Reading the *Gita*, one concludes that nonviolence is the greatest duty and an essential ethical virtue. There is no doubt that Gandhi was inspired by the *Gita* in his conception of nonviolence as a form of selflessness. Furthermore, he used the text as a cornerstone and guide of his moral conduct during India's struggle for independence. Although Gandhi based his spirituality on the

11

Gita, he was also of the belief that it was a non-dogmatic text with a universal message.

It is believed that Jainism originated in the sixth century BC, under Prince Mahavira of Bihar, though it is likely that its history goes back even further. Its roots lie in a pre-Aryan upper class of northeastern India that rejected the scriptures and traditions of traditional Hinduism.

Nonviolence serves as the foundation of Jain philosophy. The ethical value that Jains prescribe to ahimsa is that it is a tolerant means of coexistence with the universe, understanding that all that is living is treated with respect. It views the principle of living with others and killing others as contradictory. Therefore, practising ahimsa is to refrain from causing harm or injury, or using violence.

For Jainism, both violence and nonviolence are not only a question of the physical realm, but also a reality of our mind. As such, Jainism places the highest importance on the self, and it is through the self that we know. Consequently, each soul has its own view of the world, which differs from the views of others, and it is through this diversity of knowledge that one witnesses the interconnectedness of life. Jains believe that violence is the result of wrong knowledge and wrong conduct, which distort the value of self and the true vision of reality. Nonviolence, however, is seen as a combination of spirituality and equality.

Unlike Jainism, Buddhism was able to amass a significant following outside India, in the neighbouring regions of South and East Asia. It is based around the teachings, beliefs and practices of Gautama Siddhartha (born in 563 BC), who later became the Buddha. Gautama spent the majority of his life travelling in the region, preaching the message of nonviolence. For Buddhism, life is suffering (*duhkha*). The essence of living a good life is in having a pure character (*sila*), free from vice, deception and self-aggrandizement. As such, in order to destroy the causes of suffering one must live a righteous life. Of all the principles of righteousness, ahimsa is the foremost: all other virtues flow from ahimsa.

Like Jainism, Buddhism views the world as connected and interdependent. All forms of life share the Buddha nature and avoiding injury and preventing violence is part of the path of awareness that leads to awakening (*bodhi*). The path leading towards attaining awakening goes through the practice of nonviolence in thoughts, words, deeds and actions. Any intent to harm is perceived as having a negative effect on one's spiritual evolution. For Buddhism, nonviolence is not only essential in banishing evil ideas from the mind, but it is also seen as maintaining a balance between the individual and society.

Buddhism's development of ahimsa into a feeling of compassion for the whole universe is what makes it a powerful philosophy, especially regarding conflict resolution and nonviolence. Under the guidance of His Holiness the Dalai Lama, Tibet has applied these very principles of nonviolence in its struggle for independence.

Nonviolence in Hinduism

Each of the three main religions which originated in India – Jainism, Buddhism and Hinduism – developed a spiritual tradition of considerable importance in which nonviolence is a cardinal virtue. Although the centrality of nonviolence is paramount in the two philosophical streams of religious thought in ancient India, Jainism and Buddhism, the Hindu concept of nonviolence, which was brought to light by Mahatma Gandhi, finds its roots in the ethic on ahimsa that is developed in the *Baghavad Gita*, one of celebrated sacred texts of Hinduism. According to K. M. Sen (1961, p. 51), 'The Hindu belief in nonviolence (*ahimsa*) which contributed to Buddhism and Jainism, is definitely of non-Vedic origin.'

To students of the Hindu tradition the significance of the concept of ahimsa need not be argued. 'In post-Vedic literature the female term *himsa* is personified as the wife of Adharma (Unrighteousness) and *ahimsa* as the wife of Dharma, and so we might be induced to take *ahimsa* as the law (*dharma*) prescribed for everybody' (Bodewitz 1999, p. 19). Therefore, when looking at the Hindu concept of ahimsa, we should relate it to the most basic and complex concept in Hindu life and thought that is the concept of dharma. For those who consider the value dimensions of the Hindu understanding of human existence, dharma as a rule of conduct, an aim in life and duty frequently becomes the focus of discussion. Dharma is an essential rule for the ordering of human activity directed towards something conducive to good. According to the Vedas and the Sastras, whatever is conducive to the highest good and to worldly prosperity is dharma. 'Dharma is sometimes spoken of as the capstone of temporal values, providing a context of regulation for interest and desire' (Creel 1975, p. 164). Obviously, the concept of dharma as a rule of conduct is teleological.

Dharma, therefore, is a necessary stage to the attainment of individual liberation (moksa). As an ethical system, the Hindu outlook is oriented towards a spiritual goal. In the words of the Indian philosopher, Radhakrishnan (1939, p. 353) 'Ethical life is the means to spiritual freedom, as well as its expression on earth.' The ultimate justification of dharma as the ordering of life is regarded as something not imposed from the outside, but as the inner law of human beings. This finds its finest exemplification in the *Gita* where, 'acting according to one's own nature, and thereby contributing to the order and maintenance of society and the entire universe, is regarded as a form of worship of God' (Koller 1972, p. 143) Thus it would appear that in the *Gita* the pursuit of liberation does not give rise to the abandonment of one's dharma. On the contrary, the *Gita* shows that spiritual liberation requires a sense of duty and responsibility. Thus, in a clear way the *Gita* supports the doctrine of ahimsa and classifies it as knowledge, in contrast to ignorance. The *Gita* comes to us as part of the *Mahabharata*, one of the two significant Indian epics. The *Gita* takes place in the middle of the battlefield, between the two armies – those of the Pandavas, who are on the side of righteousness, and the Kauravas, who are unrighteous people – just as the war is about to begin. In his doubt and confusion, Arjuna, the greatest warrior of the Pandavas, asks for Lord Krishna's help. Recognizing his own limitations, Arjuna follows Krishna's advice on how to deal with difficult situations in life. Arjuna is transformed by the teaching that Krishna gives him and is encouraged to fight the Kauravas. But Krishna also teaches Arjuna the lessons of right action and peace. Krishna tells Arjuna that no man can know happiness without peace. As Krishna says in the *Bhagavad Gita*, 'For one who is not peaceful, from where is happiness to come?' and 'Abandoning all selfish desires, a person moves through life free from worldly longings, without the sense of "mine", without the notion of "I am acting" – that one attains peace' (Schweig 2007). Therefore, Arjuna is not counselled to bring harm to others. On the contrary, the *Gita* exhorts the path to liberation, not the intention to win and to conquer. The teachings of Krishna in the *Gita* explicitly advocate non-injury and nonviolence. Ahimsa is heralded in the *Bhagavad Gita* as one of the virtues of a person with a divine nature. The *Gita* refers to ahimsa in four places. In Chapter X, 5, Krishna refers to nonviolence as one of his qualities. 'Nonviolence, sameness, contentment, austerity, charity, fame, and infamy – in their various forms, these conditions of beings arise from me alone.' The second time, we find the concept of ahimsa in Chapter XIII, 6–12, where it is classified as a form of knowledge in contrast with ignorance. 'Absence of pride, absence of deceit, nonviolence, patience, honesty; ... This is declared to be knowledge; the absence of knowledge is whatever is contrary to this.' Moreover, in Chapter XVI, 2, nonviolence is described as one of the 26 qualities endowed with divine virtues. 'Nonviolence, truthfulness, freedom from anger, relinquishment, peacefulness, absence of slander ... These become the attributes for those of divine birth, O Bharata.' Lastly, in Chapter XVII, 14, the *Gita* advocates nonviolence as one of the austerities of the body. 'Chastity, and nonviolence – that is called austerity of the body.' As such, the *Bhagavad Gita* advocates that nonviolence is the greatest duty and a superior ethical virtue. This was well understood by Gandhi (1925, pp. 1078--9), who expressed his love for this book with the words:

> I find a solace in the Bhagavad-Gita that I miss even in the Sermon on the Mount. When disappointment stares me in the face and all alone I see not one ray of light, I go back to the Bhagavad-Gita. I find a verse here and a verse there and I immediately begin to smile in the midst of overwhelming tragedies – and my life has been full of external tragedies – and if they have left no visible, no indelible scar on me, I owe it all to the teaching of Bhagavad-Gita.

In other words, the *Gita* can be considered as a prime source of inspiration for Mahatma Gandhi's nonviolence as a form of selflessness. Gandhi (1959, p. 32) underlines this fact in his various writings on the *Gita*. 'Is the central teaching of the *Gita* selfless action or nonviolence?' asks Gandhi:

> I have no doubt that it is *anasakti* – selfless action. Indeed, I have called my little translation of the *Gita Anasaktiyoga*. And *anasakti* transcends *ahimsa*. He who would be *anasakta* (selfless) has necessarily to practice nonviolence in order to attain the state of selflessness. *Ahimsa* is, therefore, a necessary preliminary, it is included in *anasakti*, it does not go beyond it.

We can quote many other extracts from Gandhi's interpretation of the *Gita*, but this may suffice to give the reader the broad nature of the idea of ahimsa as the central message of this book. Gandhi's interpretation proves that the *Gita* is more appropriately a treatise on the duty of man in society. It is not without reason that from a multitude of religious texts, Gandhi chose the *Gita* as his guide of moral conduct; ahimsa was, for Gandhi, the infallible touchstone of moral conduct. Gandhi personalized and modernized the concept of ahimsa in the *Gita*. He put the ethical code of the *Gita* into effect in his political struggle for independence and democracy. He constantly referred to the *Gita* as his 'spiritual dictionary', but he also perceived the *Gita* as being a non-dogmatic text with a universal message. 'Since for Gandhi the essence of religion lay in ethical action, it is quite logical that for him the *Gita* occupied the highest place among the *shastras*' (Jordens 1998, p. 94). Moreover, as a necessary corollary to this view, he emphasized the basic idea of the absence of a uniform and unalterable faith in the *Gita* in particular and in Hinduism in general. Similarly, this spirit lies behind Radhakrishnan's (1927, p. 129) understanding of the *Gita* when he affirms that, 'Hinduism is a movement, not a position; a process, not a result; a growing tradition, not a fixed revelation.' Overall, Gandhi and Radakrishnan both argue that the central ethical idea of the *Gita* is to enforce dharma and a sense of duty. This was especially true because to them, as to many others, the *Gita* was the exemplification of the active ethical stance of Hinduism. This close proximity of the ethical and the spiritual in Hindu thought – with its strong emphasis on values such as kindness, truthfulness and nonviolence – brought with it the emergence of rival systems of thought and new approaches to the concept of ahimsa.

Nonviolence in Jainism

Jainism is traditionally believed to have been formulated in the sixth century BC by Mahavira, a prince born in the state of Bihar who gave up his royal household to become a monk; most probably, however, it was founded earlier. Heinrich Zimmer, the famous Indianist, considers Jainism as a religion of remote antiquity in India. According to Zimmer:

> Jainism denies the authority of the Vedas and the orthodox traditions of Hinduism. Therefore it is reckoned as a heterodox Indian religion. It does not derive from Brahman-Aryan sources, but reflects the cosmology and anthropology of a much older, pre-

Aryan upper class of north eastern India – being rooted in the
same subsoil of archaic metaphysical speculation as Yoga,
Sankhya, and Buddhism, the other non-Vedic Indian systems.
(1969, p. 217)

Nonviolence lies at the centre of Jain philosophy. The Jain ethical
imperative of ahimsa adopts the perspective that all beings are to be
treated with respect. This tolerance is rooted in the fundamental argument that all doctrines bear within themselves some level of truth.
Jainism applies the principle of non-injury to all living beings.
According to Mahavira, the great advocate of Jainism, in *Acaranga
Sutra*, a canonical text of fourth century BC,

All the worthy men of the past, the present and the future say
thus, speak thus, declare thus, explain thus, that all the breathing,
existing, living and sentient creatures should not be slain, nor
treated with violence, nor abused, nor tormented. This is the
pure, eternal and unchangeable law or the tenet of religion. (Jain
1998, p. 89)

As such, ahimsa is refraining from causing harm, injury and
violence. It is a virtue which is a precondition for all other virtues.
Ahimsa, therefore, plays its moral role not only out of respect for life,
but also as a practical self-restraint from violence.

In Jainism, violence is considered of two types – *Dravyahimsa*
and *Bhavahimsa*. The act of harming or hurting is *Dravyahimsa*,
i.e. external violence and the intention to hurt or to kill is
Bhavahimsa, i.e. internal violence ... On the basis of *drayya* and
bhavahimsa we have four alternatives of violence (1) both intention and act of killing, (2) only there is an intention of killing, not
an act of killing, (3) act of killing minus intention of killing and
(4) neither the act of killing and nor the will, though apparently
it seems an act of hurting. (*Ibid.*, p. 91)

Thus, according to commentators on Jainism, violence is not only a
physical phenomenon, but also a reality of our mind. Ahimsa, therefore, is a spiritual ideal which starts in our mind. It is not merely a
negative concept, because it has a positive meaning as a service to
other living beings. Recognizing that violence is always an immoral

act, Jaina thinkers advocate nonviolence as the best way of resisting violence and restoring peace and harmony in human society. In Jaina texts it is said, 'What is the use of fighting with others? If one wants to fight he should fight with himself because it is your passionate self which is to be conquered. One who conquers his own self conquers four passions and five senses and ultimately conquers all the enemies' (*ibid.*, p. 92). Accordingly, Jainism underlines that selfishness is at the source of all problems in life. Therefore, in order to overcome violence one needs to realize the true nature of self. For Jainism, the self is that by which we know. Capacity for knowledge is, thus, the innate character of every self. The spiritual awakening of the soul is the result of cutting the knot of ignorance and individual freedom. By holding knowledge to be self-conscious, Jainism considers that each soul has knowledge of the world it lives in. But each soul consequently has its own view of the world, which is different from the views of other souls. In other words, from a Jaina perspective, human knowledge of reality is diversified and multi-dimensional and no one can claim the right to discard the truth-value of others. This diversity of knowledge also emphasizes the interconnectedness of life. This is clear from the identification of perpetrator and victim of violence in the following text that explains the nature of nonviolence in Jainism:

> You are the one whom you intend to kill, you are the one you intend to tyrannize, you are the one whom you intend to torment, you are the one you intend to punish and drive away. The enlightened one who lives up to this dictum neither kills nor causes others to kill. (Sutra, 1981, in Chapple 2002, p. 7)

Jaina metaphysics affirms that knowledge of the reality and the self has an immense influence on passions and emotions of human beings. Therefore, wrong knowledge and wrong conduct distort the value of self and the true vision of reality and lead to violence. Viewed from this angle, the Jain ecological respect for the life of others is supported by an epistemic respect for the truth-value of others. In the words of Christopher Chapple, 'The Jaina outlook toward the ideas of others combines tolerance with a certainty in and commitment to Jaina cosmological and ethical views' (Chapple 1993, p. 85). Also, according to the Jain faith, nonviolence and religion are interrelated and cannot be separated. For Jainism, 'the real task of religion consists in removing bitterness between people, between races, between religions, and between nations' (Bhagchandra Jain, 1998, cited in Chapple 2002, p. 171). Thus, in Jain philosophy nonviolence is the result of the combination of spirituality and equality. When applied to social classes:

> nonviolence still may allow for a theory of caste, but one based on one's own deeds and not on one's birth. Mahavira said that one ought to shun all vanities in knowledge, austerities, caste, and livelihood, as they lead to disrespect for others. One who is free from these vanities and transcends caste altogether achieves the supreme state of casteless deliverance. (*Ibid.*, p. 178)

This casteless state could provide us with the basis of the Jainist concern for understanding the traditions of others as a practice of ahimsa. Jaina population are supposed to practice ahimsa in two ways: 'one for the Jaina monks, who adhere to greater vows (*mahavrata*), and another for the Jaina lay community, who follow a less-rigorous discipline (*anuvrata*). These anuvrata include nonviolence (*ahimsa*), truthfulness (*satya*), not stealing (*asteya*), sexual restraint (*brahmacharya*) and non-possession (*aparigraha*)' (Chapple 1993, p. 10). Therefore, he who renounces himsa (injury and harm) takes his ahimsa to victory. Jainism considers truthfulness as one of the cardinal virtues of nonviolence. So, untruth (*anrta*) that is powered by greed (*lobha*), anger (*krodha*), deceit (*maya*) and pride (*antimana*) has to be eliminated. Accordingly, Jains maintain the stand that the path of liberation passes through 14 stages of purification (*gunasthanas*). In this developing process the soul passes from the lowest to the highest stage of spiritual maturity. The lowest stage is that of a wrong and perverted vision of reality (*mithyadrsti*) and the highest is the perfect expression of spiritual energy and it is reached when the soul prepares for an absolute motionlessness followed by final unembodied emancipation. It is worth noting that in Jaina philosophy the success of this path to emancipation depends on the observance of ahimsa. This is how:

> the Jains made ahimsa central to their religion and took it to the extremes of avoiding killing any living thing, even insects. They wear masks to avoid inhaling any living thing that might be flying in the air. As a people they ended up gravitating to business-related occupations and away from agriculture. In the acts of

plowing and harvesting the destruction of life is unavoidable. (Rynne 2008, p. 34)

As such, like all other Indian religions, Jainism emphasizes the inseparability of ethics and spirituality. Perfect ethics is the result of perfect spiritual development and perfect spirituality cannot be had without perfect ethical conduct. Thus, Jainism could be described as being a religion of genuine austerity, without an emphasis upon the notion of a supreme being, traditionally known as God. As such, in Jainism self-purification, seen in the light of ahimsa, comes to be regarded as the primary means of release. One of the contemporary role models in this pursuit of self-purification is Mahatma Gandhi, who was heavily influenced by Jainism in his youth. Gandhi wrote:

> No religion of the World has explained the principle of Ahimsa [nonviolence] so deeply and systematically as discussed, with its applicability in life, in Jainism. As and when this benevolent principle of Ahimsa will be sought for practice by the people of the world to achieve their ends of life in this world and beyond, Jainism is sure to have the uppermost status and Bhagwan Mahavira is sure to be respected as the greatest authority on Ahimsa. (Jain Samaj Europe 2002)

Nonviolence in Buddhism

As in Jainism, Buddhism also broke away from the Vedic religion. But, unlike Jainism, Buddhism played a major role outside India. In a similar story to that of Mahavira, Gautama Siddhartha left his family and his princely life and later became the Buddha, the Enlightened One. From then until his death in 483 BC, Gautama travelled and taught his message of nonviolence around South and East Asia. Buddhism did become a universal religion, but this was the work of his followers, not of Buddha himself. Accordingly, the Buddha sought to preach his own doctrine, not only as a philosopher but also as a rebel against a number of dogmas in the Indian culture of his time. It has been a frequent charge against Buddhism that it overemphasizes suffering and is therefore a pessimistic religion. It is true that for Buddhism life is suffering (duhkha). If we examine life, says the Buddha, one thing that we cannot fail to notice is that the all-pervading fact of impermanence is the foundation of all suffering. Suffering, says the Buddha, is the result of our attachments, and attachments lead to karma and karma leads to rebirth. Karmic forces themselves are due to man's ignorance; they can, therefore, only be overcome by wisdom:

> Perfect knowledge is insight into the nature of existence and the factors that produce craving and suffering; perfect discipline, coupled with perfect knowledge, enables one to master the cravings; and perfect conduct, guided by perfect knowledge and discipline, leads to a life free from all forms of suffering and bondage. Such life is the life of wisdom, a life no longer laboring under the burden of ignorance. (Puligandla 1975, p. 58)

As such, the way to break the chain of causes of suffering would be a life of righteousness. The very fact that the Buddha recognizes an ethics of righteousness as a redemption from sorrow and suffering proves that Buddhism does not teach us a philosophy of passivity but that of courage, effort and perseverance:

> Freedom from vice, from deception, from lying and misleading people for self-aggrandizement, in short, building a pure character, or *Sila*, is enjoined by the Buddha as the most essential prerequisite of an aspirant ... Thus *Sila*, or right livelihood, means the transmutation or sublimation of the character of the individual. It is the conversion of the whole personality from the gross and ignoble life of indulgence to the pure and noble life of the saint, or Bodhisattva, who attains freedom from suffering in this life, and who goes on working for the freedom of others as long as he lives in the bodily-self. (Sharma 1965, p. 163)

If this was the settled intention of Buddha, he had to take steps to carry it out, and the idea of ahimsa was the result. Of all the principles of an ethics of righteousness, ahimsa is the foremost. In fact, all other virtues are the offshoots of ahimsa. Anyone who practises ahimsa needs to be compassionate and to have selfless love towards all other living beings:

> One indicator of the Buddhist commitment to the ethic of not injuring life forms is found in the abundant references to animals

in the teachings of both the Buddha and the later Buddhists. For instance, in the Jatakamala, didactic tales told by the Buddha drawn from his past lives, he portrays himself as a rabbit, a swan, a fish, a quail, an ape, a woodpecker, an elephant, and a deer. Animals are said to have contributed to his desire for nirvana; seeing animals and humans suffer caused Buddha to seek enlightenment. (Chapple 1993, p. 22)

On a fundamental level, the bodhi sattva (enlightenment being) exemplifies a radical form of altruism. A relevant example of this behaviour can be shown in the life of Asanga, a famed Indian Buddhist teacher:

> On the outskirts of Acinta he [Asanga] saw an old she dog whose hindquarters were raw and crawling with maggots. He felt great pity for her and wanted to relieve her suffering, but could not bear to destroy the maggots. Instead, he cut a piece of flesh from his own thigh and placed it near the dog. He then put out his tongue and prepared to transfer the larvae one by one. (Lecso 1988, p. 311)

As we can see, Buddhism clearly views the world as a network of interconnections and interdependent relations. As such Buddhism views all forms of life as sharing the Buddha nature. Thus, in Buddhism, avoiding injury and preventing violence is part of the path of awareness that leads to awakening (bodhi). Therefore, any action motivated by intent to harm has a negative effect on one's spiritual evolution. If the mind is impure, the state that follows is suffering, but, in contrast, purity of mind is conducive to happiness:

> Buddhism, like Jainism, holds to a soteriology of liberating awareness or wisdom *(jñāna, prajñā)*. When delusion is completely removed, liberation is achieved. Delusion does not merely indicate an absence of knowledge, but rather the presence of mistaken views that function to obscure one's awareness of the way events actually occur. Thus these obscurations are cognitive, while those associated with greed and hatred are emotional in nature. Of the cognitive obscurations the most fundamental is the mistaken view that accepts the existence of an independent permanent self. It is only on the basis of a deeply rooted attach-

ment to this false idea of 'self' that the emotional obscurations of greed and hatred can arise. If this basic disorientation is removed, so too are the twin possibilities of self-centered craving and antagonism towards so-called 'others'. (Adam 2006, pp. 6–7)

It is quite evident that, for Buddhism, nonviolence entails not only expelling evil ideas from the mind but also turning the attention to good ideas and therefore maintaining an ethical balance for the individual and the society. In other words, right mindedness goes hand in hand with the imperative of right action. Actions rooted in bad ideas lead to future suffering, both for the agent and for others. It is important to recognize, however, that in the Buddhist view 'actions have "natures" (*svabhāva*), albeit transitory, interdependently existing ones. Among the terms that may be correctly and usefully employed to describe them are "pure" or "impure," "awakened" or "unawakened," as the case may be' (Adam 2006, p. 7). Therefore, the path leading to the attainment of awakening goes through the practice of nonviolence in thoughts, words, deeds and actions. For Buddhists, nonviolence as a mental quality of selfless goodwill goes beyond a mere refraining from injury or killing. It is a method of developing compassion, empathetic joy and equanimity:

> Genuine *ahimsa* is thus understood positively; it does not merely indicate the absence of harmful intent, but in addition the actual presence of compassion. This compassion is the natural expression of spiritual awakening; it is likened to the feeling a mother has towards her own suffering child. This doctrine is especially developed in the Mahāyāna tradition, wherein great compassion (*mahakāruna*) generally displaces *ahimsā* as the central ethical term. (Adam 2006, p. 11)

Moreover, the practice of patience in the face of provocation leads to a habit of always drawing a veil over offences to de-escalate the feelings of those involved. The Buddha, who himself comes from a warrior-noble (*khattiya*) class, reflects on the misery of King Pasenadi, one of his followers, after he is attacked by King Ajatasattu: 'Victory breeds hatred; the defeated live in pain. Happily the peaceful live, giving up victory and defeat' (Harvey 2000, p. 250). It is interesting to note that the Indian emperor Asoka (268–239 BC) is widely known in history as a great exemplar of Buddhist compassion and righteous action, partly because of his emphasis on nonviolence:

> In the early part of his reign, prior to becoming a committed Buddhist, Asoka had conquered the Kalinga region, but his Kalinga Rock Edict 6 expressed horror at the carnage that this had caused. He therefore resolved to abandon such conquests – even though he was the head of a very powerful empire. He retained his army, though, and in one edict warned troublesome border people that, while he preferred not to use force against them, if they harassed his realm he would, if necessary, do so. He retained the goal of spreading the influence of his empire, but sought to do so by sending out emissaries to bring about 'conquests by *Dhamma*', that is, to spread the influence of his way of ruling and thus form alliances. (*Ibid.*, p. 253)

In its long history, Buddhism has used a variety of teachings on nonviolence in order to discourage the sense of division between the 'self' and the 'other'. It would be totally wrong to think that in the Buddhist tradition a person who is on the path to spiritual realization of wisdom is alone, with no consideration for others. Genuine spiritual awakening is thus understood positively as an actual presence of compassion. To attain Buddhahood one needs to practice compassion because this is a high moral ideal that will change one's life and the lives of other beings. It is possible to say, then, that 'Compassion (*karuna*), indeed is the force that holds things in manifestation – just as it withholds the Bodhisattva from nirvana. [From a Buddhist ethical view] the whole universe, therefore, is *karuna*, compassion, which is also known as *sunyata*, the void' (Zimmer 1969, p. 553). As a follower of Indian philosophy, Gautama, the Buddha, developed the ideal of ahimsa into a feeling of compassion for the whole universe. Compassion requires a fully nonviolent attitude towards others. The *Dhammapada* states: 'Let a man overcome anger by love, let him overcome evil by good; let him overcome the greedy by liberality, the liar by truth! Speak the truth, do not yield to anger; give, if thou art asked for little; by these three steps thou wilt go near the gods' (Ballou 1984, p. 135).

As such, Buddhism has much to offer regarding conflict resolution and nonviolence. Furthermore, Buddhist ethics and the practice of compassion and nonviolence could provide effective ways of building peace among individuals and communities. A few examples could highlight this point. Perhaps one of the most significant contributions of the Buddhist community in the past half a century has been centred around the moral authority of His Holiness the Dalai Lama. As a Buddhist, the Dalai Lama has made it clear that he refuses the use of violence in all situations. His emphasis reflects general Buddhist teachings, which promote the ideal of completely selfless compassion; indeed, the Dalai Lama (1984, p. 32) talks about Buddhism as 'altruism based on compassion and love'. He places Tibetan Buddhism in the framework of all Buddhist traditions: 'Buddhism is called Tibetan Buddhism, Chinese Buddhism, Indian Buddhism, Japanese Buddhism. It may look like four religions, but it is the same whether it is Tibetan or Chinese' (Singer 2003, p. 237). The idea of Tibetan nonviolence lying at the centre of the struggle for an independent Tibet (which remains the focus of attention for His Holiness the Dalai Lama) is founded on an inner strength with particular resonance in this struggle – reflecting the relationship between such strength and weathering adversity.

Aung San Suu Kyi is another striking example of the intersection between Buddhism and nonviolent action. She lays out an understanding of nonviolence which owes more to Buddhism than to contemporary modes of resistance and, in so doing, injects new meaning into the ideal of democracy. 'It is the awareness which enables her to perceive the fear that lies behind the violence of the Burmese junta and to insist on offering them dialogue. The practice of metta – 'loving kindness' – is not passive, she says, and points to the Buddha himself, who went to stand between two warring parties to protect them both at the risk of his own safety' (Bunting 2011). It is no coincidence that Aung San Suu Kyi says of herself that:

> When I am asked what sustains me in the dark nights of the political soul, I am inclined to answer: 'understanding, compassion, friendship.' This is perhaps not the kind of answer the questioners want. Perhaps they would rather hear about mysterious inner resources, some wonderful inspiration, some memorable experience that gives us the strength to withstand the hardships of the human lot. But our powers of endurance are slowly and painfully developed through repeated encounters with adversity. (Suu Kyi 1998)

Those engaged in nonviolent resistance and peace-building in today's world can draw inspiration and legitimacy from this Buddhist thought, both in- and outside Asia. Perhaps the most useful lessons Hinduism, Jainism and Buddhism have to offer spring from the celebrated and shared concept of ahimsa.

Further reading

Bhaskarananda, S. (1994) *The Essentials of Hinduism: A Comprehensive Overview of the World's Oldest Religion*.

Laidlaw, J. (1995) *Riches and Renunciation: Religion, Economy, and Society Among the Jains*. A comprehensive study that shows how renunciation and ascetism play a central part in Jainism in India.

Pauling, C. (1990) *Introducing Buddhism*. A non-technical and clear introduction to Buddhism as an ancient philosophy.

Rahula, W. (1974) *What the Buddha Taught*. A clear and faithful account of the Buddha's teachings.

Tähtinen, U. (1976) *Ahimsa: Non-Violence in Indian Tradition*. A classic on the concept of ahimsa in Eastern religions.

Chapter 2

Christianity and Nonviolence

Nonviolence in the Christian tradition has its roots in Jesus Christ's Sermon on the Mount, as detailed in the Gospel of Matthew. In the Sermon on the Mount, Jesus teaches us not to return violence with violence, but to respond with endless love to both the righteous and our enemies. Jesus's sermon defines three principles behind his ethical imperative: (1) prohibition of anger, (2) nonresistance to evil and (3) the love of one's enemies. On closer examination, it is evident that this Christian imperative to love our opponents is ultimately rooted in the love of God for human beings. As such, the love for God and the love of one's enemy is codependent, for loving our enemy is displaying love of God's children. Upon analysis of the Revelation of John it becomes clear that Christ's idea of loving our enemies is a cornerstone of the Christian community. Of course, the concept of love in the New Testament is based upon Jesus Christ's character, and the relation of the Christian to him. As such, the followers of Jesus must mould and form their love based on Christ's love. Historically, oppressed Christian communities have used their love of one another to fend off the forces pitted against them. Loving one another, Christian communities were not only able to overcome their fear, but also to establish social solidarity together.

St Paul's approach to the principle and idea of nonviolence, while similar to the classic reference of the Epistles to redemptive love, brings a new element. The Letter of Paul to the Galatians exemplifies a clear Pauline interpretation of Christ's love commandment. In Galatians, Paul claims that love precedes freedom because it serves and solidifies spiritual liberty. Furthermore, in the Letter of Paul to the Romans, Paul suggests that the law of love is different from any other earthly law in that it must manifest itself as an inner force and cannot be prescribed from the outside. Summing up all of the commandments of Jesus, Paul provides Christians with a new interpretation of the law of love and nonviolence, claiming, 'Love does no wrong to the neighbour; therefore, love is the fulfilling of the law.' Regarding nonviolence specifically, Paul teaches us that the two concepts of spirit-inspired love and neighbourly love are so bound up that they can only be separated at the expense of rejecting Christian nonviolence. Like Christ's sermon, Paul's teachings insist upon the necessity of love even for those outside the Christian community, inviting Christians to avoid vengeance and retaliation against those that persecute and curse. For these reasons the 'Love your enemies' command found in the teachings of the Sermon on the Mount and repeated by Paul have become the leading themes in the Christian ethics of nonviolence.

The overwhelming religious and moral conviction of the early Christians was that war is an absolute evil and that it was better to be killed than to kill. To kill was seen as turning one's back on God. Historically, with the political development of European Christendom and end of the Middle Ages, the strongest proponents of peace and nonviolence were Christian humanist scholars such as Erasmus. However, few Christians did so much to change the views and lives of individuals through the promotion of a nonviolent lifestyle as Saint Francis of Assisi.

Throughout the Middle Ages, many reformers had tried to solve the Church's corruption 'from within' and Francisjoined their ranks. He strongly believed in the importance of the Gospel to Christ's teaching, especially that Christian love could bring about the resolution of conflict and peace among individuals and communities. As such, Francis's notions of nonviolence were formulated by clear references to the Christian doctrine of loving your enemies.

Though Franciscan ideas on nonviolence and peace are unique, they are not the only ones in the history of Christianity. Deeply influencing the rules of war and politics, pacifism emerged among early Christians, often within sects, as an important aspect of moral and religious attitudes towards the world. The most famous and numerous of these Christians have been the Quakers. The founder of the Quakers, George Fox, believed that religious freedom went hand in hand with the practice of nonviolence. Throughout history Quakers have refused to bear arms or participate in war, seeing it as an individual decision closely related to one's personal experience of God. Quakers not only refused warfare, but they actively campaigned for peace. One of the most prominent campaigns that Quakers were engaged with was the movement for the liberation of slaves in America. By the twentieth century, Quakers were involved in protests against the escalating violence surrounding the Cold War.

The most outspoken Christian adherent of nonviolence in the twentieth century was Thomas Merton. A monk, Merton believed that a crucial aspect of being-in-the-world is that nonviolence is a meaningful attitude towards life – not only in refusal to do harm, but also in the determination to struggle for the truth. In his pioneering article of 1967, titled 'Blessed Are the Meek', Merton explores the roots of Christian nonviolence and integrates the challenge of nonviolence as a way of life for the present and future.

The roots of nonviolence in Jesus Christ

According to the Gospel of Matthew (5:43), Jesus of Nazareth told his followers:

> You have heard that it was said, 'You shall love your neighbour and hate your enemy.' But I say to you, Love your enemies and pray for those who persecute you, so that you may be children of your Father-Mother in heaven; for God makes the sun rise on the evil and on the good, and sends rain on the righteous and on the unrighteous. For if you love those who love you, what reward do you have? Do not even the tax collectors do the same? And if you greet only your sisters and brothers, what more are you doing than others? Do not even the Gentiles do the same? Be perfect, therefore, as God, your heavenly Father-Mother, is perfect.

How could we summarize Jesus's teaching on nonviolence in the Sermon on the Mount? Jesus teaches us to not return violence for violence, but instead, to offer boundless love to all. He instructs us to love those who are unrighteous and are our enemies. The three ethical principles noted above – prohibitions against anger (5:22), nonresistance to evil (5:39) and love of one's enemies (5:44) – are grounded ultimately in the love of God for human beings:

> Therefore, insofar as God's love manifested in Jesus is a model for human love, the specific ways in which it is unconditional and

indiscriminate bear on how we should treat those who have wronged us; but they have no bearing on how we should distribute our limited emotional, physical, temporal, and material resources in caring for the millions of fellow humans who can now claim to be – more or less closely – our neighbors. (Campton and Biggar 2008, p. 95)

Luke's Parable of the Good Samaritan arrives at the same conclusion in Jesus's answer to the lawyer's question, 'Who is my neighbour?' The Good Samaritan is the one who proves to be a neighbour to his enemy (Luke, 10:29). This dual love for God and love for enemies, far from presenting a conflict, actually mutually nurtures and nourishes; see 1 John 5:2: 'By this we know that we love the children of God, when we love God and obey God's commandment.' Therefore, according to 1 John 4:20–1, one who claims to love God and harbours hatred for his brothers and sisters is no less than a liar. An examination of the text reveals that the emphasis on the concept of *agape* in the Revelation to John places Christ's idea of the love of enemies as the cornerstone of the Christian community, with every Christian's approach to love modelled after Christ. According to John 13:12–17:

After Jesus had washed their feet, had put on his robe, and had returned to the table, he said to them, 'Do you know what I have done to you? You call me Teacher and Lord – and you are right, for that is what I am. So if I, your Lord and Teacher, have washed your feet, you also ought to wash one another's feet. For I have set you an example, that you also ought to do as I have done to you.

The love commandment in John appears again in 15:12–17, where the Christ says: 'This is my commandment, that you love one another as I have loved you. No one has greater love than this, to lay down one's life for one's friends.' It goes without saying that a call to love one another has always been a way for oppressed Christian communities throughout history to fend off the forces arrayed against them. This principle of love not only casts out fear, but also creates a social solidarity among the Christian community.

Nonviolence in the Epistles of St Paul

Consistent with the classic reference of the Epistles to redemptive love, Paul approaches this principle and the idea of Christian nonviolence from a new angle. The Letter of Paul to the Galatians gives us a clear picture of Pauline interpretation of Christ's love commandment. 'For you were called to freedom, brothers and sisters; only do not use your freedom as an opportunity for self-indulgence, but through love serve one another' (Galatians, 5:13). In other words, Paul claims that love has precedence over freedom because love serves and solidifies spiritual liberty. For Paul, therefore, love is the sum of the commandments of Christ, and this is possible because the law of the Spirit is nothing but the law of love. This is what appears clearly in the Letter of Paul to the Romans (5:5), 'And hope does not disappoint us, because God's love has been poured into our hearts through the Holy Spirit that has been given to us.' Paul suggests that the law of love has to come from an inner force and cannot be prescribed from outside, providing Christians with a new interpretation of the idea of love as the law of nonviolence. 'Love does no wrong to a neighbour; therefore, love is the fulfilling of the law' (Romans, 13:10). Paul tells the Galatians (5:6) that 'the only thing that counts is faith working through love'. Paul insists on the necessity of love not only within the Christian community but also among other communities: a love that manifests itself as a willingness to give oneself, as Jesus did, to one's neighbour, within or without the Christian community. At the core of Paul's vision of Christian nonviolence lies his belief in not repaying evil for evil (Romans, 12:17) and forgiveness (Corinthians, 2:7–10). Paul's response to the realities of enmity appears is founded on returning evil with goodness:

> Bless those who persecute you; bless and do not curse them ... Do not repay anyone evil for evil, but take thought for what is noble in the sight of all. If it is possible, so far as it depends on you, live peaceably with all. Beloved, never avenge yourselves, but leave room for the wrath of God ... Do not be overcome by evil, but overcome evil with good. (Romans, 12: 14–21)

Like Jesus, Paul prescribes a nonviolent attitude towards those who persecute and curse. He invites Christians to avoid vengeance and retaliation. For this reason the 'Love your enemies' command found in the Sermon on the Mount and repeated by Paul sets the central theme of Christian nonviolent ethics.

Franciscan nonviolence

The profound religious and moral conviction of early Christians was that war is an absolute evil and it is better to be killed than to kill. This Christian conception of nonviolence was usually accompanied by the conviction that human life is sacred and killing humans is somehow to turn against God. Historically, with the political development of European Christendom towards the end of the Middle Ages, the plea for peace and nonviolence and the condemnation of war found stronger adepts among Christian humanist scholars like Erasmus and, later, with Christian churches, groups or communities advocating Christian pacifism. However, few Christians did so much to change the lives and views of individuals through a nonviolent lifestyle as Saint Francis of Assisi (see Profile 2.1). Francis was born in 1182 AD to a wealthy family in northern Italy. He lived a self-indulgent life until he joined the crusades. At around this time, he became seriously ill. During his long period of recovery, which was spent in frequent prayer and meditation, Francis went on a pilgrimage to Rome. While he was away, Francis saw a vision of Jesus, who said, 'Francis, go and repair my house which has fallen into ruin.' In a dramatic moment, Francis took off his costly garments and renounced his wealth, saying he would lead the life of an ascetic. Saint Francis was not an intellectual and had no interest in Christian theology and theologians, but:

> Gradually, inevitably, a kind of doctrine emerged from Francis's antidoctrinalism. The Church was riddled with corruption; it must be reformed. Men, tempted by the devil and yielding to him, must be rescued, for the security of their souls. So men must be induced to lead apostolic lives, directed by the regenerated Church. Francis's purpose was not subversive or heretical; he proposed merely a revival of Gospel simplicity, the acceptance of Christ's teaching and the imitation of His life. (Bishop 1974, p. 58)

Francis believed that the essence of the love message of Christ was mediation of conflict and working to bring peace to individuals, communities and nations. This manifested itself in Francis as a perma-

Profile 2.1 **St Francis of Assisi**

St Francis of Assisi (1182 to 1226) was born Giovanni di Pietro di Bernardone, to a wealthy Assisian family. Francis received some elementary instruction from the priests of St George's at Assisi, but left education early to work with his father, trading clothes. At the age of 20 he went to fight the Perugians in one of the clashes so frequent at that time between the rival cities. The Assisians were defeated on this occasion; Francis was taken prisoner for more than a year. He returned to Assisi in 1203 and continued his carefree life, but, according to legend, in 1204 he became seriously ill and had a spiritual crisis. In 1205, he left for Puglia to enlist in the army, but a strange vision arrested his course. After a pilgrimage to Rome, he emptied his purse, exchanged his clothes with a mendicant and fasted among the beggars. His father, Pietro Bernardone, highly upset, dragged him back home and locked him in a dark closet. Freed by his mother, Francis renounced his father and his wealth, publicly laying aside his garments. Naked and half frozen, Francis went to a nearby monastery, where he worked for a time as a scullion. He spent two years restoring ruined chapels in the locality. On 24 February 1209 Francis heard a sermon relating how Christ told his followers to go forth and proclaim the Kingdom of Heaven and devote themselves to a life of poverty. Francis started preaching to ordinary people and was soon joined by his first follower, the jurist Bernardo di Quintavalle. Within a year Francis created the community of 'lesser brothers' (*fratres minores*). Francis went to Rome with eleven of his followers, seeking permission from Pope Innocent III to found a new religious Order. It is said that the Pope had a dream in which he saw Francis holding up the cathedral of Rome and decided to endorse the Franciscan Order. Francis tried on several occasions to take his message out of Italy, travelling to Jerusalem, Egypt and Syria, teaching a personal Christian religion that ordinary people could understand. He even went so far as to preach to animals, which earned him the nickname 'God's fool'. Many of the stories that surround his life deal with his love for animals. He died on 3 October 1226, aged 44, in Assisi. On 16 July 1228, he was pronounced a saint by Pope Gregory IX.

nent admiration and love of nature and humans as joyous spectacles of God's creation, providing the basis of the Franciscan doctrine of nonviolence and 'love of enemies'. Saint Francis wrote:

> The Lord says: Love your enemies [do good to those who hate you, and pray for those who persecute and blame you] (Mt 5:44). That person truly loves his enemy who is not upset at any injury which is done to himself, but out of love of God is disturbed at the sin of the other's soul. And let him show his love for the other by his deeds. (Francis and Clare 1982, p. 30)

Francis's boundless love, embracing poverty with peace and tranquility, carries with it not only message of humility, but also that of forgiveness. In one of the prayers that Saint Francis gave to his friars he is inspired by Christ's message of forgiveness:

> As we forgive those who trespass against us: And whatever we do not forgive perfectly, do you, Lord, enable us to forgive to the full so that we may truly love [our]enemies and fervently intercede for them before You returning no one evil for evil and striving to help everyone in You. (Francis and Clare 1982, p. 106)

These writings leave no doubt as to the nonviolent essence of Francis's thinking, linked with a love of all natural things: his sermon to the birds is a symbol of his love of nature; his poem, 'The Canticle of Brother Sun', is animated by a principled nonviolent spirit. Francis praises the godlike world and responds gratefully to the Creator:

> Praised to You, my Lord, with all your creatures, especially Sir Brother Sun, who is the day and through whom You give us light ... Praised be You, my Lord, through Sister Moon and the stars, in heaven You formed them clear and precious and beautiful. (Francis and Clare 1982, p. 38)

Francis's mystical attitude suggests that in spiritual life, working towards the goal of unity with God, the ideal of apostolic poverty is connected to the ideal of Christian nonviolence: if one disavows self-ishness, one disavows violence. Saint Francis, like the true mystics of every age, was the product of his time, but also that of his religion, defending the integrity of his faith and epitomising the ethic of nonviolence. He aimed to establish and maintain peace by the mutual adjustment of poverty and the law of Christian love. But, above all, his message of peace and nonviolence spoke against war or aggression.

Christian nonviolence in the North American context

European and American history offers several contexts where similar ideas appeared, influencing deeply the rules of war and politics. The pacifist ethic saw war and killing as sinful, involving neglect of the commandment of Christ to live at peace with one's neighbour. Although the Christian church turned away from pacifism later on, sects through the Middle Ages and to the present day have held those principles dear. These included the Albigenses, the Lollards, the Bohemian Brethren or Moravians, the Mennonites, the English Shakers, the German Inspirationists, the Russian Doukhobors, the French Camisards and the best-known and most numerous, the Quakers. The Quakers' original refusal to bear arms is based on a belief in an individual decision closely related to one's personal experience of God. Moreover, the nonviolent attitude of the Religious Society of Friends derives once again from the teachings of Jesus to love one's enemies. The Quaker sect started in the middle of the seventeenth century as an outcome of the Puritan movement. When Puritanism, initially a rebellion against the dogmatism of the established Church, turned into a new form of established dogma, George Fox turned the basic reforming spirit of Puritanism against itself and started Quakerism. It is reported that Fox, for whom religious freedom and nonviolence were inseparable, turned the other cheek when he suffered beatings by the mobs and he accepted imprisonment cheerfully. High on the list of early Quaker testimonies is the peace testimony:

> The formal Quaker Peace Testimony was written and delivered to the king of England in 1660 at a time when Quakers needed to assure the king that they had not been part of a plot to overthrow him. Entitled, 'A Declaration from the harmless and innocent people of God, called Quakers, against all plotters and fighters in

the world,' it declared in part, 'Our principle is, and our practices have always been, to seek peace and ensue it and to follow after righteousness and the knowledge of God, seeking the good and welfare and doing that which tends to the peace of all ... All bloody principles and practices, we ... do utterly deny, with all outward wars and strife and fightings with outward weapons, for any end or under any pretence whatsoever. And this is our testimony to the whole world.' But, as implied in this testimony, early Quakers not only refused warfare, they actively sought to bring about peace. (King 1988, p. 16)

Fox and the Quakers turned away from priestly authority and placed their emphasis, as we have seen, on the nonconforming principle from which Puritanism took its inspiration. George Fox's principles have proved a strong guiding light for subsequent generations of Quakers, culminating, perhaps, in the movement for the liberation of the slaves in America, in which they led the way ahead of other Christian Peace Churches. Quakers 'were the first religious group that made a sharp distinction between an other-worldly and a this-worldly gospel. This distinction is a factor in the awareness of the denominations to human problems, among which racial attitudes are important' (Fisher 1935, p. 202). The Quakers of late nineteenth-century and twentieth-century America were drawn to the pacifist and nonviolent movements by a sense of civic and moral responsibility. During international conflicts in the western world, many Quakers were active leaders in North American anti-war movements, especially in the anti-Vietnam campaigns of the 1960s – indeed, they provided medical aid to Vietnamese civilian victims. However, it should be added that during the two world wars in the twentieth century some Quakers ceased their peace advocacy and served in the military. The most famous American pacifist of the twentieth century was A. J. Muste, who was inspired by the first Quakers' struggle in the revolutionary turmoil of seventeenth- and eighteenth-century England. Muste became a Quaker and was enrolled as a minister in the Religious Society of Friends, eventually leading the Committee for Nonviolent Action, an organization whose members tried to block the launching of American nuclear submarines and sailed into nuclear test zones in the Pacific. For Muste, peace was the most important factor in the quality of life which was complementary to freedom of conscience.

A new tradition: nonviolence in the work of Thomas Merton

It would be difficult to end this chapter on Christian nonviolence without saying a word about the contribution of Thomas Merton (1915–1968). As a Christian monk, Merton was one of the most outspoken supporters of peace and nonviolence in the twentieth century. For him, as a way of being-in-the-world, nonviolence is a meaningful Christian attitude towards life. Despite having chosen a monastic life, Merton broke his silence and solitude to talk about his responsibility to dissent. He asserts:

> My solitude, however, is not my own, for I see now how much it belongs to them – and that I have a responsibility for it in their regard, not just in my own. It is because I am one with them that I owe it to them to be alone, and when I am alone they are not 'they' but my own self. There are no strangers! (Merton 1966, p. 142)

For Merton (1971), commitment to nonviolence is in the final analysis, an affirmation of the idea of wholeness as a unity that binds all humans together. According to him, 'It is not a matter of exclusivism and "purity" but of wholeness, wholeheartedness, unity and ... equality which finds the same ground of love in everything' (Merton 1971, pp. 155–6). Moreover, Merton insists that nonviolence should mean not only a refusal to do another physical harm, but also a determination to struggle for the truth and the right. In a groundbreaking article entitled 'Blessed Are the Meek', written at the request of the International Fellowship of Reconciliation's (IFOR's) Hildegard Goss-Mayr and dedicated to Joan Baez, Merton (1997) develops the Christian roots of nonviolence and attempts to synthesize the challenge of nonviolence as a way of life for the present and the future. He affirms:

> Nonviolence must be aimed above all at the transformation of the present state of the world, and it must therefore be free from all occult, unconscious connivance with an unjust use of power. This poses enormous problems – for if nonviolence is too political it becomes drawn into the power struggle and identified with one side or another in that struggle, while if it is totally apolitical it

runs the risk of being ineffective or at best merely symbolic. (*Ibid.*, p. 253)

Merton's attraction to Asian religious traditions like Taoism, Zen and Tibetan Buddhism and his deep admiration for Mahatma Gandhi opened the horizon of his Christian nonviolence to new frontiers. What significance does Gandhi have for Christianity? Merton replies to this question with no ambiguity:

> Western Christians often assume without much examination that this oriental respect for Christ is simply a vague, syncretistic and perhaps romantic evasion of the challenge of the Gospel: an attempt to absorb the Christian message into the confusion and inertia which are thought to be characteristic of Asia. The point does not need to be argued here. Gandhi certainly spoke often of Jesus, whom he had learned to know through Tolstoy. And Gandhi knew the New Testament thoroughly. Whether or not Gandhi 'believed in' Jesus in the sense that he had genuine faith in the Gospel would be very difficult to demonstrate, and it is not my business to prove it or disprove it. I think that the effort to do so would be irrelevant in any case. What is certainly true is that Gandhi not only understood the ethic of the Gospel as well, if not in some ways better, than most Christians, but he is one of the very few men of our time who applied Gospel principles to the problems of a political and social existence in such a way that his approach to these problems was *inseparably* religious and political at the same time. (*Ibid.*, p. 205)

No one seems to have had a greater influence on Merton's principled nonviolence than Gandhi. For Merton, Gandhi's principles of nonviolence and civil disobedience were important to the struggle for peace in the world of 1960s. It was in this spirit that Merton took a more responsible attitude than many Christians in regard to the nuclear arms race, which he judged to be immoral:

> We must try to remember that the enemy is as human as we are ... [We] must be reminded of the way we ourselves tend to operate, the significance of the secret forces that rise up within us and dictate fatal decisions. We must learn to distinguish the free voice of conscience from the irrational compulsions of prejudice

and hate. We must be reminded of objective moral standards, and of the wisdom which goes into every judgment, every choice, every political act that deserves to be called civilized ... History is ours to make: now above all we must try to recover our freedom, our moral autonomy, our capacity to control the forces that make for life and death in our society. (*Ibid.*, p. 96)

It was to the furthering of mutual understanding among nations that Merton devoted much energy in the last years of his life. Just as Merton recognizes the element of compassion in the lives of Jesus and Christian saints, he has a deep compassion for others. For him to live as a monk is not only to live in constant questioning of the evils of society and the world, but also to have deeper insights and expressions of love in regard to the reality of the human condition. It can be said that Merton's thought and actions have a dialogic essence that find their true expressions in Merton's Christian perspective on peace-making, nonviolence, racial justice and social concerns.

Taken as a whole, Christian nonviolence as preached by the Epistles and practised by generations of Christians is not presented as a single virtue or a single quality of life, but as an ensemble of virtues like compassion, self-sacrifice, self-renunciation, love of the enemy etc. Many Christians have advocated nonviolence in every walk of life, both institutional and individual. History, however, shows us that the success of Christian nonviolence depends largely upon the virtue and quality of Christian believers who identified themselves with the sufferings of others. What Jesus of Nazareth said and did were pointers in the use of nonviolence. Had he been alive today, he might have focused on the quest for more equality and justice in our world by turning our attention to our relations with each other.

Further reading

Chesterton, G. K. (1924) *St Francis of Assisi.* An enlightening study of the life and thoughts of St Francis by one of the best Christian writers of the twentieth century.

Maccoby, H. (1986) *The Mythmaker: Paul and the Invention of Christianity.* A well-researched study of Paul and his reworking of the nonviolent message of Jesus as the real inventor of what we now know as Christianity.

Mauser, U. (1992) *The Gospel of Peace*. A book which interlaces the meanings of nonviolence and peace with the New Testament experience of peace.

Richard, A., OFM (1989) 'Concerning Nonviolence and the Franciscan Movement', *The Cord*. An important article on the nonviolent philosophy of one of the principle monastic orders of the Roman Catholic Church.

Stassen, G. H. (1992) *Just Peacemaking: Transforming Initiatives for Justice and Peace*. An exploration of the just-peace theory according to recent biblical interpretations.

Trocmé, A. (2003) *Jesus and the Nonviolent Revolution*. A historical perspective on Jesus's call to nonviolence by a pastor of the French village of Le Chambon who is famous for his role in saving thousands of Jews from the Nazis.

Chapter 3

Islam and Nonviolence

Since the occurrence of 9/11 the image of Islam has been one constructed around stereotypes. The dominant stereotype is that to practise Islam is to be a violent fanatic. In addition, the common generalization of Islam as a faith is that it is motivated by bloodshed and violent tendencies, and that it is incompatible with secularism. Since 9/11, Muslim contributions to peace-making and nonviolence have been disregarded, overwhelmed by media images which have portrayed Islam as a religion of conflict and war.

However, Islam is not a religion that glorifies and promotes violence. Historically, Islam has shown acceptance to all religions and their respective communities. In the Middle Ages, the city of Cordoba in Andalusia – the home of Islamic civilization on the Iberian Peninsula – stood as an model for an open and tolerant society. In India, the Mogul Emperor Akbar represented Islam as tolerant and accepting of diversity. Without his coalition with the region's dominant religion, Hinduism, Akbar could not have built and sustained his empire for as long as he did.

Islamic ethics behind tolerance, violence and nonviolence derive from the Qur'an and the Sunna of the Prophet Muhammad. The Qur'an is God's message to the Prophet and, like all Holy Scriptures, it is open to multiple interpretations. As in many religions, the moral code is derived from the faith of the believer in a supreme creator. Faith in God and his justice brings all human beings awareness of righteous behaviour, but also the corrupting influence of human society. The Qur'an teaches us that all forms of violence in society are results of human wrongdoings and go against the commandments of God. As such, the Qur'an asks Muslims not to be assailants, 'do not be aggressors, God does not love aggressors' (2:190). Where Muslims are asked to fight is on behalf of the oppressed, against those that cause injustice. The call to fight against oppressors must be understood as a call to resistance against unjust rulers and unjust laws. The

Qur'an makes a distinction between an authentic form of struggle, called 'greater jihad', as opposed to the 'lesser jihad'. The authentic form does not promote violence or warfare against external enemies, but, rather, it calls on an internal effort of struggle waged against one's self. In contrast to the rhetoric used by Islamic extremism, which advocates violence against non-Muslims, the Qur'an specifically warns against religious extremism, 'do not go beyond the bounds in your religion' (4:171).

Despite this there still exist disagreements regarding the Qur'an and nonviolence. Though medieval Islamic juristic and philosophical literature was characterized by disagreements on the concept of freedom of worship in the faith and the apparent discrepancy between the Qur'anic 'verses of peace' and 'verses of sword', a closer reading of the Qur'an can solve this problem. In the Qur'an, violence is only formulated as a form of self-defence against aggression and injustice. The Meccan verses and scholars, such as Muhammad Abu Zahra, support the notion that the Prophet only fought to repel aggression.

Thus, the suggestion that nonviolent methods do not work in an Islamic context is false. Contemporarily, two leaders come to mind for their rejection of violence and support for mutual coexistence with non-Muslims: Khān Abdul Ghaffār Khān and Maulana Abul Kalam Azad. Like Gandhi, Ghaffār Khān dominated the political scene in India during her struggle for independence. Central to his conception of a spiritualized public sphere were truth, love and service, where each faith would play an important role. A significant amount of Ghaffār Khān's effort was dedicated to creating Hindu–Muslim unity, which is why he was strongly opposed to the creation of the Muslim state of Pakistan. Both Ghaffār Khān and Azad interpreted and practised Islam as a religion of patience and mutual toleration. It was Azad's fundamental belief, like Ghaffār Khān's, that tolerance was a basic value of life; he firmly believed that all religions were based on that principle and that the main goal of religion was to create peaceful unity in the world – that, although certain religious teachings differed, in the end they all converged. Moreover, Azad defines secularism not as a lack of religion and spirituality in the public sphere, but as an equal respect for all religions. As such, both leaders hoped to create a secular constitution that would maintain equal rights for all religious minorities.

Today, it is vital that the discussion of Islam and nonviolence goes beyond the question of controversy between Islamic fundamentalism and Islamic modernism. New questions should be asked regarding the

Muslim public sphere, re-examining it through a mechanism of tension management and taming violence.

Political Islam has gained an ideological reputation in Muslim societies because of historical failures of secular absolutism in the region. Too often post-colonial governments that aimed at modernization were rigidly dictatorial. Despite this, however, secularism has remained a dominant feature of national identity and it must not be undervalued. Democracy as a commitment to nonviolent social change, through dialogical mechanisms, can only flourish in an atmosphere where public issues can be discussed freely.

Nonviolence in this context must be built on dialogical mechanisms that re-examine the existing power relations in Muslim societies. In order for this to occur, a shift must be made away from 'belligerent citizenship' to 'dialogical citizenship'. Through dialogue and the nonviolent process of recognition of others a 'moral togetherness' will be constructed. This does not mean that absolute secularization should be the order of the day – exclusion of religion from the Muslim public sphere can be destructive to the social fabric of community, but neither does it mean that the Muslim public sphere should undergo a theologization. Both secular and religious dialogues pertaining to democracy should be accommodated. Promoting a nonviolent experience of Islam in this atmosphere can lead to the containment and defeat of religious fanaticism and fundamentalism.

The roots of nonviolence in the Qur'an

Many people around the world associate Islam with images of extremism and violence. Osama bin Laden and Saddam Hussein are stock characters in this association in the wake of 11 September and the 'war on terror'. The image of a fanatic and violent Muslim has become a dominant stereotype and the changing global tempo around this issue weighs on the relation between Islam and public sphere. Such an approach is in alignment with the generalization of Islam as a violent faith and the misunderstanding and misevaluation of Muslim diversity. Violence has become the symbolic image of Islam in the West. Islam, however, does not glorify violence; indeed, historically, as many examples illustrate, it has shown tolerance to all religions and communities. As mentioned above, Cordoba was once the centre of a great Islamic civilization in Andalusia – one of the most open and tolerant of its era. For hundreds of years during the Middle Ages, Cordoba witnessed a great flowering of religious freedom, which, while not perfect, was sufficient that many Jewish and Christian intellectuals lived there, writing and flourishing side by side with their Muslim counterparts in a strikingly pluralistic society. The Mogul Emperor Akbar offers another example (again, see above). Now, if it is true that Islam is a nonviolent religion, it is high time we face the question: 'How is nonviolence defined and practised in Islam?'

The Islamic ethics of violence and nonviolence are derived from the same general sources upon which Islamic law is based, the Qur'an and the Sunna of the Prophet. The first of these sources, the Qur'an, like all other revealed scriptures, is God's message to Prophet Muhammad and his followers. Though not a systematic ethical or philosophical treatise, the Qur'an, again like many other holy texts, permits multiple and hermeneutic readings. In other words, its universal applicability presents it as an ethical argument beyond its time and place of revelation. In Islam, as in all other monotheistic religions, the moral code derives from the faith of the believer in a supreme creator. It is faith in God and his justice which brings all human beings' awareness of the righteous behaviour, but also of the corrupting influences of human society. As a result, human beings discover that true peace (*salam*) and not war and corruption (*fasad*) is God's true purpose for humanity. As the Qur'an (2:208) says, 'O you who believe, enter the peace, all of you. Do not follow the footsteps of Satan. He is a clear enemy to you.' That is to say, the original and essential nature of human being is that of moral innocence; all forms of violence practised in society are the results of humans' wrongdoings and against the laws and moral commandments of God. Therefore, absence of violence is attained only when human beings submit to God's will and his commandments. In Islam, the goal of all struggles is the call to Allah and His laws, not self-aggrandizement. As such, the grounds for 'fighting' (*qital*) are separated from that of 'aggression' (*idwan*). The Qur'an asks Muslims not to be aggressors: 'Fight in the way of God against those you come upon them, but do not be the aggressors. God does not love aggressors' (2:190). Muslims are invited repeatedly by the Qur'an to fight in the path of God on behalf of the weak (*al-mustad a fun*) and against the oppressors (*zalimun*). Therefore, the prevailing attitude in Islam is not to obtain glory in violence, but to set things right against wrongs done. This ethical perspective is clearly outlined in the Qur'an: 'Permission is granted to those who fight because they have been wronged – for God is able to help them' (22:39). The Qur'an and the Sunna of the Prophet often speak of struggle against oppression and the oppressors. This, of course, should be understood as a resistance against unjust rulers and unjust laws. But the authentic struggle, which is called 'greater jihad' (*al-jihad al-akbar*), as opposed to 'lesser jihad' (*al-jihad al asghar*), is not a form of violence or warfare against external adversaries but it is rather an internal effort and struggle waged against one's self. Every Muslim is require to practise both a lesser and a greater jihad. It is interesting to point out that the ethical imperative for an inclusive and nonviolent interpretation of Islam against an extremist and exclusive interpretation of Islam has always been to stress the importance of the 'greater' rather than the 'lesser' jihad. In spite of the rhetoric on Islamic extremism which strongly advocates war and terrorist attack on non-Muslims, it is important to note that the Qur'an warns against religious extremism: 'O People of the Scripture, do not go beyond the bounds in your religion. Do not say anything but the truth about God' (4:171). Every community, we are told in the Qur'an, has been sent its guide: 'There is no community but a warner has passed away among them' (35:24). In other words, Islam recognizes differences of cultures and diversity of religious traditions. That is the reason why God has given human beings the freedom to choose: 'Had your Lord wished, all those on earth would have believed, all of them. So would you force the people to become believers?' (10:99). Muslims are, therefore, invited to respect diversity and display inclusiveness. Muslim philosophers and scholars have throughout Islamic history encouraged reciprocity and intra-Muslim dialogue. As al-Ghazālī put it:

> Those who rush to condemn people go who against ... any [particular] ... school as unbelievers are reckless ignoramuses ... For challenging others with one's knowledge is a deeply ingrained human instinct over which the ignorant are able to exercise no control. (2002, p. 120)

As al-Ghazālī's discussion makes apparent, Islamic medieval juristic and philosophical literature was characterized by fundamental disagreements on the concept of freedom of worship in Islam and the apparent discrepancy between the Qur'an 'verses of peace' and 'verses of sword'. The Qur'an, however, seems to be quite clear on the issue of freedom of worship and the idea of peace-making which goes with it. In the Sura 8, we encounter the following statements: 'If they incline to peace, you should incline to it and trust in God.' And 'there is no compulsion in religion. The right course has become clearly distinguished from error' (92: 256). Given the pivotal importance of peace in Islam, one can say that violence is only formulated as a form of self-defence against aggression or injustice. The Egyptian scholar Muhammad Abu Zahra (1961, p. 18) maintains that, 'War is not justified ... to impose Islam as a religion on unbelievers or to support a particular social regime. The Prophet Muhammad fought only to repulse aggression.' The conceptions and practices of violence existing in the Jahiliyya period undoubtedly influenced the Prophet's approach to the subject, but as the Meccan verses show clearly, despite the growing tension among his followers over the use of violence, the Prophet insisted on the virtues of patience and compassion. This nonviolent attitude is perfectly outlined in the Qur'anic verses that reflect the rejection of armed struggle. Such as: 'Endure patiently – Your patience comes only with the help of God. Do not grieve for them, and do not be in distress because of the plots they devise. God is with those who are god-fearing and those who do good' (16:127–8) and:

> the recompense of evil is the same amount of evil. Whoever turns away [from evil] and makes amends, his wage is with God. He does not love those who do wrong. Those who help themselves after they have suffered wrong, there is no way against them. The way is against those who wrong the people and act oppressively in the land without right – for them there is a painful torment. Those who are steadfast and are forgiving – that comes from determination in affairs. (42:40–3)

These verses are indicative of the practice of nonviolent resistance in the Meccan period; the Prophet's policy towards the citizens of Mecca was that of establishing the moral superiority of forgiveness over revenge. Many historians and scholars of Islam seem to agree that it was during the Prophet's time in Medina that the Islamic formulation of violence was elaborated for the first time. The Qur'anic verses of this period exhort the Prophet and his followers to fight in order to protect themselves. For example, it is said, 'O prophet, urge on the believers to fight (8:65)' or 'They will continue to fight you until they turn you away from your religion if they are able' (2:217a). But, as Sohail Hashmi observes correctly, despite his personal presence in several battles, the Prophet was always a reluctant practitioner of violence. 'On several occasions he urged the use of nonviolent means or sought an early termination of hostilities, often in the face of stiff opposition from his companions' (2002, p. 204).

It is true that the Qur'anic verses on the use of violence and nonviolent resistance contradict one another, maybe because each one of them is related to a particular event and period. But, as we have seen, the Qur'an is clear on the peace-making role of Islam and it prohibits killing since the sanctity of life is given by God: 'Do not kill the soul that God has made sacred, except by right' (6:151). This comprehensive notion of 'non-killing' has facilitated throughout Islamic history the development of Islamic nonviolent and peace-building strategies, because of its overarching emphasis on the primary obligation to fight against injustice and self-centric attitudes. As Khadduri points out:

> In the Qur'an there are over two hundred admonitions against injustice expressed in such words as *zulm*, *ithm*, *dalal*, and others, and no less than almost a hundred expressions embodying the notions of justice, either directly in such words as *adl*, *qist*, *mizan*, and others as noted before, or in a variety of indirect expressions. (1984, p. 10)

Islamic principles of peace and nonviolent resistance against injustice are, therefore, clearly compatible with the Gandhian and Christian traditions and practices of nonviolence. Thus, we can move on to a closer examination of the application of such principles and nonviolent characters in Muslim communities.

Nonviolence in the contemporary Islamic context: the case of Khān Abdul Ghaffār Khān and Maulana Abul Kalam Azad

As indicated earlier, studies of Islam in today's world often assume the incompatibility of Muslim social and political activism with nonviolence. With the coming of age of a nonviolent reading of Muslim historical and political experiences, it is now clear that earlier understanding of the Muslim public sphere as a culturally threatening issue

[]

can no longer be a theoretical starting point for thinking about the relationship between Islam and democracy. Then the real question becomes: do nonviolent methods work in Islamic context? There is no moral or political reason why Islamic society could not take a lead in developing nonviolence today and there is every reason that most of them should. In promoting the paradigm of nonviolence in Islam, Muslims can look back to the contemporary examples of leaders like Khān Abdul Ghaffār Khān and Maulana Abul Kalam Azad who – through their rejection of violence and revenge and their readiness to live, cooperate and construct with non-Muslims – left a valuable legacy in our violent times. This legacy may be of great help in the task of overcoming divisions between secular and religious citizens in the Muslim world, but also in the making of a deliberative and empathic Muslim public sphere.

Many consider Khān Abdul Ghaffār Khān (see Profile 3.1) as a Pashtun nationalist, rather than as a proponent of nonviolent Islam. Ghaffār Khān started forming his philosophy of nonviolence before he came into contact with Gandhi. His nonviolent action drew its inspiration from the Qur'an and the Prophet Muhammad, in contrast to Gandhi, whose ideals were largely inspired by the *Bhagavad Gita*, the New Testament and the writings of Thoreau, Ruskin and Tolstoy. Abdul Ghaffār Khān used to say: 'I did not learn secularism from Bapu. I found it in the Qur'an' (Sohoni 1995, p. 48). As such, Ghaffār Khān dominated the political scene of Indian struggle for independence and freedom at a crucial time, which coincided with the Gandhian era of satyagraha. Truth, love and service were central to Ghaffār Khān's conception of a spiritualized public sphere, where each faith would play an important role. Therefore, a very significant aspect of his thought and action was to bring about Hindu–Muslim unity. That is why he was firmly opposed to the creation of Pakistan as a homeland for the Muslims of the Indian subcontinent. On this as on many other issues, he shared the vision of Maulana Azad (see Profile 3.2) to build an India in which ethnic identities would flourish. Both the leaders interpreted and practised Islam as a religion of 'patience' (*sabr*) and 'mutual toleration'. Azad, like Ghaffār Khān, was a passionate advocate of tolerance as one of the basic values of life and deeply believed in the essential similarity of the main teachings of all great religions. For him the real goal of religion was not to divide but to unite. The unity of religions, as interpreted by Maulana Azad, is not the identity of religions, nor uniformity in beliefs.

Profile 3.1 **Khān Abdul Ghaffār Khān**

Khān Abdul Ghaffār Khān (1890–20 January 1988), also known as Bāchā Khān (king of chiefs). Ghaffār Khān was born in Uttamazai (now in Pakistan) to a Pathan family. His father, Bahram Khān, was a landowner in the area of Hashtnaggar. In 1911, he joined the freedom movement of Haji Sahib of Turangzai and later formed the *Anjuman-e Islāh al-Afghān* (Afghan Reform Society) and the youth movement *Paxtūn Jirga* (Pashtun Assembly) in 1927. His political activities started in 1919 during the Rowlatt Act and Khilafat Movements. He took a prominent part in the Gandhian movement of noncooperation, civil disobedience and satyagraha. From 1921 to 1949, Khan Abdul was arrested several times and spent many years in jail. During the 1920s he founded the *Khudai Khidmatgar* (Servants of God), commonly known as the 'Red Shirts' (comprising nonviolent revolutionaries who were also devoted social workers and played an active role in the nationalist movement), and forged a deep admiration for Mahatma Gandhi. Although a pious Muslim, Ghaffār Khān believed in a secular state and condemned the communal politics of the Muslim League. He was also against the idea of partition. When the referendum over accession to Pakistan was held, Ghaffār Khān boycotted the referendum. He later took the oath of allegiance to the new nation of Pakistan, but was arrested several times between late 1948 and 1956 for his opposition to the Pakistani government. In 1962, Abdul Ghaffār Khān was named Amnesty International's 'Prisoner of the Year'. He lived in exile in Afghanistan for several years. In 1969, he was invited to India on the occasion of the Gandhi centenary celebrations. In 1987, he was presented with India's highest civilian award, the Bharat Ratna. Ghaffār Khān passed away in 1988. In 2008, T. C. McLuhan produced a documentary on him titled *The Frontier Gandhi: Badshah Khan, a Torch for Peace*.

Profile 3.2 **Abul Kalam Muhiyuddin Ahmed Azad**

Abul Kalam Muhiyuddin Ahmed Azad (11 November 1888 to 22 February 1958) was an Indian scholar and one of the foremost leaders of the Indian freedom struggle. His real name was Abul Kalam Ghulam Muhiyuddin. He was born in the holy city of Mecca in Saudi Arabia. His father was a Bengali Muslim of Afghan origins and his mother was an Arab. He returned to Calcutta with his family in 1890. Azad was trained in the subjects of religion, mathematics, philosophy and history. He was also well versed in languages like Arabic, English, Urdu, Hindi, Persian and Bengali. As a young man, he was exposed to modern intellectual life in India and especially to journalism. He developed a great interest in the pan-Islamic doctrines of Jamaluddin Afghani and Syed Ahmed Khan. He visited Afghanistan, Iraq, Egypt, Syria and Turkey and met with the exiled revolutionaries. Upon his return to India in 1912, Maulana Azad developed secret revolutionary centres all over north India and started a weekly journal in Urdu called *Al Hilal*. In 1916, the British Raj banned this paper and interned Maulana Azad at Ranchi, from where he was released in 1920. Upon his release, Azad returned to politics and joined the Indian National Congress under the leadership of Mahatma Gandhi. He was also elected president of the All India Khilafat Committee. Azad grew close to the Muslim League and, in 1923, he became the youngest candidate to be elected as president of the Congress Party. Maulana Azad was again arrested in 1930 for violation of the salt laws as part of the salt satyagraha. He was incarcerated in Meerut jail for a year and a half. Maulana Azad became the president of Congress in 1940 (Ramgarh) and remained in the post till 1946. He criticized Jinnah's demand for Pakistan and the proposal that envisaged the partition of India. After the independence of India, Azad served as the Minister of Education in Pandit Jawaharlal Nehru's cabinet from 1947 and played an important role in framing communal harmony between the Hindus and the Muslims in India. He died of a stroke on 22 February 1958. He was buried in Old Delhi, near the Jama Masjid. In 1992 he was posthumously awarded the Bharat Ratna.

Religions, for Azad, are different roads converging on the same goal. That is to say, the same fundamental truths have been revealed by God in different scriptures, in different languages, through different prophets and in different nations. Therefore, as Azad says in his *Tarjuman-ul-Quran*: 'It is not proper to consider these differences as the yardstick for truth and falsehood.' In fact, Azad distinguishes between '*din*' and '*shariah*'. According to Azad '*shariah*' may differ from people to people, depending on time and place and modes of living in differing conditions, but '*din*', which is essence of religion or faith, is one among all. In other words, Azad's point (which is also that of Ghaffār Khān) is that if religion expresses a universal truth, why should there be differences and conflicts among those professing different religions? By saying this, Azad defines 'secularism' not as a lack of religion and spirituality in the public sphere, but as equal respect for all religions. This approach fundamentally criticizes a mono-religious or a mono-secular public sphere. In his pluralist approach, Azad invites Muslims, Hindus, Buddhists, Sikhs, Parsis and Christians to live together in an enlightened climate of understanding, tolerance, amity, mutual respect and regard for each other. That was also the dream of Mahatma Gandhi. For both of them, the real challenge was to ensure that the secular public sphere could uphold the constitutional rights of all religious minorities. For Muslims like-minded with Gandhi – like Ghaffār Khān and Maulana Azad – a secular public sphere meant separation of religion from the political, economic, cultural and social aspects of life, religion being treated as a purely personal matter. It meant dissociation of the state from religion. It meant full freedom and respect for all religions. It meant equal opportunities for followers of all religions and no discrimination on the grounds of religion. Most of all, it meant firm opposition to communalism of all kinds. In the current context of Islam, it is this aspect of secularism that is most critical. The real battleground for a pluralist and nonviolent Muslim public sphere is an engagement-influenced tolerance, a tolerance that is born out of constant communication and interaction between the secular and the religious. It is actually a struggle between those who wish to preserve the essence of their religious beliefs and those who seek to deliberately distort that essence into a theocratic element. To create and preserve political pluralism in Islamic societies, it is important for Muslims to learn from the experience of Muslim nonviolent thinkers and activists like Ghaffār Khān and Maulana Azad, even though their experience is far from perfect. It may take time for some Muslims to respect political pluralism as a consequence of a pluralistic society.

Islam, nonviolence and the state

As this chapter has suggested, there is an urgent need to move the discussion of Islam and nonviolence beyond the question of controversy between Islamic fundamentalism and Islamic modernism. The main issue, therefore, is not to choose between the Islamic modernists or Islamic fundamentalists, but to ask the central question: how is it possible to push the debate in the Muslim public sphere away from the 'paradigm of enmity' by generating a process of re-examination of the Muslim public sphere through a mechanism of tension management and taming violence?

Clearly, one of the main reasons that political Islam has such ideological cachet in Muslim societies is the historical failure of secular absolutism in the region. Post-colonial modernist governments founded on secular rationality were too often violent and belligerent in their project of modernization, uncompromising towards religion and, worst of all, rigidly dictatorial. However, secularism should not be underestimated in terms of its significance for national identity across the region. We should not fall prey to the simplistic conclusion that the failure of secularism in Muslim societies is somehow a failure of democratization. Those who, in the West and the East, support ongoing conflicts within Muslim societies and democracy constantly threaten violence and military invasion. Two points should be highlighted in the face of such situations: first, that tolerance and mutual respect cannot occur in a state of war and second, that democracy as a commitment to nonviolent social change through dialogical mechanisms can only flourish where public issues are discussed freely.

In this respect, it becomes theoretically fruitful to conceptualize nonviolence as a dialogical mechanism that upsets, but also re-examines the existing power relations in Muslim societies. This is captured by the shift in focus from the question of how to think about violence in Muslim societies or among Muslims and non-Muslims, to the question of how to transform the conditions which might encourage violence. Therefore, the shift from 'belligerent citizenship' to 'dialogical citizenship' in Islam affects not only the political construction of the Muslim public space, but also the scope of democratic deliberation in Islam. Thus, the nonviolent process in Muslim societies has, or should have, epistemological implications: because it defines the basic categories through which members of Muslim societies understand themselves and the others. The dialogue that nonviolent Islam generates is not only among participants in a Muslim public sphere, but also within the public sphere of other cultures and traditions. Nonviolence in the context of Muslim public sphere is a political tendency that is embedded in the idea of dialogue with others, while reconsidering and re-evaluating our understanding and application of Islam in various historical and political contexts. Related to this idea of a critical re-evaluation of Islamic history in the nonviolent process of recognition of others is the idea of 'moral togetherness' as a starting point for dialogue and action within a community of shared moral values. Nonviolent Islam is a kind of dialogical narrative which can contribute to the political achievement of this community of shared moral values. Sharing moral togetherness in an Islamic context, then, means sharing an ethical territory of interconnection and interdependence with others, without excluding religious argument from the public sphere. What is at stake here is neither an 'absolute secularization' nor a 'theologization' of the Muslim public sphere, but a dialogical governance of plurality of discourses in it. The exclusion of religious argument from the Muslim public sphere is not only unjust, but it can destroy the fabric of continuity that holds the Muslim community together and provides it with a history. The empathic accommodation of religious citizens within a secular Muslim public sphere can only take place in a critical process of self-reflection of secularism in terms of a moral togetherness. There is no single public discourse that gives public partnership its meaning and its unity – rather a diversity of criss-crossing and contested discourses through which religious and non-religious citizens participate in and identify with the Muslim public sphere. Without this reciprocity, the Muslim public sphere will remain segmented along theological-political and secular-political lines and the sharing necessary for an inclusive partnership based on a moral minimum will be impossible.

Dialogical pluralism or nonviolent governance provides a more productive solution to the inherent dilemma of ethical accommodation of secular reasoning and spiritual experience in Muslim public sphere than absolutist approaches – either 'secular absolutism', which imposes an unfair choice between 'individual rights' and 'religious traditions' through state-imposed laws, or 'religious particularism', a form of unbound and uncritical theologization of public sphere, defending complete dependence of citizenship in Muslim societies to the *nomos* of religious groups. So if the real issue is to find a third way between secular authoritarianism and Muslim fundamentalism, we need to think of joint governance that is compatible with the recognition of a minimal secular nomos and a minimal spiritual ethos as constitutive elements of a Muslim public sphere. This is how religious and non-religious citizens can understand and debate each other's perspectives in the framework of a dialogical reciprocity. In fact, in such a socio-political context 'moral recognition' of the religious mind or the secular mind consists of recognizing the impossibility of our fully knowing or accepting the point of others and therefore listening to the voice of others with a spirit of openness to learning from difference. In such a case we have to be careful not to recognize the absolute primacy of the secular reason over Muslim historical narratives. The spiritual view of Muslims is not just a stock of information, it is also a process of 'coming to know' and it is a certain experience that continues to resist translation into secular and rational discourses. From this perspective, the illegitimate exercise of secular power could be understood as a prevention of open exchange by actively excluding certain points of view from the public debate or by silencing religious voices. In contrast, in a public sphere that is committed to the nonviolent ideals of tension management and public discussion, more debate is the only effective remedy against such uses of power by secular or religious forces. Furthermore, a democratic Muslim public sphere should be understood as an ongoing process of reaching equilibrium between the religious and the secular, where asymmetries of public viewpoints can be corrected in a dynamic interaction of citizens. That is to say, if we understand democracy as a process and not an ideal then the tactics employed to attain this ideal are themselves part of the democratic process in the Muslim public sphere – not independent of it. This demands a shift in Muslim historical consciousness in order to trace nonviolence as an operating principle of shared political morality in the Muslim public sphere.

Fanaticism, fundamentalism and similar other religion-related traits may be better combated and contained by promoting a nonviolent experience of Islam. However, as mentioned previously, secularism, distanced from spiritualized politics, is not likely to achieve that desired goal. Nonviolent Islam could give a new turn to secularism in Muslim societies. It could help to steer the Muslim public sphere away from institutionalized religion, its theoretical formulations and its unlived utopias. It is in such a context that secularism should be reconceptualized, not as a principle of absolute separation between the Muslim public sphere and religion, but as a principle of even-handed treatment by the Muslim public sphere of all religions. The realization of the ideal of nonviolence is a perennial struggle for Islamic communities around the world.

Further reading

Abu-Nimer, M. (2003) *Nonviolence and Peacebuilding in Islam: Theory and Practice.* This book addresses the challenges that face the proponents of nonviolence in the Islamic context of peace-building strategies and resolving disputes.

Halverson, J. R. (2012) *Searching for a King: Muslim Nonviolence and the Future of Islam.* A comprehensive book on the Islamic conception of nonviolence and its modern actors.

Kumar, R. (1991) *Life and Works of Maulana Abul Kalam Aza.* A study dedicated to the life and works of an eminent scholar of Islamic culture, nonviolent politician and peace educationalist of repute.

Pal, A. (2011) *Islam Means Peace: Understanding the Muslim Principle of Nonviolence Today.* An illuminating book on the tradition of nonviolence in Islamic sources and in modern Muslim societies.

Chapter 4

Philosophical Foundations of Nonviolence

Some of the most notable philosophies of nonresistance were developed by Socrates, Henry David (H. D.) Thoreau and Leo Tolstoy. Both Socrates and Thoreau are considered to be defenders of conscientious disobedience. Each of these three, however, has contributed important elements to today's understanding of nonviolence and nonresistance.

Socrates offered one of the oldest statements of a philosophy of nonresistance in 399 BC. A prominent Greek philosopher, Socrates was sentenced to death for preaching critical thinking to his students. The only accounts of Socrates's teachings that we have are from his student, Plato, whose *Apology* details Socrates's trial and his defence. According to Socrates, an important characteristic of Athenian citizens was to be virtuous and maintain fidelity towards the city and its people; justice did not lie in any particular set of rules, but in the idea of knowledge, which he deemed to be central in achieving human excellence. Remarkable for this period was the fact that Socrates was able to confront and challenge the social and political institutions in a spirit of nonviolence. Together with justice, nonviolence offered the best prospect for a virtuous life.

For Socrates, the obligation that the Athenian law imposed on him was based on the ethical nature of his citizenship. Socrates's nonviolent action consisted in practising philosophy and pursuing justice. In Plato's *Crito*, Aristotle argues against the use of force and the law, or, for that matter, any legal obligations. The main charge levelled against Socrates was that he rejected the gods. Yet, during his defence, Socrates insisted that his actions were founded on obeying higher laws given to him from a divine source, although his convictions were based on his own philosophy rather than god-given wisdom. Socrates was willing to accept his punishment because he did not believe that the laws of the city-state were morally appropriate. The nature of Socrates's challenge to the unjust laws attests to his commitment to civil disobedience.

As a moral platform, Socratic nonviolence places significance on obeying higher laws. Disobeying an unjust law opens up the possibility of persuading those in authority to bring about change. Even though Socrates might not have considered himself as a nonviolent resister when facing trail, today his actions are deemed to be those of a conscientious objector.

Thoreau, like Socrates, conceived of humans as moral beings, measuring wrongfulness against a set of unjust laws. His famous essay *Civil Disobedience* opens with the following principle: 'That government is best which governs least.' As such, Thoreau viewed the government as the greatest impediment to the freedom of the individual. The essence of all of Thoreau's writings is the necessity for individual self-realization. Furthermore, he calls on everyone to follow the laws of his or her own being.

Thoreau believed that it was a moral duty to resist government and its excesses. In resisting the government, Thoreau suggested two criteria: (1) only important issues warrant resistance and (2) public support for resistance indicates a legitimate violation of moral principles. Calls for resisting government, however, should not be understood to mean he was a supporter of anarchism or traditional republicanism. Thoreau's thought was heavily influenced by Christianity, although he also found inspiration in Hindu and Muslim mystics. Thoreau formulated his views on nonviolence and respect for nature on Hindu scriptures such as the Laws of Manu and the *Bhagavad Gita*. As he strove more for nonviolence in his life, he strove for nonviolence in the political sphere.

For Thoreau, civil disobedience went beyond the private conscientious refusal to pay government taxes. Civil disobedience was a refusal to accept the ethics of utilitarianism that underpinned American government institutions. For Thoreau, these institutions were responsible for alienation, which led to citizens' powerlessness and passivity. To combat alienation, Thoreau advocated direct involvement in public affairs through the practice of participatory democracy. It must be noted, however, that for Thoreau the individual was always far more important than the government. Like Socrates, his civil disobedience pointed to the duty of resisting immoral political authorities and their commands.

Leo Tolstoy's legacy extends beyond literature and into the field of civil disobedience and nonviolence philosophy. His influence in this field was such that he became something of a mentor to Gandhi and Martin Luther King. A social reformer, Tolstoy preached messages advocating universal love and spiritual brotherhood. Focusing on the issues gripping Russia at the end of the nineteenth century, Tolstoy questioned the very essence of religion and political organizations. In regards to religion, he believed that its truth lay in God, as well as its spiritual quest for nonviolence. Tolstoy stressed the five commandments of Christ in his Sermon on the Mount and, in particular, the commandment 'Resist not him that is evil.'

Tolstoy's literal interpretation of Jesus's commandment to 'turn the other cheek', became the basis for his questioning of social, political and religious assumptions. Tolstoy's condemnation of states was centred on the violent means by which they enforce their authority. In analyzing the state, he identified four forms of violence used by states: intimidation, corruption, hypnotism and coercion by force of arms. In addition, he observed a total absence of love in state law, such as the principle of 'an eye for and eye' instead of 'turning the other cheek'. He criticized the Russian Orthodox Church, condemning it for adopting self-serving practices; he was appalled by its use of religious arguments to promote and justify state violence. People acting according to their conscience, rather than any worldly influence, he believed, would obtain truth and happiness – the precondition of realizing the Kingdom of God on earth.

Thus, Tolstoy's approach to nonviolence leads him to the rejection of violence and the idea of resistance that is respectful of the autonomy of others. He presents his philosophy of nonviolence as an alternative to both authoritarianism and liberalism. It was his argument that every action of nonviolent resistance was a way of spreading the message of love. Responding to violence with nonviolence would permeate people's consciences and become a principle that they would adopt.

Socratic nonviolence

An influential ancient Greek philosopher, Socrates was sentenced to death by the Athenian democracy for teaching his students to question authority and think for themselves (see Profile 4.1). Whether Socrates was guilty of corrupting the youth of Athens, as charged, is a question best left to history. But it is beyond doubt that Socrates holds a high place in the historical discussion of nonviolence and civil disobedience. For Socrates, justice lies ultimately not in any set of rules, however philosophically or politically framed, but in knowledge, which is essential to human excellence. Socrates is presented in Plato's dialogues as someone whose mission is not simply to contradict people, but also to get them to examine virtue. In Plato's *Apology*, Socrates maintains that he is wrongly accused of corrupting youth:

> I go about doing nothing but persuading you, young and old, to care not for body or money in place of, or so much as, excellence of soul. I tell you that virtue does not come from money, but money and all other human goods both public and private from virtue. If in saying this I corrupt the youth, that would be harm indeed. (Eliot 1980, p. 51)

Socrates is suggesting more than that he is not guilty of corrupting Athenian youth; he is suggesting that living as a citizen in Athens carries an obligation to be virtuous and to maintain fidelity to the city and its citizens. Moreover, Socrates says that, by persuading others to have a virtuous life, he is inviting them to avoid hubris through self-examination. By affirming that 'the unexamined life is not for man worth living', Socrates refuses to reduce ethics to expediency, aiming to reform the conscience of Athenians. Socrates has the power to confront the social and political institutions of his time by practising nonviolence as a premise of living as a citizen – for him, it offers the best prospect for a virtuous life.

We are sometimes told by the commentators of Plato that Socrates was a man full of paradoxes; but he pays the ultimate price for being nonviolent, as, indeed, he must – for how could Socrates engage in philosophical enquiry and debate in Athens, based on the ethical nature of his citizenship, if he tried to evade Athenian laws? The same ethics of citizenship lie behind his disobedience. Socrates's nonviolent action, then, consisted in practising philosophy and pursuing justice. Socrates argues in *Crito* that one ought never to use force against the law, or any legal obligation. He says: 'It is not holy to use force against a mother or father; and it is far more unholy to use force against your Country than against them' (Plato 1980, p. 124). Yet in *Apology*, Socrates insists that he obeys higher laws given to him by a divine voice. The truth of the

Profile 4.1 **Socrates**

Socrates (469 BC to 399 BC) was a classical Greek philosopher born in Athens. His thought was transmitted to later generations through the writings of his students Plato and Xenophon, and the plays of Aristophanes. Through his portrayal in Plato's dialogues, Socrates has become known as a master of the dialectic method of enquiry through which he invited his interlocutors to examine rationally key philosophical and political concepts such as the Good, the Beautiful and Justice. The Socratic method consisted in asking a series of questions surrounding a central concept and in making the opponents contradict themselves. Plato famously portrayed Socrates as a public philosopher questioning his fellow citizens, showing that his interlocutor's thesis was false and that the contrary was true. Explaining his mission as a philosopher, Socrates proclaimed that his goal was to help individuals to achieve genuine self-knowledge. Socrates was accused of corrupting Athenian youth and teaching new gods. The trial of Socrates took place in 399 BC. He stood before a jury of 500 Athenians. After listening to both Socrates and his accusers, the jury found him guilty by a vote of 280 to 220. Athenian law prescribed death by drinking a cup of poison. According to Plato's dialogue, entitled *Crito*, Socrates was asked by his students and followers to escape prison. Socrates considered that it was not morally right to pay off the guards and escape the city of Athens. According to him, to disobey the laws of Athens and the city of Athens would harm the citizens of Athens. Plato's picture of Socrates as a philosopher willing to face death rather than abandoning his commitment to truth and justice portrays him as a model for all future philosophers. Socrates's death was depicted in Plato's dialogue 'Phaedo'. After drinking the poison, Socrates walked till his legs felt heavy. Then the poison gradually travelled to his heart and he died. It is said that, before dying, he turned to Crito and said: 'Crito, we owe a cock to Asclepius. Please, don't forget to pay the debt.'

matter is that he presents his argument against the charge that he rejects the gods of Athens. Actually, Socrates's disobedience in the face of the legal authority of Athens is focused on challenges to his philosophical teaching, rather than the existence of gods:

> If you should say to me, 'Socrates, we will not now be persuaded by Anytus, but will let you go on this condition: you will not any longer spend your time in this investigation or philosophizing, and if you are found doing this again you shall be put to death.' If you should let me go on this condition, I should tell you, 'Men of Athens, I hold you in high regard and I love you, but I will obey the god more than you, and just as long as I breathe and am able, I will never cease from philosophizing or from exhorting you and from declaring my views to any of you I should ever happen upon.' (Brickhouse and Smith 2002, p. 235)

For Socrates, disobeying 'men of Athens' is a morally appropriate action though it is not a lawful position according to the Athenian city-state. At this point, one might concede that Socrates's understanding of the ethical nature of his action is a clear commitment to civil disobedience. Perhaps even more remarkable than this is the fact that Socrates argues repeatedly in *Crito* in favour of nonviolence and not doing evil in return for evil. 'Therefore,' says Socrates, 'we should neither retaliate nor treat anyone evilly, no matter what we have suffered from them' (*ibid.*, p. 72). Thus, Socrates's commitment to philosophy is consistent with his acknowledgment of the general principles of nonviolence. This explains why, 'Socrates rejected the notion that he might believe one thing and act otherwise, and claimed that his inner voice, his *daimonion*, consistently prevented him from acting wrongly' (Morrison 2011, p. 157). Socrates's inner 'voice' of guidance – that of self-examination and coming to know one's true self – helps him to face his accusers, revealing the falsity and violence of their beliefs and the events under scrutiny. This way of understanding Socratic nonviolence helps us to grasp another issue – that it is not enough to have knowledge (*episteme*), but rather one needs a knowledge that encompasses a capacity for justice and nonviolence. That is why Socrates famously claims in *Apology* to be engaged in a life of constant enquiry, and recommends that everyone should focus primarily on self-knowledge. One should see Socratic nonviolence, therefore, as challenging unexamined politics, making one's chief duty to improve political life in terms of morality leading to nonviolence, tying Socrates's philosophy to a transcendentalist conception of the higher laws on which he claims it rests.

The originality of Socrates's nonviolence lies in its aim to establish moral obedience to the higher laws that serve to speak the truth to the unjust and to persuade political authorities to change unjust laws:

> Just as certain enormously influential social reformers such Gandhi and Martin Luther King and their followers regarded nonviolent disobedience of the law as a way, indeed, the best way, to call attention to certain social injustices that afflicted their respective societies, so Socrates (through the Laws) is actually advocating disobedience of any law the citizen believes to be unjust. (Brickhouse and Smith 2002, p. 227)

Socrates may not have seen himself as a 'nonviolent resister' when he was facing his jurors, but history views him as a conscientious objector. Socrates appears in the *Apology* and the *Crito* to endorse an alternative view of moral obligation as a duty that could override the commands of civil authority in Athens. Though Socrates believed that he owed allegiance to the laws of Athens, his own conception of just laws and citizen's duty persuaded him to practise nonviolent disobedience, challenging the laws with philosophical rhetoric aimed at experimenting with truth and exercising the excellence of the soul. Socrates's famous trial demonstrates that there is no justice without law and that there is no law without justice. For Socrates, the path of nonviolence is clear – his conviction led to his death. He was condemned by Athens but not by history.

The transcendentalist nonviolence of H. D. Thoreau

Socrates believed that a human being is essentially a moral being and the criterion of wrongfulness lies ultimately not in the idea of justice but in the set of unjust laws. Thoreau (see Profile 4.2) starts his essay on *Civil Disobedience* with basically the same premise. Thoreau (1960 edn, p. 235) opens his essay with the motto 'That government is best which governs least', and continues by saying 'That government is best which governs not at all.' As such, Thoreau

views government as a fundamental hindrance to the creative enter-
prise of the individual:

> The essence of Thoreau's message in all his writings is the same:
> the necessity for individual self-realization. He calls upon each
> member of his audience to obey the fundamental laws of his or
> her own being, without regard for neighbours, nation, church or
> custom. (Howe, 1990, p. 21)

Thoreau was the ultimate conscientious objector. He believed that
the right to resist the government was a moral duty. However:

> Thoreau's argument contains some safeguards against anarchy.
> First of all, only important issues should be pursued this way –
> what he calls mere 'friction' in the machinery of government is
> not worth worrying about. To resist government over trivial
> matters would violate Thoreau's cardinal rule of life: 'simplify'.
> Second, either the example of resistance provokes others to
> imitate it or it does not. If it does not, then the government can
> easily deal with an isolated eccentric. But if it does, that indicates
> that the laws really may violate common moral principles and
> need changing. (*Ibid.*, p. 15)

It would therefore be wrong to identify Thoreau with either the anarchist tradition or the tradition of classical republicanism. The political
tradition most relevant to Thoreau was Christian, though he was also
very much influenced by Hinduism and some Muslim mystics. Thoreau
was an admirer of Vedic thought. Thoreau seized on the Laws of Manu
and the *Bhagavad Gita* as great spiritual texts. In his *Journal*, he wrote:

> That title, 'The Laws of Manu with the Gloss of Culluca', comes
> to me with such a volume of sound as if it had swept unob-
> structed over the plains of Hindostan; and when my eye rests on
> yonder birches, or the sun in the water, or the shadows of the
> trees, it seems to signify the laws of them all. They are the laws
> of you and me, a fragrance wafted down from those old times,
> and no more to be refuted than the wind. (*The Journal of Henry
> David Thoreau*, 1954 edn, p. 309)

The careful reader of the *Journal* becomes aware that, after the two
years spent at Walden Pond, Thoreau became more conscious about

Indian values of nonviolence and respect of nature. This interest in nature indicated that, for Thoreau, friendship with nature lay outside organized society. That is the reason why, 'the journey down the Merrimack begins as a rejection of society and as a spiritual pilgrimage. The pastoral life which Thoreau thought he saw in the woods offered a utopian alternative that renewed a sense of the social in him' (Abbott 1985, p. 188). It is characteristic of Thoreau that he was able to turn his affinity with nature into increasing attentiveness to social and political details:

> Thus, Thoreau's attitude toward government was compounded of a prevailing detachment from participation in its functionings, and, underlying this, an attachment to principles he believed it should guarantee. Non-attachment was not present in his attitude, however, since Thoreau believed that either the individual must conform to or oppose specific governmental policies. He appears to have been insensible to the feasibility of a person's actively engaging in governmental affairs without attachment to them. (Nagley 1954, p. 319)

As he strove for nonviolence in his life, he strove for nonviolence in politics. The search for nonviolence was a primary focus in Thoreau's life. It is impossible to read any of his writings at any length without becoming aware of that fact. If Thoreau was a friend to nature, he was a critical and committed political critic. As a result, 'Thoreau demanded the most severe moral commitment in the political sphere, a commitment that he knew his fellow citizens could not make' (Abbott 1985, p. 207). In this sense, for Thoreau, civil disobedience went beyond his private conscientious refusal to pay the poll tax in Concord to become a statement against utilitarian ethics as the foundation of American institutions of government. The message of Thoreau's great essay is ethical rather than political and, as such, it is congruent with the essence of his writings on nature:

> Like his contemporaries Carlyle and Marx, Thoreau was concerned about the problem of alienation in modern life ... 'Resistance to Civil Government' is about the problem of political alienation that exists even in democracy. The citizens can vote, but they still feel powerless, and tend to become passive and apathetic. Concerned as he was with the issues of slavery and the

Profile 4.2 **Henry David Thoreau**

Henry David Thoreau (12 July 1817 to 6 May 1862) was an American philosopher and abolitionist. He was born in Concord, Massachusetts, with older siblings John and Helen and a younger sister Sophia. His father owned a pencil factory. He studied at Harvard University between 1833 and 1837. In 1835 he took leave of absence from Harvard, during which he taught in a school at Canton, Massachusetts. After he graduated in 1837, he joined the faculty of the Concord public school, but resigned after a few weeks. He started a friendship with Ralph Waldo Emerson, through whom he became acquainted with Transcendentalism, a philosophy that emphasized the importance of spiritual matters. Emerson invited Thoreau to write for a quarterly periodical, *The Dial*. From 1841–4, Thoreau served as the children's tutor, editorial assistant and gardener at Emerson's house. In 1845, Thoreau built a small cabin for himself on property owned by Emerson at Walden Pond. He spent more than two years there and concentrated on simple living. Thoreau worked on *A Week on the Concord and Merrimack Rivers* (1849). The book drew from a boating trip he took with his brother John in 1839. On 25 July 1846, Thoreau refused to pay his tax because of his opposition to the Mexican–American War and slavery, and he spent a night in jail. In February 1848, he delivered lectures on 'The Rights and Duties of the Individual in Relation to Government'. 'The only obligation which I have a right to assume is to do at any time what I think right,' he wrote. He later revised and published it under the title *Resistance to Civil Government*. Thoreau continued to support abolitionism and, in 1854, he wrote an essay entitled 'Slavery in Massachusetts'. He took a stand for Captain John Brown, who led an uprising against slavery in Virginia. In 1859, Thoreau became ill with bronchitis. He finally succumbed to the disease on 6 May 1862. He was buried in the Dunbar family plot, but he was eventually moved to Sleepy Hollow Cemetery in Concord, Massachusetts.

Mexican War, Thoreau also felt that he had a more general point to make, and this must be why he thought it worthwhile to publish his essay even after the war was over, and he was (perhaps) resuming payment of his poll tax. Thoreau wanted to awaken his audience to a sense of direct involvement in public affairs – through the participatory democracy of a town meeting such as he often addressed or if necessary by defying the law. (Howe 1990, p. 31)

To recapitulate briefly, Thoreau did not advocate that we abandon politics. He simply suggested what Gandhi later called 'the spiritualization of politics' – the essence of Thoreau's experiment in his two famous essays *Walden* and *On Civil Disobedience*. Explaining in *Walden* why he went to the pond to live, he writes:

I went to the woods because I wished to live deliberately, to front only the essential facts of life, and see if I could not learn what it had to teach, and not, when I came to die, discover that I had not lived. I did not wish to live what was not life, living is so dear; nor did I wish to practise resignation, unless it was quite necessary. I wanted to live deep and suck out all the marrow of life, to live so sturdily and Spartan-like as to put to rout all that was not life, to cut a broad swath and shave close, to drive life into a corner, and reduce it to its lowest terms, and, if it proved to be mean, why then to get the whole and genuine meanness of it, and publish its meanness to the world; or if it were sublime, to know it by experience, and be able to give a true account of it in my next excursion. For most men, it appears to me, are in a strange un-certainty about it, whether it is of the devil or of God, and have somewhat hastily concluded that it is the chief end of man here to 'glorify God and enjoy him forever'. (1960 edn, pp. 62–3)

This paragraph illustrates the Romantic idealism of Thoreau, but it also stresses his proximity to nature as representing a search for some higher principles that we also find in his essay on *Civil Disobedience*. In fact, we might go so far as to say that Thoreau comes closest to other spiritual thinkers of nonviolence not because he glorifies God, but because he thinks that the free man should be lord of himself and the brother of other human beings. Thus writes Thoreau in his essay on *Civil Disobedience*: 'I do not wish to quarrel with any man or nation. I do not wish to split hairs, to make distinctions, or set myself up as better than my neighbors' (1960 edn, p. 253). It is apparent, in view of this last statement, that Henry David Thoreau clearly pursued a life of principles aimed at minimizing violence within society. Thoreau's moral insights and his Romantic responsiveness to nature's beauty can disguise his quest for nonviolence, based on a higher principle of a moral revolution primarily achieved through the exercise of an active conscience. As such, Thoreau explains, 'the individual conscience could and must be empowered to act, and not only for the individual himself, but also upon the body politic' (Howe 1990, p. 25). Thoreau believes a right to conscientious objection exists whenever the government acts immorally. Thoreau endorsed John Brown's anti-slavery rebellion in an essay on him in 1859:

> There, he took the position that slavery was large-scale institutionalized immoral violence, which could legitimately be resisted by violence, on the basis of either self-defence or altruistic principle. John Brown, about to be executed for leading an unsuccessful military raid to free the slaves, typified for Thoreau the heroism of the conscientious man. Thoreau celebrated Brown as Carlyle had celebrated Cromwell. He praised Brown as a reincarnation of the courageous spirit of Cromwell, one who rose above the trivialities of ordinary existence to act out of principle, one who by his martyrdom hastened the ultimate triumph of justice. (*Ibid.*, p. 29)

Thoreau's idea of civil resistance points, at the same time, to the right to resist an immoral political power and the duty to disobey immoral commands. He aspired to a government that fostered and encouraged moral freedom. 'I please myself with imagining a State at last which can afford to be just to all men, and to treat the individual with respect as a neighbor,' wrote Thoreau. But he continues: ' A State which bore this kind of fruit, and suffered it to drop off as fast as it ripened, would prepare the way for a still more prefect and glorious State, which I have imagined, but not yet ever seen' (Thoreau 1960 edn, p. 147).

There is no evidence that Thoreau ever declared in favour of a violent resistance against government. In fact, quite in contrast with the popular idea of Thoreau as a man who hated political constructions, he affirms his preference for nonviolent empowerment of civic consciousness against the tyranny of majority. Unlike most intellectuals of his time in America, Thoreau wanted to awaken his fellow citizens to a sense of nonviolent resistance against immoral authority and unjust laws of the state. One final word must be added on Thoreau's nonviolence: Thoreau was a nonviolent social critic, primarily concerned with the evil influence of organized religion and centralized government against individual freedom.

Leo Tolstoy and nonviolence

Only recently is Leo Tolstoy gaining recognition as an important thinker in terms of civil disobedience and nonviolence who exerted a powerful influence on Gandhi and Martin Luther King. Many still consider Tolstoy (see Profile 4.3) only as a great Russian novelist, not being aware of his nonviolent message to mankind; few social reformers have as much claim as Tolstoy to be considered as messengers of universal love and spiritual brotherhood. A proponent of nonviolent resistance at the dawn of a violent century, Tolstoy questioned the very essence of religious and political organizations in the Russian society of his time. 'Far from being a shallow rationalist unable to comprehend the real essence of religion (as Shestov and others have suggested) Tolstoy was a man for whom a religious comprehension of life as a whole was an absolute necessity' (Greenwood 1975, p. 147). For Tolstoy, religion was not a matter of dogma but a spiritual quest of nonviolence. He underwent a spiritual crisis at the age of 50 which is told in his *Confession* (written in the years 1879–80 and banned at the time in Russia). In this book, Tolstoy asks himself the reason for everything he does and can find no answer except that life is meaningless. Upon further consideration, however, he is guided to an illumination that initially supplies him with a meaning for life – that is, union with God. Tolstoy concludes his *Confession* with the idea that the truth of religion is the search for God. About the same time, he wrote the following in his diary:

> There are light people, winged, who rise easily from among the crowd and again descend: good idealists. There are powerfully winged ones who, drawn by carnal desires, descend among the crowd and break their wings. Such am I. Then they struggle with

broken wings, flutter desperately, and fall. If my wings heal I will fly high. God grant it. There are those who have heavenly wings, and purposely – out of love for all mankind – descend to earth (folding their wings) and teach men to fly. When they are needed no more, they fly away: Christ. (Simmons 1973, p. 106)

Tolstoy was led to the conviction that the teachings of Jesus contain the truth. He especially emphasized on the five commandments of Christ in his Sermon on the Mount and, in particular, on the commandment 'Resist not him that is evil'. For Tolstoy, this commandment was the fundamental reason for adopting nonresistance, abstaining from violence and loving one's enemy. Tolstoy's literal interpretation of Jesus's commandment to 'turn the other cheek' led to his questioning erstwhile social, political and religious assumptions, including the authority of the state, the credibility of the Church and the justifications of both for using violence. Yet, it also led to his broader understanding of the meaning of violence, to include not only direct violence but also the inequitable distribution of authority, power and wealth, the application of human law and punishment, and the use of hypocrisy and deception to 'hypnotize' others to ignore their conscience. In short, he defined violence against others as the disregard for the 'golden rule' ('Do unto others as you would have them do unto you'), the adherence to which centres on understanding and living the truth of love given by God. Tolstoy heavily criticized governments for the violent means through which they enforced their authority. According to him:

> All state obligations, payment of taxes, fulfilment of state duties, and submission to punishments, exile, fines, etc., to which people appear to submit voluntarily, are always based on bodily violence or the threat of it. The basis of authority is bodily violence. (1894, p. 94)

He identified four forms of violence used by states: intimidation, corruption (in the form of taxing the population and using such funds to satisfy the greed of officials), hypnotism (in the form of controlling the moral development of citizens in line with the interests of the state and through the use of patriotic and religious superstitions) and coercion by force of arms (particularly forced conscription into a national army). He argued that all four forms of violence, which are also forms of slavery, combine in a cyclical process that reinforces the authority of the state and the slavery of the masses. He opposed wars and state preparations for them, and was heavily critical of conscription, which he viewed as an extreme abuse of power and form of slavery. For him, compulsory military service destroyed social life, particularly the scope for mutual cooperation towards collective welfare. He also heavily objected to attempts by the state to deceive citizens into obeying government instructions before those of God – into behaving in ways that are inconsistent with one's conscience – a conscience that follows the Christian law of the brotherhood of men: 'the whole power of the army and the state is based in reality on this delusive emancipation of men from their duty to God and their conscience, and the substitution of duty to their superior officer for all other duties' (*ibid.*, p. 167). Tolstoy worried that, even though they are morally responsible for their own actions, people, including self-professed Christians, have grown so accustomed to this inconsistency between their God-directed conscience and their actions that they blindly accept and do not question governments' use of violence, nor the complicity in it. Tolstoy also opposed the absence of love in state law. He believed that where legislative institutions should apply the principle of 'turning the other cheek', they instead apply the doctrine of 'an eye for an eye':

> Christ says, 'Do not resist evil.' The purpose of the courts is to resist evil. Christ prescribes doing good in return for evil. The courts retaliate evil with evil. Christ says, 'Make no distinction between the good and the bad.' All the courts do is to make this distinction. Christ says, 'Forgive all men; forgive, not once, not seven times, but without end; love your enemies, do good to those who hate you.' The courts do not forgive, but punish; they do not do good, but evil, to those whom they call enemies of society. Thus it turns out, according to the meaning, that Christ must have rejected the courts. (Tolstoy, 1904, p. 22)

Tolstoy (1894) was also very critical of the Russian Orthodox Church. He was of the opinion that rather than believing Jesus's teachings, people had come to believe in what the Church ordered them to believe. As a result, he pointed out that the Epistles do not contain any mention of a Church with its sacraments, miracles and infallibility (*ibid.*, p. 51). He accused the Church of adopting self-serving prac-

Profile 4.3 **Lev Nikolayevich Tolstoy**

Lev Nikolayevich Tolstoy (28 August 1828 to 20 November 1910) was a Russian writer and political thinker. Tolstoy was born in Yasnaya Polyana, the family estate in the region of Tula, Russia. Tolstoy received his primary education at the hands of French and German tutors. In 1843, he enrolled in an oriental languages programme at the University of Kazan, but excessive partying meant he left without a degree. He was convinced by his brother Nikolay to join the army as a Junker. He was transferred to Sebastopol in Ukraine in November 1854, where he fought in the Crimean War through August 1855. During this period, he worked on an autobiographical story called *Childhood*. After completing this book, Tolstoy started writing about his day-to-day life at the army outpost in the Caucasus. *The Cossacks* was completed in 1862. After the war ended, Tolstoy left the army and returned to Moscow, where he married Sofya Andreyevna Bers. He travelled to Paris, where he met Victor Hugo and was deeply influenced by the political and literary currents of his time. Full of enthusiasm, Tolstoy returned to Yasnaya Polyanna and founded several schools for his serfs' children. He began his masterpiece, *War and Peace*, a historical account of the Napoleonic wars, combined with the lives of fictional characters. Following its success, in 1873, Tolstoy started working on the second of his best-known novels, *Anna Karenina*, the tragedy of a married aristocrat and her affair with the affluent Count Vronsky; in a parallel story-line, Konstantin Levin, a country landowner, desires to marry Kitty. According to the literary critics, Levin is a semi-autobiographical portrayal of Tolstoy himself. Despite his success as a literary writer, Tolstoy suffered a spiritual crisis and grew depressed. In addition to his fiction, Tolstoy continued to write political and spiritual pamphlets. One of his most successful later works was the novella *The Death of Ivan Ilyich*, written in 1886. During the last 30 years of his life, Tolstoy established himself as a nonviolent moral and religious leader. His ideas about nonviolent resistance to evil influenced Gandhi, with whom he had a short correspondence. In 1910, Tolstoy's spiritual beliefs created tensions in his home life. Anxious to escape his wife, Tolstoy embarked on a pilgrimage. Unfortunately, old and ailing, Tolstoy died in a train station in Astapovo, Russia. He was buried at his family estate in Tula.

tices, such as obscuring the true meaning of the teachings of Jesus in order to reinforce the need among laymen for the Church. And he criticized its use of incorrect religious arguments to justify the use of, particularly state, violence (*ibid.*, p. 47) For Tolstoy, the only authority was that of God; therefore, he rejected the self-serving methods of the Church. For him:

> The churches as churches, as bodies which assert their own infallibility, are institutions opposed to Christianity. There is not only nothing in common between the churches as such and Christianity, except the name, but they represent two principles fundamentally opposed and antagonistic to one another. One represents pride, violence, self-assertion, stagnation, and death; the other, meekness, penitence, humility, progress, and life. (*Ibid.*, p. 43)

Unsurprisingly, Tolstoy's adoption of the nonviolent teachings of Christ led him away from and into conflict with the very principle of the modern state. Tolstoy believed that the modern state was violent, unjust and un-Christian, but he also argued that it could not be stopped through the use of force. From a practical perspective, any revolution to overturn a government, he argued, only resulted in further and subsequent violence at the hands of the new authority. 'Every conflict', he affirmed, 'only strengthens the means of oppression in the hands of those who happen at a given moment to be in power' (*ibid.*, p. 109). Resistance, he explained, was futile. However, more importantly, from a religious perspective he explained that Jesus's teaching prohibits resistance to state evils by force. It also provides a new way of life and a paradigm for ending conflict between all people:

> not by making it the duty of one section only of mankind to submit without conflict to what is prescribed to them by certain authorities, but by making it the duty of all – and consequently of those in authority – not to resort to force against anyone in any circumstances. (*Ibid.*, p. 105)

He called for nonresistance and nonviolence, but he also encouraged activities of noncompliance. In 'The Kingdom of God is Within You', he argued that the Epistles forbid the taking of oaths; thus, he suggested that readers should not take an oath or pledge allegiance to the state. He suggested not paying taxes that are subsequently used to fund un-Christian actions, such as war and imprisonment. He argued against carrying passports, as they are recognition of one's dependence on a state, which exists by means of force. He was against joining the police because it is un-Christian to 'put any man in fetters, lock him up, or drag him from place to place' (*ibid.*, p. 124). Likewise, he encouraged non-participation in juries because doing so would condone a law of vengeance rather than the Christian law of forgiveness and love. Similarly, he supported the avoidance of entering military service because to do so is to be complicit in violence. He underlined this by saying:

> Governments assert that armies are needed above all for external defence, but that is not true. They are needed principally against their subjects, and every man, under universal military service, becomes an accomplice in all the acts of violence of the government against the citizens without any choice of his own. (*Ibid.*, p. 99)

He explained that while a government can punish those who attempt to, or actually, use violence against it, or can incentivize people to use violence on its behalf (e.g., by working in the army or the police), it cannot force citizens to undertake actions, such as participating in government, that are against their conscience. He argued that if a government punished people for following their conscience, it could not then claim to be good and benevolent. For him, the whole power of government rests on these obligations, so states are rendered helpless when confronted with a strong spiritual conviction against the use of violence. Tolstoy emphasized the need to give up the 'social theory of life', which is intrinsically violent and based on the authority of social groups, and instead move towards the 'divine theory of life', which is based on the love, authority and truth of God, suggesting that the transition from the social to the divine life would not be a passive event but would require considerable effort on the part of humanity. Tolstoy explained that, rather than using force, which would merely result in greater opposition, this change would occur through a modification in public opinion based on the growing prevalence among people of the Christian virtues of patience, meekness, endurance, purity, brotherhood and love. Such virtues would be reflected in the growing use of nonresistance and nonviolence. In this way, people could strive to attain truth and happiness by behaving according to their conscience rather than any corrupt, worldly influence, and would ultimately experience the realization of the Kingdom of God on earth:

> Tolstoy's approach is clearly one in which Christianity is to be lived rather than believed, but the Christian life he promotes is hardly one of abundance. For Tolstoy rejects what many see as the good things of life: the pleasurable, the beautiful, the creative. The good is to be found in this life, but it is to be found in giving up all the apparent goods of this world. There is only this life on Earth, but it is to be lived in a way that shows that no importance whatsoever is attached to the things of this world. Not only does Tolstoy attribute no significance to earthly goods, but the spiritual life, to which alone all meaning and value is ascribed, is a stark one. It is a life of poverty, chastity and nonviolence that, however brief, impoverished, and violent, is its own reward. (McKeogh 2009, p. 73)

Tolstoy's approach to nonviolence seems to him a simple and straightforward one, which leads him to a rejection of violence and an idea of resistance which respects the autonomy of the 'other'. He presents his nonviolence as an alternative to both authoritarianism and liberalism. For Tolstoy, a nonviolent society is a harmonious community where the ethical questions replace the political ones, because Christian love and forgiveness will reign. According to him:

> Christians can never rule, subjugate others, and do violence to them, Christians will humble themselves, love their enemies, forgive offenses, and not resist evil with force. Therefore, they cannot take part in any government activity, hold any public office, serve as witness or on a jury in a court case, voluntarily pay taxes, accept any government money, make use of any government institution or service that is supported by taxes collected under threat of violence, or appeal to government force for the protection of one's person or possessions. These to Tolstoy, are the political implications of Christ's command to resist not evil. (*Ibid.*, p. 139)

Central to Tolstoy's argument is that every action is an opportunity to spread the message of love and nonviolence to others and that, by responding to violence in a nonviolent manner, such a philosophy will permeate people's consciences and become the principle that they adopt. Tolstoy argued that, from a moral perspective, it is never certain that any attempt to prevent a potentially violent future act will be morally better and less violent than allowing that possible action to happen. Therefore, pre-empting violence with violence is unacceptable. Furthermore, Tolstoy argues that all of God's teachings are absolute but possible to perform and that their fulfilment will ultimately result in greater brotherhood, unity and love in the world. Despite apparent weaknesses in his Christian nonviolence, Tolstoy's philosophy of nonresistance to evil and the need to love one's enemy have had a major impact on the nonviolent resistant movement to this day. For example, following correspondence with Tolstoy and after reading his book, *The Kingdom of God is Within You*, Mohandas Gandhi applied his concept of 'satyagraha' in pursuit of independence through nonviolent political and social reform in colonial India. Likewise, Martin Luther King, Jr adapted Tolstoy's nonresistance to evil, with its religious justifications, during the civil rights movement in the 1960s in America. Since Tolstoy's death in 1910, the relevance of his Christian nonviolence seems to have been obscured in a world in which prophetic imagination has no place. Nevertheless, certain features of Tolstoy's nonviolence are still alive through the relevance of Gandhian doctrine in India and around the world.

Further reading

Alton, C. (2010) 'Tolstoy's Guiding Light', *History Today*. An in-depth study of Tolstoy's spiritual thoughts.

Brock, P. (1992) *A Brief History of Pacifism From Jesus to Tolstoy*. An illuminating exploration on the philosophical and historical roots of war resistance.

Martin, R. (1970) 'Socrates on Disobedience to Law', *Review of Metaphysics*. An original study on one of the most influential thinkers in the history of the West and his view on law and nonviolent disobedience.

Myerson, J. (ed.) (1995) *The Cambridge Companion to Henry David Thoreau*. A valuable resource for understanding Thoreau's mind, offering new insights into his brief but original life.

Richardson, R. D. (1986) *Henry Thoreau: A Life of the Mind*. A study which casts new light on Thoreau's life and his thoughts through a re-examination of Thoreau's writings.

Taylor, C. C. W. (2001) *Socrates: A Very Short Introduction*. An introduction to the engaging life of Socrates, both as a historical figure and as a character in Plato's dialogues.

Chapter 5

Gandhi and Nonviolence

Mahatma Gandhi continues to inspire many with his practical ideal of nonviolence. Although India has produced many gurus, Gandhi was the only spiritual figure who has able to merge spirituality and politics together to covert politics from a subjugation of power into a pursuit of truth and nonviolence. Gandhi admitted that his philosophy of nonviolence was not unique, since it was proclaimed in ancient scriptures. His conception of nonviolence was that it was a unifying force of loving and caring that connects humans among themselves and with nature, a means of seeking the sacredness of life: truth.

By 1909, Gandhi had picked up where Tolstoy, Thoreau and Ruskin had left off in offering a moral critique of modern civilization. In arguing for the unity of ethics and politics, Gandhi insisted on the balance of means and ends, unlike the conventional dictum of politics, 'the ends justify the means'. It was these principles that Gandhi applied to his struggles to undermine the moral, cultural and political authority of the British Empire.

In his famous work *Hind Swaraj*, Gandhi called for the moral rejuvenation of Indian politics through the method of satyagraha. The word is based on two of Gandhi's guiding principles satya (truth), which implies love, and *agraha* (firmness). Together these words are supposed to serve as a synonym for force. Prior to arriving in India to challenge imperial British authority, Gandhi's South African experience with satyagraha perfected his guiding principles of truth and nonviolence, expressing the conquest of hatred by love. Therefore, practising nonviolence contained the universal ethical imperative of active love of others. This pluralist understanding of nonviolence had important consequences for his project of spiritualizing politics. However, Gandhi was not so innocent to think that political victory through nonviolence could come about easily. He was well aware that its dynamic could only be fully realized with radical social and political changes.

As much as nonviolence was conceptualized spiritually, it did not imply an ascetic way of life, but rather, a moral strategy with social implications. In preaching nonviolence, Gandhi suggested to Indians, and later to the world, that it represented an active struggle for freedom and human dignity. The three pillars of Gandhian nonviolence – swaraj, satyagraha and swadeshi – were conceived as practical methods of political struggle against injustices in an effort to bring about freedom and socio-political changes. The concept of swaraj not only related to the terms 'freedom' and 'independence', but also to a form of deliberative democracy intrinsic in the consent of the people. Satyagraha, then, implies a technique of fighting earthly and political evils and is deeply rooted in the law of love, self-sacrifice and self-suffering. And, finally, the term 'swadeshi' was considered by Gandhi to represent as self-discipline and capacity of service. Therefore, Gandhian nonviolence meant not only liberation of the masses from authoritarianism, but also a strategy of constructive work based on pure moral authority.

Gandhian democracy stressed the importance of an active democracy, where citizens would be enlightened, disciplined and self-reliant. Far too often, he noted, democracy was plagued by disempowered and passive citizens. Under Gandhian democracy, individual liberty of opinion and action was as important as minority freedoms. Hoping for a decentralized democracy, he believed that, eventually, political representatives would not be necessary because life would become so perfect as to be self-controlled. This, he argued, would be a state of enlightened anarchy, where everyone would conduct himself or herself in such a manner that their behaviour would not adversely affect their neighbours.

Gandhi's decentralized government aimed to serve as means of resisting bureaucratic procedures and institutions that create a wall between the people and their government. As a model, Gandhi favoured a system based on the panchayat raj (village republic), where citizens would be empowered to make decisions at the local level. Gandhi built his campaigns on behalf of the untouchables in Indian society on this model. He considered the concept of untouchability to be the ultimate example of sin against God; his social actions were aimed at altering the consciences of higher castes by proclaiming no distinction on the grounds of caste in his personal life.

Gandhi's technique of nonviolent social and political change is a systematic combination of resistance and reconstruction. This is why he speaks of nonviolence as the recognition of the irreducible present of others for self-transformation. He conceives nonviolence as denoting the self and society as two interdependent elements of the same dynamic process. Gandhi believed that with the principle of disinterested performance duty the world would not be able to exist. Rejecting the distinction between politics and ethics, and between economics and welfare of all, he hoped that moral values would rise above self-interest, believing that a decentralized economy could be based on values such as trusteeship, self-sufficiency and harmony. In this way, Gandhian nonviolence performs a dual role in combating injustice and awakening in others a sense of moral and spiritual self-development. Gandhi's main critique of modern civilization was that it disregarded moral values and promoted violence and self-interest. That is why Gandhian nonviolence turned out to be more than a departure from engagement in violence, but became the essence of democracy and social equity in India. For Gandhi, there could be no such thing as separation between spiritual and political development of nations; his vision was clear, to elaborate a doctrine of nonviolence that could span across time and space.

Gandhi's conception of nonviolence

In 1944, Albert Einstein, paying a tribute to Mahatma Gandhi, wrote:

> As a leader of his people, unsupported by any outward authority; a politician whose success rests not upon craft or mastery of technical devices, but simply on the convincing power of his personality; a victorious fighter who has always scorned the use of force; a man of wisdom and humility, who has devoted all his strength to the uplifting of his people ... a man who has confronted the brutality of Europe with the dignity of the simple human being, and has at all times risen superior. Generations to come, it may be, will scarcely believe that such a one as this ever in flesh and blood walked upon this earth. (Nanda 1995, pp. xvi–xvii)

About 70 years has elapsed since Einstein wrote these words and yet Mohandas K. Gandhi (see Profile 5.1) remains greater than ever as a 'great soul', Mahatma, who continues to inspire many around the world with his practical ideal of nonviolence. India produced many gurus, ascetics, saints and politicians in Gandhi's time. Yet, Gandhi was the only figure who brought spirituality to politics and converted politics from a conquest of power into a quest for truth and nonviolence. He summarized his philosophy in the following words: 'I have nothing new to teach the world. Truth and nonviolence are as old as the hills. All I have done is to try experiments in both on as vast a scale as I could do' (Gandhi 1936, cited in Nanda 1995, p. 113). Though Gandhi admitted that his philosophy of nonviolence was not original, since it was proclaimed in the scriptures of human civilization, he did not describe it in a metaphysical way, nor did he understand it as a religious truth. For him, nonviolence was an education against hatred, greed and lies. In other words, in Gandhi's philosophy of life nonviolence stands as a unifying force of loving and caring that interconnects humans among themselves and with nature. He saw it as as a means of struggling for the sacredness of life and seeking for truth. By drawing upon the central theme of the Vedas, Gandhi affirmed that truth is higher than all religions, frequently expressing his view of religion in terms of 'God is Truth'. He then 'went a step further and said that Truth is God. You will see the fine distinction between the two statements, viz., that God is Truth and Truth is God.' Gandhi's use of the terms 'God' and 'Truth' interchangeably was consistent with the *advaitin* – the essential unity of all existence. Yet, he repeatedly explains to his readers that, 'Nobody in this world possesses absolute truth. This is God's attribute alone. Relative truth is all we know. Therefore, we can only follow the truth as we see it.' According to Gandhi, human beings as spiritual beings can, at most, experiment with truth as a moral mode of action and, above all, as nonviolent compassion. Nonviolence was, therefore, in Gandhi's eyes, a practical situation that set as its goal the pursuit of truth.

Asserting the unity of ethics and politics, Gandhi insisted on the balance of means and ends. Unlike the conventional political motto that the ends justify the means, Gandhi believed that 'the means may be likened to a seed, the end to a tree; and there is just the same inviolable connection between the means and the ends as there is between the seed and the tree'. Contained in this idea is Gandhi's higher spiritual perspective, which provides the rationale for his nonviolent campaigns in South Africa and India. By 1909, Gandhi, echoing Tolstoy, Thoreau and Ruskin, was undermining the moral, cultural and political authority of the British Empire by formulating a moral critique of modern civilization.

Profile 5.1   **Mohandas Karamchand Gandhi**

Mohandas Karamchand Gandhi (2 October 1869 to 30 January 1948), also known as Mahatma (meaning 'great soul'), was the political and spiritual leader of the Indian Independence movement who masterminded nonviolent civil disobedience against British rule. Gandhi grew up in the town of Porbander, in Gujarat, going to school in nearby Rajkot. At 13 he was married to Kasturbai, and in 1888 set sail for England to study law. In London, Gandhi was introduced to British theosophists and vegetarians, and started studying the texts of the Christian and Hindu religious traditions. Despite being called to the bar in 1891, he returned to India, to a short, unsuccessful career in law in India. Gandhi decided to accept an offer from a Muslim Indian businessman in South Africa, where he was confronted with racism for the first time in his life. From this experience, Gandhi emerged as a political leader in search of truth and nonviolence. He coined the term 'satyagraha' to signify holding firmly to truth; his 1921autobiography was titled *The Story of My Experiments with Truth*. In 1909, on a trip back to India, Gandhi authored a short pamphlet entitled *Hind Swaraj* [*Indian Home Rule*], elaborating his critique of modern civilization. Gandhi returned to India in early 1915 and, after travelling widely around the country, started his nonviolent campaign of noncooperation against the British Raj, which led the great Indian poet, Rabindranath Tagoreto give him the title 'Mahatma'. Gandhi suspended his campaign of noncooperation in February 1922 when several Indian policemen were killed by a large crowd at Chauri Chaura, but was arrested and sentenced to six years' imprisonment. Subsequently, Gandhi worked to preserve Hindu–Muslim unity, launching a new resistance movement against British rule in 1931, organizing a 'salt' march to Dandi. He represented the Indian National Congress at the second Round Table Conference in London. On his return to India, he was arrested again. In 1942, Gandhi led the Quit India movement and was placed in confinement in the Aga Khan's Palace in Pune. On 15 August 1947, India gained independence, but Gandhi declined all political positions, focusing instead on improving relations between Hindus and Muslims after the partition of India. On 30 January 1948, Gandhi was shot at point blank range by a Hindu fanatic, Nathuram Godse. Before dying, Gandhi blessed his assassin: *He Ram! He Ram!*

Nonviolence in the Hind Swaraj

In his famous book, *Hind Swaraj*, Gandhi called for the moral regeneration of Indian politics through satyagraha, a name that he adopted early in his struggle against the repressive South African regime. Explaining his choice of the word 'satyagraha', Gandhi (1938b, p. 172) wrote: 'Truth [satya] implies love and firmness [agraha] and therefore serves as a synonym for force. I thus began to call the Indian movement satyagraha, that is to say, the force which is born of truth and love of nonviolence.' Gandhi's South African experience of satyagraha honed his two principles of truth and nonviolence and prepared him for far more challenging struggles in India. Identifying satyagraha as a courageous and active force, Gandhi affirmed:

> It is a most powerful expression of a soul's anguish and an eloquent protest against the continuance of an evil state. An out and out civil resister simply ignores the authority of the state – disregards immoral state law, refuses to pay taxes, disobey laws, but he never uses force and never resists force when it is used against him. He invites imprisonment because he finds the bodily freedom he seemingly enjoys, to be an intolerable burden. He argues to himself that a State allows personal freedom only in so far as the citizen submits to its regulations. It is the price paid for personal liberty. (Cited in Nanda 1995, p. 50)

Thus, Gandhi expressed the ethical core of his satyagraha movement in South Africa as the conquest of hatred by love and later, when he launched his mass noncooperation campaign in India against the extension of emergency powers in the 1919 Rowlatt Bill, he continued to emphasize the moral importance of his nonviolent strategy. 'There cannot be any trace of violence in my plans or in my thoughts, he said. 'A nonviolent person has a complete faith in God' (Gandhi, 1999, pp. 159–60). Emphasizing that nonviolence contained the universal ethical imperative of active love of the other, Gandhi's pluralist understanding of nonviolence had important ramifications for his project of spiritualization of politics. Of course, Gandhi was not so naive to think that victory through nonviolence would come about easily, being all too aware that the transformative dynamic of nonviolence went hand in hand with radical social and political changes. According to him,

'Nonviolence is not a cloistered virtue to be practiced by the individual for his peace and final salvation, but a rule of conduct for society if it is to live consistently with human dignity' (Iyer 1987, p. 237).

Gandhi defines nonviolence not as an ascetic way of life, but as a moral strategy with social implications. What Gandhi had in mind was to suggest to Indians, and later to the world, that nonviolence should be pursued as an active struggle for freedom and human dignity. He was convinced that nonviolent resistance was far superior to violent defence. Gandhi extended the traditional concept of ahimsa, as defined by Hinduism and Jainism and applied it to all fields of life, to cover moral and political values such as bread-labour, non-possession and a constructive programme. In fact, Gandhi believed that 'when nonviolence reigns, materialism takes a back seat, avenues are changes and in a nonviolent war there is no waste of efforts, property or moral fibre' (Dhawan 1990, p. 140). Therefore, the three principal offshoots of Gandhian nonviolence – that is, swaraj, satyagraha and swadeshi – cannot be confused with simple passive resistance or an ascetic attitude in life. All these Gandhian concepts are practised as methods of political struggle against injustice, attaining freedom and autonomy and bringing about social and political changes. As it has been mentioned, for Gandhi, satyagraha, as a technique of fighting political evil, was deeply rooted in the law of love, self-sacrifice and self-suffering. As for swaraj, it is defined by Gandhi as self-rule and self-restraint. However, considered it not only in terms of freedom and independence, but also as a form of deliberative democracy administered by consent of the people. Thus, from a political point of view, swaraj means self-government, not good government. According to Gandhi:

> Real swaraj will come not by the acquisition of authority by a few but by the acquisition of the capacity by all to resist authority when abused. In other words, swaraj is to be obtained by educating the masses to a sense of their capacity to regulate and control authority. (Dhawan 1990, p. 293)

But one must hasten to add, here, that Gandhi's idea of people's progress towards swaraj encompasses all spheres of life and is vitally connected with progressive self-realization and self-reliance of the individual and the society. Gandhi considered swadeshi as self-discipline and capacity for service. He believed that:

A man's first duty is to his neighbor. This does not imply hatred for the foreigner or partiality for the fellow countrymen ... If everyone of us daily performed his duty to his neighbor, no one in the world who needed assistance would be left unattended. Therefore, one who serves his neighbor serves all the world. As a matter of fact, there is in swadeshi no room for distinction between one's own and other people. (Mathai 2000, p. 141)

As such, for Gandhi, nonviolence meant not only liberation of the masses from the yoke of authoritarian and colonial powers, but also a strategy of constructive work based on pure moral authority. That is the reason why Gandhi was seriously concerned with the question of nonviolence as a way of empowering politically the individuals and the masses. He wrote: 'To me political power is not an end but one of the means of enabling people to better their condition in every department of life' (*ibid.*, p. 205). It is useful to recall that Gandhi admitted that democracy could not exist if citizens remained disempowered and passive. Therefore, in Gandhian democracy every man and woman had to be enlightened, disciplined and self-reliant. That is why he cautioned us: 'Democracy is not a state in which people act like sheep. Under democracy individual liberty of opinion and action is jealously guarded. I, therefore, believe that the minority has a perfect right to act differently from the majority' (*ibid.*, p. 209). This exposition suggests that Gandhi recognized the priority and necessity of self-regulation and self-control in politics. He was against the monopolization of political action and decision-making and hoped for a decentralized democracy in which small-scale communities could regulate their political and economic affairs. For Gandhi political power was not the ultimate aim. He argued that changing social order was not divorced from changing the notion of power in general. In his writing in 1939, Gandhi went back to Thoreau's appeal to the presence and need for democratic self-rule:

Political power, in my opinion, cannot be our ultimate aim. It is one of the means used by men for their all-round advancement. The power to control national life through national representative is called political power. Representatives will become unnecessary if the national life becomes so perfect as to be self-controlled. It will then be a state of enlightened anarchy in which each person will become his own ruler. He will conduct himself in such a way that his behaviour will not hamper the well-being of his neighbours. In an ideal state there will be no political institution and therefore no political power. That is why Thoreau said in his classic statement that government is the best which governs the least. (Iyer 1987, pp. 496–8)

What Gandhi wants to resist are the bureaucratic set of procedures and institutions that create distance between people and their governments; decentralizing government is a way to humanize modern democracy and make it the end result of popular decision-making. To address this problem, Gandhi argues for political, social and economic conditions that eliminate inequalities while favouring individual autonomy. Emphasizing an ethically coherent political life, Gandhi suggests a system of political arrangement by the name of panchayat raj (village republic) in order to empower citizens rather than the state. A panchayat is a five-member assembly elected by the villagers that functions as a cooperative and participatory community, giving citizens the opportunity to participate in the management of their own affairs. Moreover, if the source of power lies in the hands of the people and not in the government, the constructive programme would be translated as real politics. This was the foundation of Gandhi's wide-ranging campaigns on behalf of the untouchables in Indian society.

Gandhi considered the practice of untouchability as a sin against God and a humiliation to the whole of mankind; he wanted to eliminate untouchability, concentrating on social justice. In this respect, 'Gandhi believed that untouchability was a religious matter, that it had no religious basis but was a late accretion to Hindu tradition, and that it was deeply destructive of Hinduism. Therefore, his strategy was accordingly fashioned to touch the consciences of the higher castes – by example, for he permitted no distinctions on grounds of caste in his personal life and in his *ashrams*, by speaking and writing, and ultimately by fasting' (Brown 2006, pp. 249–50). Set at this level of practicality, Gandhi's nonviolence appears a strategic pattern of autonomy, where self-governing agents are empowered as they meet their multiple needs and duties.

As already indicated, the Gandhian technique of nonviolent social and political change is a systematic combination of resistance and reconstruction. As such, nonviolence is a strategy of transformation that Gandhi evolved for translating the grand vision of unity and oneness of all life (*advaita*) into a practical social and political programme. In this context Gandhi brought in a new argument about the performance of duty at the individual and social levels. That is why Gandhi speaks of nonviolence as the recognition of the irreducible presence of others for self-transformation. Needless to say, Gandhi's conception of nonviolence denotes the self and the society as two interdependent elements of the same dynamic process. Gandhi went on to say that the world cannot subsist for a single moment without the principle of the disinterested performance of duty; for him, nonviolent action was equated with sacrifice (*yajna*), that is, a selfless action in benefit of others. As Gandhi (1960b, p. 13) says, 'sacrifice (yajna) means exerting oneself for the benefit of others, in a word, service. And when service is rendered for service's sake, there is no room for attachment, likes and dislikes.' Rejecting the distinction commonly made between politics and ethics, and between economics and welfare of all, Gandhi goes on to say that constructive nonviolence should be guided by moral values and rise above all forms of self-interest. Therefore, if the search for truth is the goal of economic and political activities, self-sacrifice and self-suffering should become the mental requisites for nonviolence. It is in view of these considerations that Gandhi suggests the idea of self-contained villages. As he says, 'You cannot build nonviolence on factory civilization, but it can be built on self-contained villages. Rural economy as I have conceived it, eschews exploitation altogether, and exploitation is the essence of violence' (Roy 1985, p. 136).

Moreover, Gandhi believes that a decentralized economy is based on values such as trusteeship, self-sufficiency and harmony. Thus, Gandhian nonviolence performs a dual role of combating injustice and awakening in oneself and in others the awareness of moral and spiritual self-development. It is clear, therefore, that the main reason why Gandhi denounced modern civilization was the fact that it ignored and disregarded moral values and promoted violence and self-interest. Gandhi's objection to the modern idea of multiplication of wants goes hand in hand with his idealization of voluntary simplicity and a society without poverty based on nonviolence. More than 100 years ago, Gandhi wrote *Hind Swaraj* on his way back to South Africa. This book is, in the words of Anthony Parel (1997, p. xiv), 'the seed from which the tree of Gandhian thought has grown to its full structure'. Conceived later as a conceptual framework to the Gandhian creed of nonviolence, *Hind Swaraj* was Gandhi's prescription regarding the course that a free and independent India should take. As Gandhi's experiments with truth progressed, nonviolence turned out to be more than a mere reaction against violence. It became the alpha and omega of democracy and social equality in India. Although Gandhi is remembered today as the nonviolent leader of modern India, his goal was to educate humanity in the spirit of nonviolence. In Gandhi's mind the spiritual and political development of Indians and that of other nations was inseparable. His doctrine of nonviolence can be universally applied today.

The technique of nonviolent resistance that Gandhi used in his struggle for the independence of India led the way, in the twentieth century, to leaders like Martin Luther King Jr, Nelson Mandela, the Dalai Lama, Lech Walesa and Aung San Suu Kyi. Debate regarding whether there is such a thing as Gandhism is superfluous; Gandhi himself did not believe in it. One of the first things Gandhi ever did was to ask others to look into their own soul and become greater than him. This is where Gandhi's greatest contribution lays – in practicing nonviolence in one's own life and culture. What Gandhi taught humanity was to stand for truth and to practise it according to the light of nonviolence. This light was no ordinary light. It has illuminated the political and social actions of men and women around the world for nearly 70 years.

Further reading

Brown, J. M. (1991) *Gandhi: Prisoner of Hope*. A rich biography of Mahatma Gandhi within the context of his time.

Chadha, Y. (1997) *Gandhi: A Life*. A well-balanced sketch of Gandhi which reveals the transformation of Mohandas into Mahatma.

Dalton, D. (1993) *Mahatma Gandhi: Nonviolent Power*. A study of Gandhi's political thought and his views on key ideas such as freedom and power.

Gandhi, R. (2006) *Mohandas: A True Story of a Man, His People and an Empire*. A remarkably researched and detailed chronological account of Gandhi in his daily life and in his closest relationships.

Merton, T. (ed.) (2007) *Gandhi on Nonviolence*. An essential compendium of Gandhi's philosophy of nonviolence chosen by a great figure of nonviolence.

Chapter 6

Pragmatic Nonviolence

Two forms of nonviolence exist: principled and pragmatic. The previous chapters have dealt heavily with principled (secular and religious ethical ideals) forms of nonviolence. In contrast, pragmatic nonviolence is a method of struggle concerned with the results nonviolence can achieve. Nonviolent principles are often used by individuals, not necessarily because they are believers in nonviolence from a philosophical standpoint, but actually to achieve practical advantages. Some scholars link pragmatic nonviolence with Machiavellianism, for its understanding that means justify the ends. It is for this reason that supporters of principled nonviolence argue that their struggle is more 'worthy' because it attempts to equate the means with the ends, without compromising one in favour of the other. Furthermore, they might claim that pragmatic nonviolence only leads to a half-hearted acceptance of the principle. However, proponents of such pragmatism argue that nonviolence is a far more effective 'weapon' than the use of violence.

The most notable scholar of pragmatic nonviolence is Gene Sharp, whose works detail the practical and realistic uses of nonviolent action in bringing down dictatorial regimes. Committed to pragmatic principles as Sharp is, he does not believe that nonviolent struggle is an absolute answer, nor does he believe it to be quick and easy. The difficulty is in the widespread assumption that the only possibilities for change are violence and negotiation. Therefore, Sharp's work tries to develop nonviolent political action that can serve as a third alternative.

Alternatives such as coups, elections and foreign interventions are all deemed problematic, however. The shortcomings of a coup primarily arise from the misdistribution of powers between the population and the new elite assuming power (Sharp 2010, p. 5). A truly democratic system exhibits a redistribution of power and strong civil society, both of which are absent in regimes that come to power through coups. From Sharp's perspective, elections too are deemed insufficient because if a government is truly oppressive faith in elections can be misplaced. Established dictatorships are not inclined to allow elections that could spell the demise of their power. Finally, foreign interventions are also unsuitable, not only because behind them lie third-party interests, but also, most importantly, because a dictatorship's continued existence is based on internal factors, which foreign interventions do not take into account.

To understand what Sharp's pragmatic teachings target, and in what way, it is important to know what dictatorial power rests upon. Sharp identifies six sources of political power from which dictators draw their powers: authority, human resources, skills and knowledge, intangible factors, material resources and sanctions. The very population the dictatorial regime suppresses supplies all these sources of power. Sharp's nonviolent struggle aims to identify a regime's most crucial sources of power and slowly works on eliminating them in an effort to undermine the regime's rule and authority.

In his work *There are Realistic Alternatives*, Sharp lists just fewer than 200 specific methods of nonviolent action. However, all these methods can be classified under three characteristic classes: nonviolent protest and persuasion, noncooperation and nonviolent interpretation (Sharp 2012, p. 338). The first consists of symbolic acts used to demonstrate disagreement and attempt to persuade the oppressor. The primary goal of these acts is to change the ideology of the population and incite them to action. Therefore, nonviolent protest and persuasion seek to actively undermine a government or to force a certain action, and provide the best results in society where these actions are deemed illegal. The second class, noncooperation, can be categorized as three fields: social, economic and political. All three of these forms of noncooperation seek an active withdrawal from participation in the oppressive system. The final class, nonviolent intervention, is an action defined by the fact that it affects the situation actively and directly. It intervenes in a situation both positively, by establishing new behaviours, policies, institutions etc., and negatively by destroying existing ones.

In *From Dictatorship to Democracy* (2010), Sharp identifies four mechanisms of change that occur as a result of methods of nonviolent action. These are essential in understanding how nonviolent action changes situations where it has been applied. The first of these mechanisms of change is conversion. Conversion is the process whereby members of the regime are emotionally moved by the suffering and the repression of nonviolent protesters. The second mechanism is known as accommodation. This mechanism occurs as a result of withdrawal from economic and/or political cooperation by the resisters, which forces opponents to agree to compromise. It is important to understand that both conversion and accommodation are attempts at engaging with the opposition in the hope that they will voluntarily change. When no voluntary change can be expected of the opposition, the third mechanism, nonviolent coercion is followed. This method strips the dictator of their power, although so that they might still be ruling, they become nothing more than a figurehead, unable to control government and society. Finally, the most extreme mechanism of change that results from nonviolent action is known as disintegration. This mechanism goes even further than nonviolent coercion because it means the regime and its proponents are not only stripped of their power, but of their positions as well. This leads to the eventual collapse of the regime and establishment of a new government.

However, before any nonviolent action can be taken there must exist certain preconditions, and knowledge is the most basic and primary of these conditions. The first type of knowledge required is of the conflict situation, the opponents and the needs of the society. The second is that of the operation and the techniques of nonviolent action that will have to be employed in the specific situation; understanding and comprehensive study of nonviolence are absolutely necessary for any strategic plan to be successful. This is why outside intervention can never work, because those oppressed have a far greater understanding and familiarity of the regime and its political system. While outsiders may offer financial support, they do not have the intimate knowledge of the historical context needed to deliver a successful campaign.

Finally, in addition to knowledge, a strategic plan must exist, based on realistic and pragmatic considerations. These considerations are: (1) sources of power of the opponent; (2) balance of dependencies; (3) status of civil society; (4) whether the campaign objectives and activities aggravate weaknesses of the oppressive system; (5) the importance of initiative in the conflict.

Gene Sharp and pragmatic nonviolence

The difference between principled and pragmatic nonviolence can be understood quite simply. Proponents of principled nonviolence are those 'whose principles (whether secular or religious ethical ideals) preclude their use of violence under any circumstances' (Spencer 2012a, p. 13). Pragmatic nonviolence is the position where violence is not shunned in principle – rather, nonviolence is used as a method of struggle simply because it is effective. Moreover, a major feature of pragmatic nonviolence is that, unlike in its principled cousin, 'people didn't have to have the belief in order for them to act' (Spencer 2012b, p. 8).

It must not be forgotten that nonviolent struggle can be a very powerful and effective tool, one whose 'tough nonviolent actions are commonly chosen by pragmatic people who are not "believers" in nonviolent principles but who see their practical advantages' (Spencer 2012a, p. 14). Metta Spencer (2012a, p. 15) praises this approach as balancing 'two irreducible factors – strict nonviolence and pragmatic effectiveness'. This however, is not the universal view. Scholars such as Bharawadj offer alternative understandings, and claim that pragmatic nonviolence is self-defeating.

Some scholars claim that it succeeds 'because it sacrifices everything on the altar of success' (Bharadwaj 1998, p. 80). They see such a compromise as devastating, sacrificing all morality in favour of success and jeopardizing the very use of nonviolence as a means of struggle. They believe that 'the focus on success is bound to lead to an opportunistic or half-hearted acceptance of nonviolence, with the result that the temptation to use other means will lead to the eventual corruption or destruction of the good end' (*ibid.*). It is for this reason that principled nonviolence tries to equate means and ends, without compromising one in favour of the other, and tries to keep them both 'purer' (*ibid.*). However, pragmatists would dispute these scholars' views on this 'half-heartedness', pointing out the ultimate ends of such nonviolent action.

Among the most notable proponent of pragmatic nonviolence has been Gene Sharp, whose works outline the practical and realistic uses of nonviolent of action. Before an exposition of Sharp's thought on the subject, it is necessary to clarify certain easily misunderstood points. Sharp does not believe that nonviolent struggle is an absolute answer. He does not believe that it is always quick and efficient. Neither does he believe that nonviolence guarantees success. Most of all, Sharp does not believe that nonviolence is easy. These reminders are constantly present in Sharp's work, and ought to be born in mind. He puts forward a strong case for nonviolence as the most powerful method of struggle. He tries to show that it is just as, or even more, effective than any other tool in a democrat's arsenal.

Sharp outlines several reasons why the use of violence to change a repressive form of government into a democratic one may be unwise; he does not deny that 'conflict in society and politics is inevitable, and, in many cases, desirable' (2003, p. 1). However, he states that it is unreasonable to assume that conflicts can be resolved with words when basic and fundamental issues are at stake (*ibid.*). The difficulty is in widespread assumption that the only available alternatives are either violence or negotiation. Sharp (*ibid.*, p. 3) suggests the further option of nonviolent political action as having 'the chance of success equivalent or greater than the violent option', especially against a government that has violent force at its disposal.

Upon reflection, it seems that the use of violence against an oppressor is, effectively, 'placing confidence in … the very type of struggle with which the oppressors nearly always have superiority' (Sharp 2010, p. 4). Having had a monopoly over the use of force, a dictatorial government is able to use their vastly superior technical knowledge and tools to wage a violent conflict against dissidents, often resulting in severe civilian losses – thus, the use of violence often plays into the hands of those in power.

Moreover, alternatives such as coups, elections and foreign interventions are equally problematic. Insofar as change might be brought about through a coup, assuming that a violent struggle against an oppressor is successful, the new government is faced with the fact that there is still a misdistribution of power; any change must be accompanied by a redistribution of power and a disjuncture with the past power dynamic. For a true democracy to exist, there must be a strong civil society which would be absent in a scenario where a regime comes to power through a coup d'état (*ibid.*).

Some may place their faith in the idea that elections can help bring about the required change in a way that is neither violent nor radical. However, if the government in question is truly oppressive, then such faith might be misplaced, as 'Dictators are not in the business of allowing elections that could remove them from their thrones' (*ibid.*, p. 6). Finally, fearing no other solution and with no confidence in their own abilities, some may believe that pleading for help to the international community would be the only effective and quick way to bring about a change in government. Unfortunately, private interests make it quite difficult to gauge whether an action is truly being taken out of humanitarian considerations (Sharp 2010). Additionally, Sharp argues that a dictatorship's continued existence is primarily based on internal factors. As such, while it may be weakened through sanctions or condemnations from the international community, only an internal struggle can truly destabilize such a regime.

Negotiations are often an attractive route for democrats, as, on the surface, they present the option for everyone to work together towards a better and united future, especially in face of the clear superior military capacity of the oppressor (*ibid.*). In fact, negotiation with a dictator can be quite dangerous, and Sharp dedicates a detailed discussion on the shortcomings of negotiations.

He is sceptical about the potential of negotiations to end an oppressive regime, believing it to be unrealistic when fundamental issues are at stake;, the danger often lies in the ulterior motives of the participants. In fact, when the resistance is only a nuisance to the dictator, negotiations can be a way to 'negotiate the opposition into surrender under the guise of making "peace"' (*ibid.*, p. 11). Negotiations may also be used as a stalling technique, allowing the oppressor to regroup their forces, or to 'salvage as much of their control or wealth as possible' if the resistance movement is a very successful and powerful one (*ibid.*). Aside from such disingenuousness, the content and outcomes of negotiations rarely reflect what is just. Rather, they are very often the product of calculations of the other's power capacities (*ibid.*). A strong dictator may refuse to discuss certain issues altogether, thereby limiting the content of negotiations, and may only make concessions based on the relative strength of the resistance movement.

Moreover, one must take into account why a dictator is in power and why they wish to stay in power. Sharp identifies certain of these underlying motives as power, position, wealth, reshaping society etc. Democrats would enter negotiations with the desire of stripping a dictator of these privileges as they are simply not compatible with a democratic system (hence the fundamental nature of the disagreement), but, the hope that they might be used in order to bring about substantial democratic change is perhaps unrealistic in many cases.

Negotiations are also strategically problematic according to Sharp. Engaging in negotiations with an oppressor is often the result of a successful campaign of resistance, where the dictator is forced to come to the bargaining table or engage in a long, drawn out and difficult suppression – thus, they aim at reducing the precise force which brought the dictator to the bargaining table. As such, the cessation of resistance by democrats and the 'collapse of popular resistance often removes the countervailing force that has limited the control and brutality of the dictatorship' (*ibid.*, p. 13). Once the democrats engage in negotiations and cease their struggle, the dictator has carte blanche to oppress once again. For these reasons, Sharp has some difficulty in accepting negotiations as a reasonable option to change society for the better. He also outlines the potential benefits of using nonviolent action beyond the strategic.

The use of nonviolent methods of struggle should also be praised for its democratizing effects. The major difference is a comparison drawn between a democratic nonviolent movement and an oppressive dictatorship. While a dictator can easily coerce using violence or the threat of violence, 'leaders of a political defiance movement can exert influence and apply pressures on their followers, but they cannot imprison or execute them when they dissent or choose other leaders' (*ibid.*, p. 37). Therefore, the initial rejection of violence as a tool contributes to the democratizing effects of nonviolent struggle.

Beyond this, using nonviolence has an empowering impact. It allows a people to use the tools of nonviolent struggle to achieve liberation and, furthermore, it 'provides the population with a means of resistance that can be used to achieve and defend their liberties against existing or would-be dictators' (*ibid.*) – thus offering a guarantee to prevent future attempts at the establishment of a dictatorship. Nonviolent struggle is, therefore, a safeguard of democracy.

Yet in light of the obvious flaws with violence, and the great potential benefits of nonviolent alternatives, violence is still often seen as the ultimate factor in determining the strength of an opponent, with negotiations thought to be the 'right way' – and nonviolence to be slow, unrealistic and ineffective.

These are some common misconceptions which Gene Sharp argues against. In fact, Sharp (2003) outlines several attributes of nonviolent action, chiefly: that it does not require a central charismatic leader; it is not restricted to a certain culture; it can be entirely secular and has no requirements for deference to religion; it has been effective to the point that it has yielded results against oppressive regimes such as those in the Eastern bloc; and that it has, in the past, brought about the disintegration of entire systems of oppressive governance. It is this view of the relationship between the rulers and the ruled, a precarious and dependent relationship, that lies at the foundation of Gene Sharp's case for the use of nonviolent action.

The misconceptions concerning nonviolence are greatly due to the underestimation by a people of their own political capacity and power. Gene Sharp (2010, p. 18) uses the example of the monkey master fable attributed to Liu-Ji:

> In the feudal state of Chu an old man survived by keeping monkeys in his service. The people of Chu called him 'ju jong' (monkey master).
>
> Each morning, the old man would assemble the monkeys in his courtyard and order the eldest one to lead the others to the mountains to gather fruits from bushes and trees. It was the rule that each monkey had to give one-tenth of his collection to the old man. Those who failed to do so would be ruthlessly flogged. All the monkeys suffered bitterly, but dared not complain.
>
> One day a small monkey asked the other monkeys: 'Did the old man plant all the fruit trees and bushes?' The others said: 'No, they grew naturally.' The small monkey further asked: 'Can't we take the fruits without the old man's permission?' The others replied: 'Yes, we all can.' The small monkey continued: 'Then, why should we depend on the old man; why must we all serve him?'
>
> Before the small monkey was able to finish his statement, all the monkeys suddenly became enlightened and awakened.
>
> On the same night, watching that the old man had fallen asleep, the monkeys tore down all the barricades of the stockade entirely. They also took the fruits the old man had in storage, brought all with them into the woods, and never returned. The old man finally died of starvation.

Liu-Ji says, 'Some men in the world rule their people by tricks and not by righteous principles. Aren't they just like the monkey master? They are not aware of the muddle-headedness. As soon as their people become enlightened, their tricks no longer work.'

What is to be taken from this story is not that overthrowing an oppressive regime is simple, rather, that the imagined strength and total domination of a dictatorship is precisely that, imagined. The monkeys understood this and as soon as they withdrew from the system which they themselves helped perpetuate, the monkey master's rule over them unravelled.

Sharp furthermore identifies certain necessary sources of political power. These are foundations from which the dictator draws his powers. Sharp (*ibid.*, pp. 18–19) identifies six of these:

- *Authority*: the belief among the people that the regime is legitimate, and that they have a moral duty to obey it.
- *Human resources*: the number and importance of the persons and groups which are obeying, cooperating, or providing assistance to the rulers.
- *Skills and knowledge*: needed by the regime to perform specific actions and supplied by the cooperating persons and groups.
- *Intangible factors*: psychological and ideological factors that may induce people to obey and assist the rulers.
- *Material resources*: the degree to which the rulers control or have access to property, natural resources, financial resources, the economic system and means of communication and transportation.
- *Sanctions*: punishments, threatened or applied, against the disobedient and noncooperative to ensure the submission and cooperation that are needed for the regime to exist and carry out its policies.

Much like in the monkey master fable, these sources of power are effectively supplied by the very population that are repressed by the dictator. In fact, the existence of the dictator is predicated on the acceptance, submission and cooperation of the ruled subjects. Sharp (*ibid.*, p. 19) outlines that these are not guaranteed: 'without the availability of [these] sources, the rulers' power weakens and finally dissolves'. In fact, nonviolent struggle aims at identifying the most crucial sources of power of a dictator and slowly eliminating them, thereby suffocating the dictator's ability to command authority and rule.

Pragmatic nonviolence in practice

However, if nonviolent struggle is to be successful, there are two essential processes which need to be present. First there has to be an ability to 'defy and at times to reverse the effects of repression' and, second, 'an ability to undermine and sever the sources of power of the opponents' (Sharp 2003, p. 10). These two characteristics are common in every successful nonviolent struggle. If a population seeks to use nonviolent methods of action, it is, first, necessary for them to be able to reject oppression and stand up for themselves and, second, to identify and attack the primary sources of power of a dictator in a well thought-out and strategic manner. These two preconditions make successful nonviolent struggle possible. There are other conditions that can make it probable.

While it might be possible to carry out this political starvation, its success is not as simple as it might initially appear. Sharp (*ibid.*, p. 21) states that there are three primary considerations which will determine to what degree this action might work. The first is the 'relative desire of the populace to impose limits on the government's power'. Second is the amount of decentralization of the state, or as Sharp (*ibid.*) says 'the relative *strength* of the subjects' independent organizations and institutions to withdraw collectively the sources of power' (emphasis original). In fact, these organizations and institutions carry out a very important function. The existence of such 'centres of power' allows for spaces beyond state reach and thereby creates a forum for resistance (*ibid.*, p. 22).

Third is the population's '*ability* to withhold their consent and assistance' thereby carrying out the necessary actions for political starvation (*ibid.*, emphasis original). If these three primary considerations seem to be balanced in favour of the democrats, then there is a good chance that a well thought out and strategically implemented nonviolent struggle would be able to achieve the goal of the democrats and resisters.

After considering the relative probability of carrying out a successful campaign of nonviolent struggle, there still remains the task of developing and implementing a strategic framework of specific actions. First, it must be noted that dictatorships have certain weaknesses that may be exploited. Among these are the fact that they are often opposed by intellectuals and students; that the general public, given time, may become disenchanted with, and indeed hostile to, the regime; that the segregations of society, between gender, ethnicity, race or religion, may become even more pronounced; and, finally, that social mobility is very limited and is entirely subject to the whim of a supreme ruler. Of course, these are only a few examples, and Sharp identifies at least 17 in his *From Dictatorship to Democracy* (2010, pp. 26–7). These weaknesses must then be exploited by the resistance. They can be deliberately exacerbated in order to 'alter the system drastically or to disintegrate it' (*ibid*., p. 27); the exploitation of these 'Achilles heels', injustices to which dictatorships are prone, can lead to a situation in which the general oppressed population can rise up and partake in the struggle for liberation.

Furthermore, nonviolent actions can lead to the dynamic that Sharp identifies as political Ju-Jitsu (assuming that there has been some form nonviolent resistance which has been met with an iron fist). Sharp (2003, p. 10) argues that 'repression and even brutalities do not always produce a resumption of the necessary degree of submission and cooperation to enable the regime to function'. The importance of this is twofold. First, it means that even if there is a supressed nonviolent uprising, it does not necessarily mean the defeat of the democrats – it may even cause irreparable damage done to the regime. Moreover, when a government meets a nonviolent resistance group with violence, then it 'creates a special, asymmetrical, conflict situation' (*ibid*.). This conflict situation has to do with the implicit moral dimension of nonviolence.

When an oppressor brutally represses a group who are resolute in their refusal to resort to violence, an imbalance arises in favour of the proponents of nonviolence. According to Sharp (*ibid*., p. 11), 'the contrast in types of action throws the opponent off balance politically, causing their repression to rebound against their position and weaken their power'. The different nature of actions does not even allow for a comparison to be drawn, and therefore blocks the idea that there can be a proportional use of force.

This can increase the resolve of the opposition, turning the general population against the dictator, as well as third parties not directly involved in the struggle. Political Ju-Jitsu may even have the effect of fomenting disillusionment within the oppressors' camp (*ibid*.). Indeed, this may even lead to greater and more coordinated nonviolent action against the dictator, and when this grows to 'a significant scale, the opponents' repression will clearly have weakened their relative power position and contributed to their possible defeat' (*ibid*.).

Thus far, we have seen how a dictator obtains his power and what ought to be done in order to suffocate his power. We have also seen the importance of certain preconditions which make nonviolent struggle possible and can make success probable. We then identified specific weaknesses of dictatorships which can be exploited in order to increase the strength of the opponents. Finally, we also examined the dynamics of political Ju-Jitsu and the destabilizing nature of using nonviolence against a violent regime. Now let's turn to more specific methods of nonviolent action.

As mentioned above, in his work *There are Realistic Alternatives* (2003), Gene Sharp lists just under 200 specific methods of nonviolent action. This list is also found in his much more comprehensive work, *Politics of Nonviolent Action* (1973). He does not claim that these lists are exhaustive. In fact, he states quite the opposite, that throughout the history of political struggle, other methods have likely been used. However, no matter the exact number of methods that have been used in the past or will be used in the future, 'they have the characteristics of the three classes of methods: nonviolent protest and persuasion, noncooperation, and nonviolent intervention' (Sharp 2012, p. 338). Sharp separates his 198 methods into these three classes. There are classes and subclasses and so devising a visual representation along with this reading might prove to be beneficial.

The first class consists of nonviolent protest and persuasion, which 'are largely symbolic demonstrations, including parades, marches, and vigils' (Sharp 2010, p. 31). These are symbolic acts used to demonstrate disagreement and attempt to persuade the oppressor, 'stopping short of noncooperation or nonviolent intervention' (Sharp 1973, p. 117). These can be directed at the political opponent, as a means of showing them the amount of public disagreement for a certain action, either in the hope of changing their views or making it clear that without immediate remedy the demonstrations may escalate to other forms of struggle. Protests and persuasion may also be directed at the public, so as to 'arouse attention and support for the desired change' (*ibid.*, p. 118).

It is, however, important to note that nonviolent protest and persuasion aim at disseminating a view and hoping to change the ideology of others or to incite them to action, while noncooperation and nonviolent intervention seek either to actively undermine a government, or to force a certain action. Moreover, the efficacy of nonviolent protest and persuasion will differ greatly depending on the situation. Sharp states that in situations where such actions have never been taken before, they may have a greater impact than where they are commonplace. As such, protesting under a dictatorship where such forms of action are illegal might attract much more attention and be more dramatic – simply due to the rarity of the event and the courage of the participants – than in democratic conditions where protests are much more frequent and face virtually no danger of repression by the state (Sharp 1973).

The second class of methods is noncooperation. There are three categories of noncooperation: social, economic and political noncooperation. Noncooperation is the active withdrawal from participation in perpetuating the oppressive system. This can take many forms, from refusing to go to work, to disobeying laws deemed unjust (*ibid*.). As Sharp (*ibid*., p. 183) states, 'noncooperation involves the deliberate discontinuance, withholding, or defiance of certain existing relationships'. Social noncooperation, the first of the three categories, involves stopping all social activities with a person, group or institution deemed as having acted wrongly, or seen to perpetuate the oppressive system. It can also involve a refusal to continue institutionalized behaviour if that is seen to perpetuate the same oppressive system (Sharp 1973). Social noncooperation has been further divided into three categories: 'ostracism of persons, noncooperation with social events, customs and institutions, and withdrawal from the social system as a means of expressing opposition' (*ibid*., p. 184) These three methods all aim at making clear that, insofar as a dictatorship requires the tacit acquiescence of its people in order to rule, this consent is not guaranteed and can be revoked at any time.

The second means of noncooperation is economic. There are numerous forms of economic noncooperation; it 'consists of a suspension or refusal to continue specific economic relationships' (*ibid*., p. 219) and can be divided into two. The first category deals with economic boycotts, and aims at restricting or eliminating trade and economic relationships through market activities. The second set consists of various forms of striking, with the aim of slowing down and hindering the economic activity and capacity of a state machine (*ibid*.). Let's consider economic boycotts first.

There are two forms of economic boycotts, primary and secondary. Primary boycotts are applied against the direct and immediate opponent. Secondary boycotts are aimed at any third parties who carry on market activity with the direct and immediate opponent in the hope that they too will join in the primary boycott (*ibid*.). Let's imagine a simplified model. There is group 'O', the oppressor, and group 'R', the resister. They are in direct conflict. All the other 24 letters are third parties. Primary economic boycotts consist of group 'R' refusing to carry out any trade with group 'O'. Secondary boycotts are more severe, and consist of 'R' refusing to carry out any trade with 'O', and any other group who carries out trade with 'O'. Economic boycotts must be well researched before they are applied. The economic consequences must be understood, both for the resisters and the boycotted group, especially if the target of the boycott is one of the few or the only producer of a necessary product. Realistic considerations of economic power must be central to deliberations considering the application of this method of nonviolent action. Economic noncooperation may also be defined by the group who implements them (consumers, workers and producers, middlemen, owners and management, holders of financial resources, governments); however, these are not rigid groupings (*ibid.*, p. 221). Moreover, the specific actions specified by Sharp can be used both for primary and secondary economic noncooperation purposes, depending on the circumstances.

The second category of economic noncooperation is the strike. Sharp (*ibid.*, p. 257) defines this method of noncooperation as 'a refusal to continue economic cooperation through work'. This method of action is typically used when economic issues are the central focus of the disagreement; however, this is not exclusively the case (Sharp 1973). Resisters generally achieve their goals by listing a certain set of conditions which must be met for the strike to cease, and it is important to note that the collective nature of the strike is what lends it power (*ibid.*). For striking to be effective, there has to be a large number of strikers, enough to 'disrupt seriously or to make impossible continued operations of at least that economic unit' (*ibid.*, p. 258). Should there be a large enough group, often a threat of striking will be sufficient. The sheer number and collective threat of ceasing activities and impairing the productive capacity of that particular economic unit is often enough to make the oppressor either cede to the demands of the resisters or at least to bring them out to the bargaining table.

Among the different categories of striking, there are symbolic strikes, agricultural strikes, strikes by special groups, ordinary industrial strikes, restricted strikes (small and immediately undetectable methods of reducing efficiency in the workplace), multi-industry strikes and a combination of strikes and economic closures. As with economic boycotts, there are several ways in which this method may backfire if the situation in which it is applied has not been adequately studied. The number of strikers and solidarity among workers, the ability to replace workers (and thereby the value and skills of the strikers) – all must be considered before applying this method of noncooperation.

The third and final method of noncooperation is at a political level. Political noncooperation involves 'refusals to continue the usual forms of political participation under existing conditions' (*ibid.*, p. 285). They can have extremely application – used by one person or by larger concerted efforts. Furthermore, they may be applied to achieve varying goals – anything, from personally dissociating 'from something seen as morally or politically objectionable', to producing the disintegration of the regime (*ibid.*, pp. 285–6). What they have in common is the desire to prevent the political operation of an opponent, and to discourage certain political actions and behaviour.

The specific methods of political noncooperation include the rejection of authority, citizens' noncooperation with the government (refusing interactions with the government, from state schools to refusing the dissolution of existing institutions), citizens' alternatives to obedience (ranging from intentionally slow compliance to the total civil disobedience of 'illegitimate' laws), action by government personnel, domestic governmental action and international governmental action.

The third and final method of specific nonviolent action is known as nonviolent intervention. This class of action is defined by the way it affects the situation actively and directly. It intervenes in the situation – positively by establishing new behaviours, policies, relationships, or institutions which are preferred, or negatively by destroying existing ones (Sharp 1973). Their directness and intervening nature also presents certain challenges in their application. Sharp (*ibid.*, pp. 357–8) notes that 'if successful, the victory is likely to come quicker by the use of methods of this class than with the use of methods of the previous classes, because the disruptive effects of the intervention are harder to tolerate or to withstand for a considerable period of time'. This means that the actions of the resisters will instigate a quicker and possibly stronger response by the oppressor. This is to be expected as this method of action engages more directly with the oppressor, especially since these methods of intervention may be used defensively, or offensively in order to actively weaken the oppressor's position (Sharp 1973). It is important to note, as Sharp (*ibid.*, p. 358) does, that the 'result is not necessarily a more rapid success; precisely because of the character of intervention, speedier and more severe repression may be a first result – which, of course, does not necessarily mean defeat'.

Political intervention can be separated into five subclasses; they are psychological, physical, social, economic and political (Sharp 1973). It is important to note that these subclasses are less clearly defined than the other two forms of nonviolent action, and that they are intimately linked. One form of action can have repercussions of another nature and therefore, these subclasses are somewhat arbitrary as Sharp readily admits.

These examples of nonviolent struggle ought to be seen as tools to bring about change. Nevertheless, they should not be used blindly, hoping that they will achieve the intended result on their own. As Sharp (2012, p. 338) warns, 'it is necessary to know what kinds of pressure are to be used before choosing the precise forms of action that will best apply those pressures'. This requires a strategy into which these actions may fit, but, more immediately, an understanding of the processes and mechanisms by which they may bring about change.

Sharp's four mechanisms of change

In order for these methods to be as efficient as possible, there needs to be a clear understanding of how change may take place through their use. In *From Dictatorship to Democracy* (2010), these are identified as the four mechanisms of change. In *There are Realistic Alternatives* (2003), they are known as the four ways to success. These terms can be used interchangeably. While the methods we have discussed explore a wealth of specific forms of action to be taken, these mechanisms are to be understood as the 'how' behind the action of nonviolent action. Essentially, they are an answer to the question: how does nonviolent action change the situation in which it is applied? It does so in four ways.

The first mechanism of change is *conversion*. Conversion is the process whereby 'members of the opponent group are emotionally moved by the suffering of repression imposed on courageous nonviolent resisters', and relies heavily on the hope that the opponent is emotionally and rationally accessible (Sharp 2010, p. 35). This will then lead the oppressors to 'make concessions voluntarily because it is right to do so' (Sharp 2003, p. 15). This can be a product of political

Ju-Jitsu, where a clash between the methods of struggle shifts the balance in favour of the resisters. These instances are rare, and only occur when the polarizing effect of nonviolent action is not felt. Unfortunately, this is not often the case, so other mechanisms of change must also be examined.

The second such mechanism is known as *accommodation*. This is when 'withdrawal of economic or political cooperation has forced the opponents to agree to a compromise' (ibid., pp. 13–14). This usually can only take place under certain definite circumstances, where accommodation can diffuse the tension between the oppressors and the resisters. As Sharp (2010, p. 35) states, such mechanisms of change are only applicable if:

> the issues are not fundamental ones, the demands of the opposition in a limited campaign are not considered threatening, and the contest of forces has altered the power relationships to some degree, the immediate conflict may be ended by reaching an agreement, a splitting of differences or compromise.

This, of course, is dependent on the idea that the opposing factions can come to some form of stable peace, each by making concessions. These are often seen as the resolution to strikes and other similar forms of action, where there is room for compromise, and the ideals and aspirations motivating the struggle are not absolute. However, this is not frequently the case under dictatorships. Often a dictatorship will not be willing to make concessions as there are very often fundamental issues at hand which make compromise impossible. This leads us to the third method of nonviolent action.

Conversion and accommodation are attempts at engaging with the regime through nonviolent action in the hope that there may be voluntary change. The third mechanism of change, *nonviolent coercion*, is a method which is used when no voluntary action can be expected of the opponent. It is the weapon left to those 'who have no other option but to capitulate' (Sharp 2003, p. 14). This method strips the dictator of their power and their actions of their potency. Their sources of power have been cut off, and, while they remain in position as rulers, they become nothing more than a figurehead, as their 'ability to control the economic, social, and political processes of government and the society is in fact taken away' (Sharp 2010, p. 36). Finally, the most extreme form of change is known as *disintegration*. It is the suffocation of a dictatorship to such an extreme that the entire system collapses upon itself. The six sources of power are severed to such a degree that the dictatorship is not only unable to govern, but also unable to sustain its own existence. This mechanism goes further than nonviolent coercion as the dictator and oppressing class are stripped of their power as well as their position, the regime crumbles and a new one is established (Sharp 2010). This is such a powerful mechanism, and its effects so absolute, that the opponent does 'not even have sufficient power to surrender. The regime simply falls to pieces' (*ibid*., p. 36).

Knowledge of the relationship between the oppressor and the oppressed and how this dynamic is changed through nonviolent struggle is necessary before applying any of the specific methods discussed above. Moreover, beyond understanding the 'four ways to success' and a familiarity with the specific methods of change, a well thought out and meticulously designed strategic plan can dramatically increase the chances of nonviolent action being successful.

Necessary preconditions to change

The development of a strategic plan can be, and often has been, the deciding factor in whether or not nonviolent struggle is successful. Specific methods used reactively and without a long-term vision can be counterproductive and allow for suppression of a democratic uprising. The development of a sound strategic plan is dependent on certain preconditions.

Knowledge is the most basic and primary precondition, and Sharp divides it into three kinds. According to him, 'the analytical capacity that is capable of producing a wise grand strategy must involve the integration of these three types of knowledge and thinking' (Sharp and Raqib 2009, p. 16). These are all relevant and complementary to one another and form a cohesive understanding necessary to develop and implement a successful strategic plan.

The first type is of required knowledge is 'of the conflict situation, the opponents, and the society and its needs' (*ibid*.). This kind of knowledge is centred on the need to understand the 'strengths and weaknesses of both sides, their sources of power, and the likely impacts of the use of the power of both sides in an open conflict' (*ibid*., p. 19). Sharp clarifies that this kind of knowledge is known to those who live under an oppressive system. This knowledge of the current system and state of affairs then lends a certain 'power potential', a currency of power, to the oppressed, for if they are to use this knowledge and apply it in a strategy, it would 'enable the group to wield significant power' (*ibid.*, p. 18).

In *Self-Liberation*, Sharp (*ibid.*) identifies certain questions to be asked in order to clarify and understand this type of knowledge: how easy or difficult would it be for each side to make concessions to the other? Are the possible concessions beneficial or harmful to the resisters against the oppression? How can the real issues be used to advance mobilization of resistance, to shrink support for the opponents and to change loyalties within the opponent group and third parties? This reflects Sharp's approach to strategic planning which is realistic, pragmatic and decidedly non-reactionary while allowing space for adapting to the changing circumstances in a struggle.

The second kind of knowledge is the 'in depth knowledge of the nature and operation of the technique of nonviolent action' (*ibid.*, p. 18). It is precisely what you, the reader, are undertaking right now. An understanding and comprehensive study of the means of nonviolent study are required in order for any strategic plan to be successful. The mechanisms of change, the methods of struggle, the preconditions for nonviolent struggle, the need for nonviolent alternatives, the conditions and specifics of the society in which this struggle is to be applied are only some of the seemingly simple but deeply complex practical and theoretical issues which must be considered before the development of a strategic plan. Sharp (*ibid.*, p. 20) advises readers of his works that 'recognizing what one does not know can be very helpful in guarding against simplistic and dangerous presuppositions that can lead to problems and disasters'. This underlines the point that, beyond the fact that no one would be capable of devising a well-planned grand strategy without intimate knowledge of the technique, this strategy can be not only inefficacious, but also deeply dangerous for the members of the group and the movement itself.

This is why it is perhaps unwise to accept and rely on outside help. As stated, part of the reason why an oppressed people have such great power is their familiarity with the regime and the political system which is forced upon them. They are in tune with society and therefore draw great power potential from this knowledge. Outsiders, while they may have financial means, expertise in regime change and even political influence, do not have the 'intimate knowledge of the particular conflict situation, nor the current political situation, nor the historical background', all of which are crucial to a successful campaign (*ibid*., p. 22).

There are also other dangers linked with accepting foreign and outside help. It is rare that gifts are made out of the goodness of hearts or out of principle. It is much more often the case that the motivation of those offering help from outside the conflict situation are driven by concealed and private desires, which may evolve to conflict with those of the democrats (Sharp and Raqib 2009). Moreover, it is an enabling mechanism rather than an empowering one (*ibid*.). Nonviolent and autonomous struggle is a phenomenon where the population rises against their oppressor, leading to the self-determination of a people, giving them the necessary political power in order to face their challenges and protect against any future internal or external domination. Relying on foreign assistance has the opposite effect. It denies the right to self-determination, and prevents the democrats from acquiring the tools to safeguard their newfound liberty, as nonviolent struggle can be used in the future against aspiring dictators or invaders. Sharp (*ibid*., p. 26) identifies two such processes whereby the power which was once concentrated in the hands of a small elite is diffused throughout society:

- The population becomes experienced in the application of this type of action that can, with care, be used against any present or future oppression.
- The application of nonviolent struggle strengthens, and helps to create, independent institutions outside the control of the state. These institutions and groups can be called loci of power, 'places' where power resides and from which power can be applied. These institutions can when needed serve as bases for organized resistance. Individual protests and defiance may be noble and heroic, but successful resistance to end oppression requires corporate resistance and defiance.

While necessary, this is still insufficient for the development of a successful strategy to lead the resistance campaign against a dictator. This additional requirement is the third type of knowledge outlined by Sharp.

The ability to think and plan strategically is the third piece of the puzzle, enabling the formation of a coherent and effective strategic plan. This is a necessary mindset, which can be summarized as the ability to think ahead and design each stage of the struggle to increase the chance of success, while keeping in mind the realities of the situation in which the actions are located. Far from being reactionary, this third type of knowledge merely demands malleability to changing circumstances while keeping the long-term goals in mind and designing strategies so as to attain those goals (Sharp and Raqib 2009). This demands thinking both long and short term, being malleable when required but inflexible in principle. Bearing in mind that the long-term struggle is made up of limited campaigns, it is important that the 'long-term grand strategy will need to pay keen attention to the several anticipated future limited campaigns of the long-term conflict' (*ibid.*, p. 27). Another consideration is 'how the long term conflict is to begin, how the activities are to develop, and how sub-strategies and individual campaigns for limited issues should contribute to achieving finally the main goal' (*ibid.*). Together, these three types of knowledge are required to develop the crucial strategic plan. While such a plan does not guarantee success, it increases its probability significantly.

In the previous section, there was a discussion of the need to be able to adapt to changing situations and thereby come closer to a final victory with each action. In order for this to be possible, there are several basic considerations that must also be born in mind, to increase the likelihood of success, as any strategic plan must be based on realistic and pragmatic considerations.

1 *Sources of power of the opponent.* An important issue to take into consideration is the sources from which a dictator draws power and how those sources may be eliminated (Sharp and Raqib 2009). As stated earlier, there are six sources of power that feed a dictatorship (legitimacy, human resources, skills and knowledge, intangible factors, material resources and sanctions). These are supplied to a tyrant by explicit as well as tacit acts, by 'the support, assistance, obedience, and cooperation of the population and institutions of the society' (*ibid.*, p. 28). An effective strategy must target these sources, causing the regime's stranglehold on power to slowly disappear.

2 *Balance of dependencies.* What Sharp calls the balance of dependencies is an elaboration of the previous idea of restricting the supply of power. While there are certain dependencies which can be restricted as a powerful form of struggle, they are not necessarily unilateral. There are certain sources of power on which the regime relies for its existence, and those can be targeted effectively in order

to bring down a tyranny. However, the democratic resistance may also be dependent on those particular goods, services and sources of power (Sharp and Raqib 2009). Moreover, one side may depend on the other for access to these sources. In order to clarify these relations, Sharp points to certain questions that ought to be asked:

- Which side depends on the other for its necessary goods, services and sources of power, and to what degree?
- Are the dependencies all in one direction, or do both sides depend on the other in significant ways?
- Does the dependent side, or do the dependent sides, have, or can they create, alternative goods, services and sources of power to replace those that have been shrunk or severed by noncooperation by the other side?

One must be aware of how an action may affect the opposing side, but also one's own camp, and whether a particular form of nonviolent struggle can effectively suffocate a regime's power sources, or whether it simply has a 'scorched earth' effect.

3 *What is the status of civil society?* The groups and institutions within a civil society are essential and act as '*loci* of power', meaning that they offer a space outside the reach of the government (*ibid.*, p. 28). Moreover, they serve important functions, and the 'power potential of these loci of power may be simply enlightening (as in educational), or may shake the system (as in noncooperation by the civil service), or may even end the oppression (as in disintegration of the opponents' administration and enforcement)' (*ibid.*). It is therefore crucial to know the status of civil society and whether it can weather the storm and help in the process of nonviolent regime change.

4 *Do the campaign objectives and activities aggravate weaknesses of the oppressive system?* Sharp argues that there are pre-existing weaknesses in a dictatorship's claim to power, and that these may be exploited (*ibid.*, pp. 29–30). The efficiency of action is therefore linked to whether or not it targets a pre-existing and inherent weakness in the structure of a dictatorship.

5 *The importance of initiative in the conflict.* This consideration rests on the idea that a successful campaign ought to be based on action

rather than reaction. Instead of responding to a dictatorship and therefore allowing the opponent to dictate the terms of the struggle, 'it is important that the resisters both seize the initiative at the beginning and also maintain it throughout the conflict' (*ibid.*, p. 31).

Beyond the five basic strategic considerations, there is advice in Sharp's work about how to approach the planning and implementation of a strategy. These are practical and pragmatic words of caution so as to avoid making certain basic mistakes. Primarily, one must consider the state of the democratic movement, whether it is strong or timid, and how to help this movement grow. This can often be done with a series of smaller campaigns to increase the confidence of the democrats incrementally until more ambitious campaign may be considered (Sharp and Raqib 2009). It is not realistic to try and achieve disintegration with a quick campaign in a society that is not yet ready to face government forces in direct conflict. Smaller campaigns can empower the population, which is why Sharp (ibid., p. 33) advises that 'when struggling against great oppression it is often wise to fight on a limited specific expression of the large problem'. When the movement has grown, more direct and confrontational methods of nonviolent struggle may be used if they are judged appropriate. However, the guiding principle for action must be that whatever means are chosen, they must be done in order to attack 'the opponents' weakest points in ways that make victory more likely' (*ibid.*, p. 37). However, just as the movement and ambitions for achievement grow, 'the regime's counter measures, especially repression, may become harsher' (*ibid.*, pp. 38–9). This is a very real possibility which the democrats must face.

Assuming that the instructions of nonviolent action have been followed successfully and that the democratic movement has achieved its long-term goals, then the dictatorship would have been abolished or transformed. However, it is not enough to simply hope that there will be a better future after this victory. The period of political transition is a severely volatile one and it is necessary to 'calculate how to prevent an initial success from being stolen by a coup d'état' (*ibid.*, p. 40). Coups may come about from several directions. They may stem from inside the very dictatorship that is facing a resistance movement, or they may be a revolutionary force which seizes power and establishes their own dictatorship, much like the Bolsheviks during the October Revolution (Sharp and Raqib 2009). Therefore, the initial period after the downfall of a dictatorship is one where several steps must be taken to ascertain that it is the democratic movement that flourishes. Such efforts may include precautions against a possible threat of a dictator attempting to seize power, helping the development and growth of the loci of power in civil society and ensuring the creation of 'new, more equitable, institutions and strengthening the capacity of civil institutions generally to meet the needs of the society outside the State structure' (*ibid.*, p. 40). However, the tools used in nonviolent action are empowering and allow for these safeguards to be established. Most of all, they remain within the collective history of a people and allow them to draw upon this specific chapter in their history should there ever be another similar oppression.

Further reading

Ackerman, P. and Duvall, J. (2000) *A Force More Powerful*. A critical study of the use of nonviolent action to achieve social change in the twentieth century.

Holmes, Robert L. (ed.) (1990) *Nonviolence in Theory and Practice*. An insightful collection of writings by some of the leading theorists and practitioners of nonviolence.

Satha-Anand, C. (1991) 'From Violent to Nonviolent Discourse', in Elise Boulding (ed.), *Peace Culture and Society: Transnational Research and Dialogue*. A theoretical discussion of the subject of transforming radical extremism with principles of nonviolent action.

Steger, M. and Lind, N. (eds) (1999) *Violence and Its Alternatives: An Interdisciplinary Reader*. A collection of essays by specialists in the fields of politics, psychology, sociology, gender studies and race studies on violence and nonviolence.

Chapter 7

Critiques of Nonviolence

Many Marxists believe violence to be a necessary and inevitable phase in tearing down the capitalist system. According to traditional Marxists, there is a historically determined revolution that will reconstruct the relations of production and put in place socialism. From this Marxist tradition stem the works of more contemporary theorists such as Georges Sorel and Slavoj Žižek, who believe in some way that a violent revolution is necessary. Post-colonial theorists such as Frantz Fanon apply Marxist conceptions of class struggle in a colonial framework. They argue that the nature of the colonial system is such that it legitimizes the use of violence as the only way of reaffirming the humanity of the colonized.

Many scholars, such as Christopher Finlay, as well as others mentioned above, accept the Marxian claims that violence may be used legitimately. Debate does exist, however, regarding the necessity of violence in the works of Marx, with some scholars suggesting the possibility for a bloodless revolution. One of the most insightful, and most popular, works by Marx, *The Communist Manifesto*, is important because it describes the relation between the proletariat and the bourgeoisie and how the forces of history lead towards a revolution.

General to this book is the argument that a revolution will eventually take place and transform the relations of production, thus establishing a new social dynamic. Marx believed that capitalism would come to a breaking point when the exploitation endured by the proletariat became unbearable. Marx believed that, since there was a natural process to history, the socialist revolution could not be created, but, rather, it would naturally occur when society reached its maturity. The first step towards the liberation of the proletariat is the formation of trade unions, which is in itself the first manifestation of class struggle. It is the mobilizations made under the trade unions that will lead the proletariat towards an eventual confrontation with the bourgeoisie.

Scholars such as Finlay argue that Marxist theory explicitly justifies and excuses violence because in the process of the revolution it is creating new ethical values and its primary aim is the abolition of injustices. More interesting, however, is the scholars' acceptance that Marxist theory legitimizes violence. Since there is an assumption that a new social order will be created, along with a new set of moral and ethical codes, then the current ones may be discarded. Finlay sees future violence – carried out in the hope of a future absolution, based on a hypothetical social order able to create its own universal system of ethics – as a 'permissive doctrine'. That is to say, he sees this as a *carte blanche*, and therefore dangerous and unethical.

There are other scholars, such as Rustam Singh, who argue that violence is integral to Marx and that any reading of Marx must include a non-negotiable use of force in the forthcoming revolution. In contrast, others such as philosopher Adam Schaff were of the belief that a violent revolution was avoidable and underlined instances where Marx explicitly refers to the possibility of a peaceful transition. Schaff's understanding of Marx's conception of the role of violence is a nuanced one. According to him, Marx believed that, under the right conditions, such as England, America and the Netherlands, a peaceful transition could take place. Therefore, as long as a country had a developed parliamentary democracy a violent revolution could be avoided.

However, Singh disagrees with Schaff's assessment. He points to writings from Marx that argue for violence as a purging quality, claiming that only violence can destroy the remnants of a previous regime. Singh, however, does acknowledge the desire in Marx to avoid a bloody revolution. He notes that the early writings of Marx, up until 1848, alluded to the possibility of achieving a nonviolent transformation. However, this all changed after 1848 when social upheavals across Western Europe were brutally put down by governments.

Mikhail Bakunin and Sergei Nechaev's seminal work, *Catechism of a Revolutionary* (1871), provides insight into the role of violence in the anarchist movement. The most cited section of the text looks at the attitudes of a revolutionary and is divided into four parts. The first part focuses on the relationship of the revolutionary with himself. Furthermore, it states that the revolutionary is one who surrenders all personhood, attachments and considerations for public opinion or morals. The revolutionary is ready to use force in attainment of a revolution. The second segment describes the relations between the agent of the revolution and others working towards the revolution. It prescribes that there is no place for the self within the revolution. But it is the third and fourth sections that deal explicitly, and justify, violence. They state that the revolutionary must be ruthless and capable of destruction without any sense of remorse in order to destroy everything built up by capitalism.

Following in the footsteps of anarchism, Georges Sorel's work focuses on the preservation and defence of the revolution against parliamentary socialists. In Sorel's view the revolution was neither historically determined nor imminent. He was a fierce opponent of making concessions with the bourgeoisie because he feared that it would lead to a decadent and dysfunctional socialist society. Sorel gives violence a central role in his theory. According to him, small-scale violence was crucial for two reasons. First, it would provide impetus and accelerate the clash between the two classes. Second, he believed that violence would contribute to breaking bourgeois values and ethics, thereby creating new ones.

In the same manner, Frantz Fanon builds on Marxist thought by applying it to a colonial context. In his major work, *The Wretched of the Earth*, produced in 1961 at the height of the Algerian War of Independence, Fanon opened his work with the following line; 'Decolonisation is always a violent event' (2004, p. 1). Fanon's work argues for the necessity of violence in the emancipatory battle between the colonized and the colonizer. The violence employed by the colonized derives, and is a direct response, to the traumatizing effects of violence at the base of the colonial system. Furthermore, the need for violence stems from the fact that there can be no other alternative, psychologically, in purging the marks of violence left on the colonized. In an all too similar argument, Fanon is convinced that the morality of this revolution is entirely secondary and that the violence is justified due to the historic grievances of the colonized.

Of contemporary Marxist theorists, no one has gained more interest in the past decade than Slavoj Žižek. Similar to previous theorists, Žižek sees the purpose of violence to antagonize the working and bourgeois classes. As such, Žižek considers violence to have an empowering effect on the oppressed and to be an important tool as they demand reparation. Perhaps the most intriguing aspect of Žižek's theory is its concern with finding a form of subjectivity from which an authentic revolutionary violence can confront the violence of the state.

In doing so, Žižek argues for a new path of revolutionary action that does not run the risk of becoming a new order that establishes another form of domination advocating unfocused and excessive violence. In efforts to distinguish authentic versus inauthentic revolutionary violence, Žižek establishes a criterion which he labels 'criteria of the enacted utopia'.

The role of violence in Marxism

Many Marxists believe that violence is a necessary or inevitable phase in the construction of politics or social transition. According to them there is a historically determined revolution which will take place to reshape the relations of production, changing society from a capitalist system to a socialist one. Such a belief is also present in the anarchist thought of theorists such as Bakunin, who, while denying that such a revolution is a historical necessity, admit that it is an end that ought to be pursued. From the Marxist tradition stem the works of several more contemporary theorists, such as Sorel and Žižek, who understand in some way the necessity of a violent revolution, thus drawing a justification of the use of violence. In other words, since there is no alternative, it can be defensible. Moreover, Fanon applies the Marxist class struggle in a colonial framework and legitimizes the use of violence as the only way of reaffirming the humanity of the colonized, while also providing a psychological explanation for the necessity of violence.

For many scholars, such as Finlay as well as other theorists like Fanon, Sorel and Žižek, Marxist doctrine supports the idea that violence may be used legitimately. The necessity of violence in the works of Marx is, however, debated, as some scholars argue that there is the possibility of bloodless revolution. Perhaps one of the most insightful works of Marx is his *Communist Manifesto*, in which he describes the relation between the proletariat and the bourgeoisie and how the forces of history will lead to a revolution.

Central in this book is the indication that a revolution will necessarily take place and change the relations of production, thereby forming a new society with a new social dynamic. In Marx's view, capitalism will lead to a breaking point, where the system at hand becomes destructive to the proletariat, which is integral to the very same capitalist system. According to Marx:

in the development of productive forces there comes a stage at which productive forces and means of intercourse are called into existence which, under the existing relationship can only cause mischief, and which are no longer productive but destructive forces. (Heiss 1975, p. 355)

Marx believed that, since there was a necessary process to history, the socialist revolution could not be carried out at any time. Rather, a society must reach its proper maturity in order for socialist revolutions to be successful. In other words, until class conflict and the obsolescence of the relations of productions under a capitalist society became manifest, a socialist revolution would not be fruitful. The obsolescence of capitalist society is demonstrated by the fact that it becomes destructive for the proletariat. Therefore, the bourgeoisie becomes 'unfit to rule because it is incompetent to assure an existence to its slave within his slavery because it cannot help letting him sink into such a state, that it has to feed him, instead of being fed by him' (Marx 1994, p. 169). At this point, there is no other option than to liberate the working classes.

The first step towards the liberation of the proletariat is the formation of trade unions, and this is also one of the first manifestations of a class struggle, where the proletariat expressly defends its interests against that of the bourgeoisie. These unions are, furthermore, only made possible by the technological advance of the capitalist system as 'it furnishes the proletariat with weapons for fighting the bourgeoisie' (*ibid*., p. 167). It is the mobilization of the proletariat by these trade unions that leads an eventual confrontation with the bourgeoisie. The purpose of the confrontations will be the abolition of 'all previous securities for, and insurances of, individual property' (*ibid*., p. 168). The conclusion of this inevitability is that this 'more or less veiled civil war, raging within existing society … breaks out into open revolution, and where the violent overthrow of the bourgeoisie lays the foundation for the sway of the proletariat' (*ibid*.). Here, Marx makes an open and express appeal for a violent revolution as the only way by which the modes of appropriation may come under the ownership of the commons. Yet the question remains, is the use of violence, in principle, illegitimate, inexcusable and unjustifiable?

Finlay argues that Marxist theory explicitly justifies and excuses violence. Moreover, the role of the proletariat in creating ethical values may seek to legitimate the use of violence. This however, is a discussion which will also be present in the works of Sorel, Fanon and Žižek.

Finlay, like Arendt, uses the terms 'justify' and 'excuse' in specific ways. He uses the former to mean 'according to conduciveness to attaining just ends from "legitimacy" which claims validity according to the appropriateness of origins', and the latter when an action is demanded out of necessity, regardless of its nature as just or even legitimate. Finlay understands Marxism as justifying the use of violence, since it is a means that is used to bring about the abolition of injustice. Moreover, Finlay (2006) argues that Marxist theory also excuses the use of violence. First of all, it is essential to remember the historicity in Marx, and the necessity of the socialist revolution. This would excuse the use of violence, because as it 'forms a necessary part of successful, materially progressive revolutions, it is to be regarded as part of the natural process of human historical progress' (*ibid.*, p. 377). As such, not only is there no alternative to the use of force, from this necessity also stems the reason why revolutionaries are excused of their actions.

Most interesting, however, is Finlay's argument that Marxist thought, beyond justifying and excusing the use of violence, also legitimates it. Finlay (*ibid.*, p. 378) argues that this is done by 'undermining existing moral norms and suggesting that new ones will be created to suit a new proletarian order'. Marx argues that norms and ethics are determined by the dominating class of the time, as can be illustrated in Lenin's statement that 'Honesty is a bourgeois virtue', meaning that honesty is crucial to the existence of bourgeoisie, as other virtues such as loyalty and obedience were necessary virtues during the reign of the feudal aristocracy. This impacts the concept of justice in war dramatically.

As there is the assumption that a new social order is to be created, along with a new set of moral and ethical codes, then the current ones may be discarded. Therefore, Finlay (*ibid.*) states that it would be conceivable for revolutionaries to commit atrocious crimes in bringing about a socialist system, with the belief that their crimes will be retroactively absolved by the new system of ethics put in place by the proletariat. Finlay also addresses an alternative opinion, that of Shlomo Avineri, who believes that this may be a non-issue when one takes into account the universality of the proletariat. This universality means that it has no active class-based or sectarian interest, or, rather, that its interests represent those of all society. Its major interest is simply to 'eliminate all other special interests on the basis of which it suffers oppression' and is an entirely negative entirely (*ibid*., p. 379). Therefore, our conception of ethics and morality – the product of a capitalist society – is inaccurate. Being based on the interest of the bourgeoisie rather than a true and authentic reflection of the ethics of a universal class, its contravention is not something to be lamented. Finlay understands Avineri as drawing two conclusions. First, that:

> whatever the bourgeoisie with its individualistic and rights-based conception of political ethics and legality has to say about the morality of violence is likely to be invalid since it reflects the particular class interests and therefore the perverted humanism of its proponents. (*Ibid*., p. 370)

and, moreover, that only ethical claims of the proletariat are valid, insofar as they are true reflections of 'the perspective of the last social class, at its final, revolutionary stage of oppression' (*ibid*.). It is only then that morals and ethics can be created authentically, and all other systems ought to be considered as arbitrary. However, this creates a major difficulty for Finlay and, as Marx has inspired many other theorists (Žižek, Fanon, Sorel, etc.), this is a difficulty which he identifies in each of their works as well.

Understanding that revolutionary violence is carried out in the hope of future absolution based on a hypothetical social order able to craft a universal system of ethics, Finlay sees this as *carte blanche* for revolutionists to carry out any action, however atrocious, so long as it helps bring about this imminent revolution. Finlay's 'permissive doctrine' is a 'philosophical framework within which the possibility of using violence is validated but without setting any clear limits to how much violence can be used and against whom'. Finlay also argues that there is a tendency for excess, as Sorel, Fanon and Žižek all see the use of violence as beneficial, since it may act as a spark for the revolution. Finlay sees the total legitimation of violence in revolution, with no principle of restriction, to be both dangerous and unethical.

Robert Heiss contrasts Marx's position to that of Proudhon. Where the fourth part of the *Communist Manifesto* is 'an open declaration of war', Heiss states that Proudhon, in his rejection of dogmatism, also rejected revolution as a motor for social change, as revolution is 'an appeal to force, to arbitrary action' and as such cannot be seen as 'means of social reform' (Heiss 1975, pp. 359–60). Nonetheless, some scholars argue that the transition to a socialist state described by Marx may allow for a pacific transfer.

Finlay presents a compelling argument, highlighting the predisposition of Marxist revolutionaries not to restrict the use of violence in revolution, making it a potentially devastating affair. However, he proceeds from the assumption that Marxist thought allows for the transition to a socialist society to be possible only through revolution, and that this revolution is necessarily violent. There is debate as to whether or not Marx allowed for the possibility of a peaceful transition to socialism. If he did, then the subsequent theories of Sorel, Fanon and Žižek, extensions of the Marxist tradition, all lose a great deal of their thrust, as they are built on the assumption that violent revolution is the only way to overthrow a capitalist or colonial oppressor.

There are other scholars who argue that violence is integral to Marx, and that any statement about the possibility of a peaceful resolution to class conflict made by Marx is only the result of practical and historical considerations. One such scholar is Rustam Singh. In his article *Status of Violence in Marx's Theory of Revolution* (1989), he takes the position that any reading of Marx must include a non-negotiable use of force in the imminent revolution.

Adam Schaff is of the belief that such a violent revolution is avoidable, and underlines the instances where Marx makes explicit references to the possibility of peaceful transition. Schaff (1973, p. 265) argues that 'when the relations of production no longer fit the needs of the productive forces, the former begin to act as a brake on the latter' yet overcoming this dynamic does not need to 'always culminate in a violent revolution that results in the use of arms'. He does not attack the historicity in Marx, nor the idea of class struggle, but simply believes that the bringing about of a socialist order is possible through the peaceful expression of a class struggle.

Schaff's understanding of Marx's conception of the role of violence in revolution is a nuanced one. According to Schaff (*ibid.*, p. 266), Marx always 'approved of the possibility of a violent, armed revolution as the culminating point of class-struggle ... but he did not glorify it, either, and he did not preach it to be the only possible path to victory'. Marx thought that, under the right conditions, a peaceful transition could take place, and he points specifically to the example of England, America and, perhaps, the Netherlands. In Schaff's (*ibid.*, p. 267) words: '[Marx] claimed that it could be imagined that an old society could turn into a new one in those countries in which popular representation has all the power in its hands, where everything can be achieved constitutionally if one is supported by the majority of the nation'. Essentially, so long as a country has a (relatively) just representative democracy with parliamentary supremacy, then there is no need for the use of violence.

Singh (1989, p. 9), however, would disagree. He quotes Marx saying that:

> the revolution is necessary ... not only because the ruling class cannot be overthrown in any other way, but also because the class overthrowing it can only in a revolution succeeded in ridding itself of all the muck of ages and become fitted to found society anew.

Singh makes a principled argument: that Marx saw the use of violence, even when it is avoidable, as required insofar as that it has a purging quality, believing that only by using violence can all elements of the previous regime be eradicated. Moreover, Singh (*ibid.*, p. 14) considers Marx's references to the use of bourgeois democratic institutions to bring about social change only as 'hinting to the possibility of the working class coming into power, in England, through universal suffrage'. Furthermore, he quotes Engels in a letter addressed to the Communist Committee in Brussels in October 1846. In this letter, Engels states that there cannot be any means of carrying out the communist agenda 'other than a democratic revolution by force' (*ibid.*, p. 10). Singh, however, does acknowledge the desire in Marx to avoid a bloody revolution.

Singh (*ibid.*, p. 11) notes that most Marxist writing that alluded to the possibility of this transition being carried out peacefully took place before the events of 1844–48, which 'showed that a peaceful change was not even remotely possible'. After 1848, Singh notes a return to advocating a violent revolution due to what Singh identifies as the 'practical considerations' of being unable to overcome the existing obstacles to a peaceful transition. Singh (*ibid.*, p. 13) writes that, in 1848, Marx published an article titled *The Victory of Counter-Revolution in Vienna*, where he states: 'there is only one means by which the murderous death agonies of the old society and the bloody birth throes of the new society can be shortened, simplified and concentrated – and that is by revolutionary terror'.

Despite this, Schaff (1973, p. 268) endeavours to show that to break with the assumed violent tradition of Marxist thought does not '"betray" the principle of social revolution'. In other words, one may be a Marxist without the unequivocal call for a violent revolution. In fact, according to Schaff, admitting the possibility of a peaceful transition to socialism is perfectly in line with revolutionist thought, as the emphasis placed on the requirements for such a transition outlines the need for revolution should such prerequisites be absent. This conception does not eliminate class struggle. Indeed, Schaff (*ibid.*, p. 269) feels the need, later in his text, to mention once more that 'it would be naive to think that radical changes in social life would take place ... without resistance, protests, and even determined struggle on the part of the reactionary groups of the bourgeoisie'. Schaff shows that the acceptance of the possibility of peaceful resolution to class struggle is possible in Marxist theory while still being considered a revolutionary rather than a reformist.

Singh (1989, p. 10), however, sees the manifestation of class struggle as anything but peaceful, 'for the aim of this struggle will inevitably be to demolish the bourgeois mode of production and, thereby, the bourgeois social order which stands on its shoulders'. While Schaff admits the difficulty in assuming that bourgeois interests will not present an obstacle to the peaceful introduction of socialism, Singh views it as impossible to imagine that bourgeois interests will not lead to the use of violence against the proletariat. Singh (*ibid.*, p. 16) argues that, while a bloodless change is ideal, nowhere does Marx claim that this change can be brought about exclusively with the use of peaceful means. He further develops his point by showing that, although Marx would like to see a peaceful transition, communists would not shy away from the use of violence should there be obstacles presented in the path of progress (Singh 1989), with many of the determining factors as to whether or not violence was used in bringing about a socialist government resting on historical and contextual elements. Whether or not violence is an absolute necessity in the work of Marx, it is clear that is has a privileged role. There are other theorists, however, who depart from Marxist thought with the belief that violence is not only a practical requirement to bring about a revolution, but that it also holds therapeutic or pedagogic roles in shaping the consciousness of the proletariat.

Violence in anarchism

One of the most interesting of Bakunin's texts is the *Catechism of a Revolutionary* (1871). There is some debate regarding to whom this work is attributed; whether it was Bakunin, Nechaev, or both, the *Catechism* provides a significant insight into the attitude of the revolutionary. The second part of the text, the most famous part, is divided into four segments. The first deals with the revolutionary's view of himself, essentially surrendering all personhood (particular interest, sentiments, personal attachments etc.) and motivated only by one thought – that of the revolution. The revolutionary is a hard individual, with no emotions, attachments, or consideration for public opinion or morals that could prevent him from his ultimate goal. He is essentially a machine with one purpose, and that purpose is revolution (Confino, Bakunin and Nechaev, 1975). Already we can see that there is a necessary readiness for the use of force. The revolutionary must be prepared to sacrifice his life for the revolution and, at the same time, disregard the bourgeois system of ethics as he is effectively at war with capitalist society.

The second segment describes the relation of this agent of revolution with other members working towards achieving revolution. It is equally as dehumanizing as the previous section. Here it states that friendships are not born out of any consideration other than their utility towards furthering the goals of the revolution (*ibid.*). This is extended to the point that, if his friend faces danger, the revolutionary must weigh his friend's utility to the revolutionary cause, and the damage caused by his rescue, and make his decision based on this. There is effectively no room for the self in this conception of 'the revolutionary'.

The third segment discusses the relationship of the revolutionary with society. Again, the revolutionary must be ruthless, capable of destruction without hesitation, even of those nearest to him. Yet, at the same time, the revolutionary must be able to be a chameleon and exist in society should it be required of him. Moreover, in light of the injustice present in society, revolutionaries must make lists of those upon whom to exercise their violence. These lists are comprised of members of society that subjugate the rest, and perpetuate the unjust system of capitalism (*ibid.*).

Finally, the fourth segment discusses the relationship of anarchist society towards the people. Here is the first hint of a moral consideration. The first line says that 'the Society has no other goal than the liberation of the people, that is to say, the workers' (*ibid.*, p. 104). Bakunin further states explicitly that this is not possible through any other way than a popular revolution that would destroy everything.

We can also see a similarity to Marx, as he advocated that a revolution can be only achieved by 'developing and spreading all the misery and pain which will finally exhaust the patience of the people and push them towards a general uprising' (*ibid.*). However, this concept of class antagonism differs from Marx's as Bakunin is calling for the active reduction in the standards of life of the workers, whereas thinkers in the Marxist tradition support class antagonism as a reaction by the state to an action of the workers. Bakunin seems to advocate the active and direct targeting of the same people who he endeavours to rescue.

The *Catechism* delineates the case for violence in Bakunin. Like many others, he laments that 'humanity has not yet invented a more peaceful means of progress', but suggests that any other path is not realistic (in Abbey 1959, p. 22). Moreover, in his description of the revolutionary, who 'is depicted as a complete immoralist', despite him being cold, unattached and shunning society, there is a hidden morality to this (Avrich 1974, p. 11). One must not forget that this soldier of revolution is only in existence himself as a means to inflict violence on and destroy the structures of the bourgeois state, for no other purpose than the liberation of the people.

Kropotkin's essay, translated in English as 'Must we Occupy Ourselves with an Examination of the Ideal of a Future System?', provides an insightful view into his thought about the place that violence would take in his anarchist thought. It is interesting particularly for its differences with Marxist thought in relation to the necessity of violence, and its similarities concerning the necessity of class antagonism. First and foremost, it must be said that part of Kropotkin's rejection of attaining the goal of revolution is his disagreement with Marx on the subject of historical determinism. Kropotkin (1970, p. 75) argues that those who favour peaceful means 'proceed from that utterly unproven position that every people must inevitably pass through all those phases of development which other peoples have passed through'. What is interesting, however, is that by his comment he seems to imply that there is space in Marxist thought for a peaceful transition to socialism. He states that those who think in this way are approaching the issue mistakenly. What ought to be asked, is 'What condition most hastens social insurrection?' (*ibid.*, p. 76). This question carries with it a background assumption, that 'social transformation cannot occur by peaceful means, but inevitably it must occur by means of insurrection' (*ibid.*). It should be noted, however, that Kropotkin neither dismissed nor glorified violence, but always assumed that a certain level would be required in the revolution. Rather, Kropotkin was of the belief that if there is a clear and defined goal towards which the revolution strives then there will be a reduction in bloodshed due to the efficiency of the revolution; Kropotkin saw it as a duty to reduce the violence in revolution.

Furthermore, he states that a revolution is tantamount to the self-sacrifice of the revolutionist, and that there have to be conditions which make this self-sacrifice seem to be a valid alternative. Kropotkin states that, for a revolution to begin, there have to be four conditions present. First, there must be a widespread realization and dissatisfaction with the current state of affairs. Second, it must be acknowledged that such conditions are otherwise eternal and, third, that they cannot be remedied by conventional means. Finally, these prerequisites must create the condition where the people are prepared to take risks, namely, that they are willing to make that self-sacrifice. This can be equated to Marx's class antagonism, as the more oppressed a person is, the greater is their hatred for the state. Moreover, Kropotkin argues that political rights will dampen the revolutionary spirit. Much like Sorel's social order to be discussed later, there has to be great and widespread alienation between the individual and the state.

Political rights carry with them a secondary difficulty as well: the same political rights must be granted to each individual. This is problematic in that freedom of speech, while allowing those such as Kropotkin and other anarchists to spread their views, also allows for a panoply of other conflicting views to be spread as well, thereby preventing 'less developed people the possibility to confront matters squarely' (*ibid.*, p.79). As such, rights such as free speech are the enemy of the worker on two counts, for, in addition to preventing the expression of their revolutionary desires, it 'enfolds a man in the midst of a world foreign to him', mesmerizing him and preventing his participation in revolution (*ibid.*).

The role of violence in the work of Georges Sorel

Georges Sorel wrote in the Marxist tradition during the early years of the twentieth century. His major concern was that 'parliamentary socialists', those who tried to bring about socialism through parliamentary methods, would bargain with the bourgeoisie and obtain certain concessions (such as higher wages, better working conditions and other labour laws), which would then 'sap the proletariat of its energy and rob it of its revolution' (Finlay 2006, p. 381). This fear was exacerbated due to the fact that Sorel rejected the historical determinism of Marx. For him, the socialist revolution was not imminent and guaranteed. Yet social peace was not in and of itself sufficient to worry Sorel, as he believed the act of giving concessions by the bourgeoisie would show the concepts of scarcity and social duty to be entirely artificial, leading the proletariat to further question the logic of capitalism. What did preoccupy Sorel was the idea that, if this bargaining took place, it might lead to a decadent Europe. Combined with the conservative nature of revolutions (that a new regime will conserve certain aspects of the one it replaces), Sorel feared that this might lead to a decadent and dysfunctional socialist society. It is in light of this belief that Sorel argues against any *rapprochement* between the bourgeoisie and capitalists.

By this line of thought, Sorel gives violence a central role in his theory. To Sorel, violence was crucial as it served two major purposes. First, it would accelerate the clash between the two classes by antagonizing them and showing their clear divisions. Second was Sorel's belief that bringing about a socialist order would have to be the product of the 'creative spontaneity of an advanced proletarian consciousness entirely divorced from the old bourgeois order' (*ibid.*, p. 382). Violence, in Sorel's view, contributed to creating this break with values and ethics of the establishment. In essence, anything that would contribute to the segregation of the bourgeoisie and the proletariat would be beneficial insofar as it helped create a genuinely proletarian state, unsullied by established bourgeois values. In practice, this meant the use of violence on a small scale, which would then give force to the idea that there is an inevitable and violent clash between the classes. The use of violence on a small scale would create further separation between the classes, giving way to the actual violent manifestation of the final class struggle.

This is why Finlay ascribes a moral dimension to Sorel's use of violence. He states that the use of violence is not primarily motivated by practical considerations. As the purpose of violence seems to be to antagonize classes, inspire revolutionary spirit and educate, it therefore takes the role of a 'key element in the moral transformation of humanity' (*ibid*., p. 383). Indeed, Sorel's view of violence is one which helps shape the subjectivity of the proletariat by antagonizing the proletariat and the bourgeoisie, therefore allowing for a more genuine construction of a socialist state.

Finlay, always cautious when it comes to legitimating the use of violence, highlights the difficulties that other major theorists such as Georg Lukacs have with Sorel's conception of violence. Lukacs, says Finlay, sees the use of such violence to be in contravention of legal and moral standards. This is a formulation of a similar problem in other theorists who have been influenced by Marx, whereby the 'responsible revolutionaries are torn between the limits of an old, bourgeois ethics and the ethics of a future society which may or may not be about to emerge', which may lead to justifying a wide array of brutal crimes (*ibid*., p. 384). Moreover, this confusion between ethical systems is inescapable, as 'by its very nature revolution in this sense cannot be linked to an already established set of criteria of justice' (Frazer and Hutchings 2009, p. 57). This only exacerbates the issue, as the criteria of justice of the old regime are void; however, the criteria of the new one are not yet established. As such, there 'are no limits in principle on what that violence may entail in practice' (*ibid*., p. 60).

Lukacs therefore argues that any acts of violence that are committed should not be considered a priori justified. At the same time, however, these necessary acts of violence ought to be carried out in the hope that the new system of ethics which emerges from the proletariat consciousness will, in fact, legitimate them (so long as they are carried out with the direct goal of bringing about a socialist revolution). Lukacs concludes that the proletarian revolutionary would do well to avoid the bourgeois definitions of legal and illegal, and carry out their necessary actions 'courageously' with the awareness that they are not justified.

Frazer and Hutchings agree with Finlay in that there seems to be a fundamental problem with the issue of the promise of legitimating certain acts of violence in the future. They identify the root of the issue as mistakenly applying 'scientific means – end reasoning to an inherently unpredictable world in order to realise the blueprint of justice' (*ibid*., p. 55). This promise of retroactive absolution is again problematic, as it becomes 'easy to slip into the mistake of justifying all kinds of means in terms of future justice' (*ibid*.).

The role of violence in the work of Frantz Fanon

Frantz Fanon wrote his major work *The Wretched of the Earth* in 1961, during the closing years of the Algerian War, which lead to the independence of Algeria from France. Fanon builds on Marxist thought by applying it to a colonial context, where the bourgeoisie is replaced by the colonists and the proletariat is colonized. The preface was written by Jean Paul Sartre and deserves a closer examination. Sartre outlines many themes in Fanon's work which have to deal with the very system of colonialism. Fanon endeavours to show that such a system cannot be remedied, and cannot be rationalized. Only its utter destruction can lead to the emancipation of the colonized, and this unequivocally requires the use of force.

Before a discussion of the necessity of violence in Fanon, we must examine how Fanon sees the dynamic present in colonial states. Fanon sees the world inside the colony as a fundamentally confrontational and resentful one. The use of legal force is concentrated within the hands of the colonists. Moreover, while the system is composed, necessarily, of two entities – the colonists and the colonized – one of them 'is entirely superfluous', rendering any kind of discussion or dialogue impossible. This is in spite of the fact that the 'superfluous' entity is the aboriginal, the native and authentic population, while the second is an outsider, 'the other' (Fanon 2004).

Sartre, in the preface, brings up the issue of the hypocrisy of European humanism, which, on the one hand, elevates the human being to a universal status and yet, in practice, marginalizes an entire population as the colonized. This leads to a basic assumption, that the system of colonization is a dehumanizing one, an assumption later made explicit in Fanon. Through practice, it is made clear that since a colonist can, without crime, rob, subjugate or kill his similar, therefore it is posited in principle that the colonised is not equal to a human' (Fanon 1961, p. 51) . It is in response to this view, to this intolerable dehumanization, that the colonized react and understand the need to cast off the domination of the colonist. The dynamic may be described thus: 'the work of the colonist is to make even the dreams of liberty impossible for the colonised. The work of the colonised is to imagine every possible method for annihilating the colonist' (Fanon 2004, p. 50).

Additionally, what marks this work as astounding is its decidedly non-eurocentrist (or rather colonist-centred) approach. There is no engagement with the colonist; there is no dialogue or discussion. This book strips the European colonizer of a privileged position as the subject of a discussion, to a mere object. And the only way to deal with the colonist as such, a member of a corrupt system aimed solely at racist exploitation, is through the use of violence.

Fanon states outright, in the first sentence of his work, that 'decolonisation is always a violent event' and the aboriginal can only regain human status after a 'murderous and decisive confrontation between the two protagonists' (*ibid.*, p. 1). The necessity of the use of force in Fanon is derived primarily from the violence to which the colonized has been subjected. Bearing in mind that the 'colonist's only resort is the use of force' (Fanon 1961, p. 13) and this force is used to dehumanize, Fanon manages to provide a psychological account of what takes place once force is used.

According to Fanon, when the colonist subjects an aboriginal to violence, that has a traumatizing effect. The impact of the use of force does not stop at the same time as the colonist stops the immediate blows, but, rather, has a lingering impact. The aboriginal absorbs this violence which will, in turn, 'incite in their bodies nothing else than a volcanic rage with a strength equal to that of the pressure exercised upon them' (*ibid.*, p. 16).

Already we are able to see that, for Fanon, there is no other alternative than the use of force directed against the colonist. Given that a colonist necessarily subjects an aboriginal to violence, and that this violence is not absorbed and erased, but rather retained to an explosive degree, and that violence can only be repaid in the same way, then the use of force, a bloody uprising against the dominant force, is the only option available to the colonized to regain their humanity.

The immediate outcome of this subjection to violence will be that the colonized will express this absorbed violence towards one another, looking for an outlet by which they can expel this dehumanizing force. However, this is not a perpetual state. According to

Fanon, 'violence continues to progress, the colonised subject identifies with his enemy, puts a name to all of his misfortunes, and casts all his exacerbated hatred and rage in this new direction' (Fanon 2004, p. 31). Using Finlay's vocabulary, violence can be directed towards the colonist when there is an attainment of 'revolutionary subjectivity'. We can see clearly the unifying aspect of violence; it dissolves all artificial segregations in colonized societies (based on clans, tribes, religion, regionalism etc.) and leaves nothing but a sense of community and the consciousness of a national struggle in the colonized people .

The need for violence stems from the fact that there can be no other alternative, psychologically, to purge the marks of violence than the use of violence directed against the initial aggressor. As such, 'the colonised can only be healed of the colonial neurosis by chasing out the colonist with arms' (Fanon 1961, p. 20). The use of violence, the very act of revolt against the oppressing presence of the colonists, requires the act of killing European colonists. To do so is:

> to kill two birds with one stone. It eliminates at the same time an oppressor and an oppressed: leaving behind one dead man, and a free man; the survivor, for the first time, feels a *national* soil under his feet. (*Ibid.*, p. 20)

The national consciousness is therefore born out of the violent revolt against an oppressor.

Moreover, Sartre states explicitly that nonviolence is simply not a reasonable option. He claims that if it were the case that domination and exploitation were recent phenomenon, if it were the case that they did not condition the very essence of the regime, then perhaps nonviolence might have had a chance of diffusing the situation. However, since violence is entrenched in the structure of the regime, then there can be no remedy to it other than violent revolt. Furthermore, the peaceful coexistence of these two separate and opposing forces is impossible, due to the fact that 'the colonist is no longer interested in staying on and coexisting once the colonial context has disappeared' (Fanon 2004, p. 9). Fanon (*ibid.*, p. 23) criticized the 'colonized intellectual', the colonial bourgeoisie and the path of mediation and nonviolence, as he claims that the system of colonialism is 'not a machine capable of thinking, a body endowed with reason. It is naked violence and only gives in when confronted with greater violence.' Negotiating in the colonial context is therefore not possible. Even if it were, the goal is not to make the context more agreeable, to obtain 'better life and improved wages', but the 'radical overthrow of the system' (*ibid.*, p.22). The national bourgeoisie is working to prevent this national struggle from reaching its full and authentic expression, while 'enlightened by violence, the people's consciousness rebels against any pacification' (*ibid.*, p. 52).

Fanon's work states outright that the use of violence is not only a necessity, but that it is also desirable, that it will lead to an infinitely better society. According to Finlay, there are three important ethical conclusions in Fanon's work. First, it is implied that 'violence against the colonist is *just* because it enacts *just* retribution against European colonists whose violence is thus revenged' (Finlay, 2006, p. 384, emphasis original). Moreover, it has been shown that violence takes a necessary and inevitable role if the desired outcome is the end of colonialism. Finlay sees this as potentially dangerous as Fanon is thereby removing any moral responsibility from the use violence, having equated it with a natural process. Finally, Finlay (*ibid.*, p. 385) states that 'the violence of a native against a coloniser is presented as a necessary part of the preparation of true revolutionary subjectivity', since it is only through violent expression that the evil of colonialism may finally be purged.

For Fanon, the morality of this revolution is entirely secondary, and implicitly justified due to the historic grievances of the colonized as well as the necessity for this use of force. However, Finlay outlines that there are certain important consequences of Fanon's thought. Finlay argues that Fanon's view has important consequences for Europeans. First, there is the idea that due to the unilateral dynamic between Europe and the colonies, colonists 'cannot say anything that has any meaning beyond their own culture about the morality of violence as it confronts them in the colonies' (*ibid.*, p. 386). Second, and this is stated explicitly both by Fanon and Sartre, there is no such thing as an innocent colonist. Any moral outrage or disagreement with the system does not erase the collective guilt placed upon all members of the 'metropolis' who have, in some way benefited from the system of colonialism. This means that there can effectively be no restraint on violence, that, in light of the arbitrary or foreign moral standards in place, any act can be committed to pursue the cause of revolution. Just as in Marx, this is done with the belief that the system that will be established in its place may retroactively absolve them of any wrongdoing.

The role of violence in the work of Slavoj Žižek

Slavoj Žižek is the most recent and one of the most interesting theorists who anticipates the reproaches made thus far to Marx, Sorel and Fanon. His theory begins with an exposition of the dynamic of the use of force between the dominated and the dominator. Žižek believes that the 'effectiveness of the master's rule … is based on the subject's masochistic desire to be ruled' (*ibid.*, p. 387). If this is the case, then how can there be any authentic revolutionary action? The subject's 'libidinal' investment in the relationship seems to prevent the possibility of forming an actual revolutionary subjectivity. The subject does so by directing violence at himself. By assuming the role of the master, by effectively rendering the master superfluous, the subject is able to reach closer to a revolutionary subjectivity.

Here Žižek separates two paths of action. One is defined as 'substituting-dominating solicitude' and the other is 'anticipatory-liberating solicitude' (*ibid.*). This can best be explained by understanding the former to be 'enabling', and the latter to be 'empowering'. Substituting-dominating solicitude is the act of providing 'short-term partial relief', much like in Sorel's social peace, which calms the revolutionary spirit and extends the life of the bourgeoisie. An anticipatory-liberating solicitude on the other hand, 'is one which helps oppressed subjects to help themselves, leading to autonomous liberation' (*ibid.*).

Here, the role of violence becomes clear. Similar to previous theorists, the purpose of violence is to antagonize the classes, and leads to confrontation between the proletariat and the bourgeois state. Most importantly, however, 'violence by the oppressor, paradoxically, is better than charity because it openly confesses itself and compels the oppressed to confront themselves in the reality of their situation' (*ibid.*, p. 388). As such, violence has the effect of empowering the oppressed to realize their situation and demand reparation through confrontation with the state. Both of these processes allow for the awakening of a revolutionary subjectivity, what Finlay defines as 'an attitude tending towards true liberation' (*ibid.*).

Perhaps the most interesting part of Žižek's theory is the question of finding a form of subjectivity from which an authentic revolutionary violence may 'confront the inauthentic, excessive and illegitimate violence of the state' (*ibid.*). The answer to this question will also provide a reply to Finlay's critique of Marx, Sorel and Fanon. The importance of finding such an authentic form of subjectivity is that it would allow for locating a path of action which simultaneously escapes the danger of becoming a new order (establishing another form of forceful domination), as well as the general, unfocused and abusive use of violence so abhorrent to Finlay. To answer this dilemma, Žižek constructs the only criterion which can effectively distinguish authentic and inauthentic revolutionary violence. This he calls the 'criteria of the enacted utopia' (*ibid.*). Žižek recognizes that while the 'utopian future' is not yet realized, it is not quite as far as Finlay might think. It is as if 'we are ... briefly allowed to act as if the utopian future is (not yet fully here but) already at hand, there to be seized' (Žižek 2002, p. 259). Legitimizing the act of revolution is not based on the outcome of the struggle, nor is it based on the ethical system that will be established after this struggle takes place. According to Žižek (*ibid.*), 'it is, as it were, *its own ontological proof,* an immediate index of its own truth'. Finlay (2006, p. 389) is still unsatisfied with this response, however, and writes somewhat grimly 'in the absence of any independent criteria, recognition of its legitimacy must rest on our trust in the good faith of the revolutionaries themselves'. This is not adequate, as there is no other perspective than that from within the revolutionary subjectivity where its legitimacy may be understood and evaluated.

Running through this article was Finlay's analysis of Marxist theory of revolution, and how it shaped the subsequent theories of Sorel, Fanon and Žižek. Finlay understands that this school of thought justifies and excuses the use of violence. However, each of the theorists provides a space, based on the future state established after a revolution, which brings with it its own ethics, where any act of violence contributing to bringing about the revolution can actually be legitimated. Such an understanding eliminates the possibility of a principle of restraint, and can be used to legitimate any crimes committed during a revolution. This also applies in part to the anarchist theorists, who saw violence as an important tool for class antagonism, leading to revolt. In Bakunin there was a particular use of violence, enacted by the revolutionary who seems to be accountable to no one, simply having a vague admiration of the working people and a strong commitment to the revolutionary cause.

Further reading

Bernstein, R. J. (2013) *Violence: Thinking without Banisters*. A study of the thoughts on violence of Carl Schmitt, Walter Benjamin, Hannah Arendt, Frantz Fanon and Jan Assmann and their significance for our times.

Finlay, C. J. (2006) 'Violence and Revolutionary Subjectivity: Marx to Žižek', *European Journal of Political Theory*. An exploration of the relationship between revolution and violence in Marxism and in a series of texts drawing on Marxian theory.

Gordon, L. R. (1995) *Fanon and the Crisis of European Man: An Essay on Philosophy and the Human Sciences*. A book that is rare in analyzing the work of Fanon as a liberation philosopher and a thinker of violence.

Leier, M. (2006) *Bakunin: The Creative Passion: A Biography*. This book provides the best information about Bakunin's life, words and thoughts.

Chapter 8

Nonviolence in the Twentieth Century

The twentieth century witnessed a few remarkable figures that employed nonviolent rhetoric and practice in efforts to combat injustices and oppression. Gandhi's nonviolence, due to its spiritual and political applicability, influenced a number of other prominent political leaders such as Martin Luther King, Jr, Nelson Mandela and the Dalai Lama.

Symbolically, Martin Luther King, Jr was the undisputed leader of the Civil Rights movement – even after his assassination – from 1950 through to the 80s. A scholar of theology and devout Christian, King received his source of strength and belief in nonviolent practice from his faith. Like Gandhi, King's spirituality played an important role in his political action. Heavily influencing King's relationship with people were two fundamental religious qualities: fellowship and goodness. Through the notion of God's love of humanity, King believed that God was a personality that could be encountered in any individual who expressed these attributes. Furthermore, he believed that a unique way to relate to God was through Jesus Christ. Christ's figure was central to King because he was a constant source of love. In Christ King saw an inspirational figure that was concerned with social justice.

The centrality of Christ for King was affirmed in his sermon titled 'Can a Christian be a Communist?'. In this sermon King came up with three explanations of what it means to establish a connection with Jesus Christ. Therefore, in order for one to connect with Christ they must: (1) talk about the life and death of Jesus Christ, (2) live out their words and (3) have the will to die for the cause of Jesus. The conclusion King reaches through his work is that a follower of Christ must emulate his image, striving for love and justice above everything else. Wherever one meets injustice one must rise above hatred and violence.

As such, with the willingness to suffer, nonviolence becomes a choice of love that every strong individual must make. Because nonviolence calls for suffering, it is therefore an act of abandoning the internal violence of the spirit.

For King, embracing love had three main functions. First, it drove out hate and allowed individuals to develop the highest good. Second, love had the power to achieve dialogue and eventually reconciliation. Lastly, love could overcome both evil and spiritual blindness. Therefore, in order for one to understand King's conception of nonviolence they must study the philosophy of love.

In the same way that King applied Christian teachings of nonviolence in his struggles, retired Anglican Archbishop Desmond Tutu applied Christian nonviolence to the conflicts of South Africa. In the aftermath of the South African apartheid regime, Tutu played a central role in the 1995 Truth and Reconciliation Commission (TRC). Using Christian nonviolence philosophy as the main instrument in the Commission, his conception of truth was linked to the concept of reconciliation. Under the vision of Christian nonviolence, the key to revealing and accepting the truth was offering forgiveness, redemption and amnesty. Through reconciliation, Tutu applied the Christian doctrine of universal salvation whereby all sinful souls will ultimately be reconciled with God. Therefore, one can argue that Tutu's notion of fellowship is closely linked to Gandhi's communitarian ethos of interfaith dialogue and communal harmony. In addition, his conception of nonviolence, naturally, resembles that of King's centrality of love as a means for spiritual and material transformation.

Tutu's teachings are important because they analyze the community as a forum for differences and otherness. In confronting the racism of the apartheid regime, Tutu not only sought to bring clarity and solidarity to the South African community, but to restructure justice and peace. The dominant view in the TRC was created through the combination of transnational human rights values and a Christian ethic of forgiveness and salvation. This dominating ethic blocked the possibility of violence in the form of punishment and retribution.

Similar messages of peace, love and nonviolence are a staple of Mother Teresa's teachings. Mother Teresa believed that her duty was to serve the poor regardless of public acknowledgment, except if that promoted funds being raised for her cause, and that this work should not be monopolized by Christians or Catholics, but that it was everyone's responsibility, regardless of their creed. Her immense influence was possible because of her limitless passion and devotion for the cause of nonviolence. In fact, her notion of nonviolence derived from her notion of love, which was profoundly linked to her Christian religion. According to Mother Teresa, those that were not loved could not be expected to return their love. As such, words of love were not in themselves enough – rather, love as action, through work, was crucial. Like all Christians practising nonviolence, Mother Teresa believed that love required sacrifice from within. The highest example of love as sacrifice lies in loving those who cause us harm, our enemies, by means of avoiding revenge. As such, Mother Teresa used her faith to link the suffering of Christ with the suffering of the poor.

Despite the fact that Mother Teresa was a religious figure, she realized that political activity was necessary in promoting nonviolence. It was for this reason that Mother Teresa appealed to heads of state rather than Catholic priests. Her 'love in action' promoted public awareness of the violence of poverty.

As mentioned earlier, the Buddhist tradition has also produced figures that have been deeply committed to the cause of nonviolence, for example, His Holiness the Dalai Lama. It is the Dalai Lama's belief, however, that nonviolence is contrary to human nature, which is interdependent with the self and on a quest for happiness. As such, the Dalai Lama provides his followers with a number of reasons to reject violence, ranging from ethical to strategic. Like Gandhi, the Dalai Lama's actions are a result of his path towards truth. This truth is not represented as an intellectual or theoretical quest, but as a concrete attitude towards life.

To lead a life of nonviolence is to share life among human beings, with their miseries and problems. It is in this sense that nonviolence is presented as a quest for truth. The social philosophy of the Dalai Lama is one of kindness and compassion, which is revealed in the connection the between the personal, socio-moral transformations, and a traditional Tibetan approach in training the mind and heart (Timm 1997). In supporting nonviolence, the Dalai Lama calls for the elimination of any notion of otherness in social relations, as it is seen as contradictory to universal harmony. A central concept of universal harmony is the idea of interdependence, as signified in the Buddha, suggesting that every element in the universe is linked together and that nothing has a disconnected existence. Just like other species, humans must maintain their harmony with one another through compassion and nonviolence.

These ideas are exemplified in the Dalai Lama's struggles for an independent Tibet. The first step in this struggle is to offer forgiveness, for it is the only way to have hope for a true reconciliation. For this reason, for the past 55 years His Holiness has urged his Tibetan followers to endure suffering and self-discipline in the face of Chinese aggression.

In neighbouring Burma, Aung San Suu Kyi has employed Buddhist teaching such as compassion and self-strength in her battle to bring the country democracy. Suu Kyi's spirituality strengthened her resolve to withstand years of house arrest and isolation. Her nonviolent philosophy emanates from her support of democratic institutions that are founded in respect for justice and peace. Above all, Suu Kyi envisions the ordinary people, or the 'power of the powerless', as the cornerstone of the nonviolent revolution to usher in democracy.

Martin Luther King

In the vast landscape of the twentieth century, only a handful of individuals stand out as prophets of nonviolence. Gandhi's nonviolence, in being both spiritual and political, set the stage for leaders like Martin Luther King, Jr, Nelson Mandela and the Dalai Lama to fight for freedom, equality, justice and independence. Gandhi's campaigns in India inspired them to employ nonviolence as a strategy. The fact that Martin Luther King (see Profile 8.1) was a theology scholar and a believer in Christ had a great impact on the way he saw life in general and nonviolence in particular. For King, it can be seen that nonviolence was both spiritual and political, arising out of his religious beliefs. King believed in a personal and Christian God, who bestowed dignity to all human beings, and was, therefore, convinced that love was the only thing that could bring about a true transformation of American society. 'From Personalism, King came to believe that there is worth in all people, and that a personal God exists' (McElrath 2008, p. 58). King (1986, p. 40) rejected any understanding that presented God as a distant entity. According to him:

> To say God is personal is not to make him an object among other objects or attribute to him the finiteness and limitations of human personality; it is to take what is finest and noblest in our

consciousness and affirm its perfect existence in him ... So in the truest sense of the word, God is a living God. In him there is feeling and will, responsive to the deepest yearnings of the human heart: this God both evokes and answers prayers.

For King, God's fellowship and goodness – two fundamental religious categories – could only be applied to a person. Another argument King used as a rationale for personalism was that God's fellowship was especially expressed in his love for humanity, and that only a person can express love. Therefore, God was a personality who could be encountered, present throughout the universe, comprehensible to any individual, to whom people could relate. According to King, a very unique way to relate to God was through Jesus Christ. As the embodiment of King's belief in a personal God, Christ was a central figure because he was a constant source of inspiration and a model of love. Christ was particularly important in King's quest for social justice. For King, one of the main concerns of the Christian religion was a passionate concern for social justice, and every Christian, like Jesus himself, should be a committed person. King (*ibid.*, p. 38) affirmed:

> Any religion that professes to be concerned about the souls of men and is not concerned about the slums that damn them, the economic conditions that strangle them and the social conditions that cripple them is a spiritually moribund religion awaiting burial.

The centrality of Christ for King is clearly expressed in a sermon he gave on 30 September 1962 called 'Can a Christian be a Communist?'. During the sermon, King provides three definitions of what it means to be witness of Christ according to the New Testament. The first meaning is to talk about life, death and resurrection of Christ. The second meaning is to live out what one talks about. The third meaning involves the willingness to die for the cause of Jesus Christ, and King emphasizes the importance of this dimension by explaining that if one is not ready to stand up for what one believes in, one is already dead. For Martin Luther King, through Christ it becomes clear that God maintains a personal interest in all human beings. Therefore, King comes to the conclusion that as a follower of Christ who believes in a God who personally loves all human beings, the only attitude in life is love and justice. 'Those of us who call the name of Jesus Christ find something at the centre of our faith which forever reminds us that God is on the side of truth and justice' (*ibid.*, p. 88). For King (*ibid.*) 'the universe is on the side of justice', therefore the ideal of brotherhood is a reality and not an illusion. But one cannot rise against injustice with hatred and violence. Nonviolence, for King, is a choice of love made by strong individuals and as such it requires 'every bit as much preparation, discipline, sacrifice, courage' (Hanigan 1984, p. 182). Thus, the purpose of nonviolence is to gain the opponent's friendship and understanding, not to cause bitterness and chaos by humiliating the adversary. As such, in King's philosophy, nonviolent resistance requires a willingness to suffer. One must accept violence without retaliating and must be willing to accept any consequences brought about by nonviolent resistance. 'To suffer in a righteous cause is to grow to our humanity's full stature' (King 1986, p. 487). Nonviolence is, therefore, an abandonment of internal violence of spirit. Before any struggle for justice, a certain amount of interior struggle and hope is required. In other words, the nonviolent resister must have faith that justice will occur in the future, even if he or she will not be present to witness it.

However, to bring nonviolence into another dimension and make it a way of life, one has to embrace the crucial ethics of love. In forming his views on nonviolence, and his whole worldview in general, King was influenced heavily by the concept of love, and specifically by the form of love known as agape. For King, agape is the centre of the universe and the ultimate principle of life:

> Agape is disinterested love. It is a love in which the individual seeks not his own good, but the good of his neighbor. ... It springs from the need of the other person – his need for belonging to the best of the human family ... It is not a weak, passive love. It is love in action. Agape is love seeking to preserve and create community. It is insistence on community even when one seeks to break it. Agape is a willingness to sacrifice in the interest of mutuality. Agape is a willingness to go to any length to restore community. (*Ibid.*, pp. 19–20)

More specifically, King saw love as having three main functions. First, it drove out hate. This is important because hate brings severe damage to its victims, and love allows us to drive it out and develop the highest good. Second, it had the power to achieve reconciliation between enemies and create mutual respect among communities. Third, and finally, love overcomes spiritual blindness and evil. To avoid blindness, one needs to have a right mind and a right heart, and there cannot be a right heart without love. Therefore, in order to understand King's views on nonviolence as a way to face injustice, one must first study his philosophy of love. According to King (*ibid.*, p. 83), 'Love is a transforming power that can lift a whole community to new horizons of fair play, good will and justice.' King, however, believed that love, as nonviolence, could be achieved by committed people. Further he noted that love was a powerful instrument in transforming the whole world. He affirmed, 'What is the *summum bonum* of life? I think I have discovered the highest good. It is love. This principle stands at the center of the cosmos. As John says, "God is love." He who loves is a participant in the being of God. He who hates does not know God' (*ibid.*, p. 11). From King's point of view, the reason why we should love our enemies is because hate intensifies the existence of evil in the universe and distorts the personality of the hater. King held that individuals should not lower themselves to the level of their oppressor by retaliating with violence. Instead, one should show his or her moral strength with love, because love has within it a redemptive power that transforms the enemy. For King this is the creative power that people like Jesus and Gandhi discovered and that the world so desperately needs to discover if it is to avoid complete destruction. King (*ibid.*, p. 16) relied heavily on this analysis and argued, 'I had come to see early that the Christian doctrine of love operating through the Gandhian method of nonviolence was one of the most potent weapons available to the Negro in his struggle for freedom.'

It is clear that King embraced nonviolence both as a strategy and as a philosophy, but it is necessary to understand how he actually used nonviolence in order to influence and to transform American society. King, following his successful leadership of the Montgomery boycott, became a national figure and a symbol of nonviolent resistance in North America. Inspired by his own success, he found it easier to shift his attention from the local struggle in Montgomery to a more global struggle for justice and nonviolence in and outside America. King's work extended beyond American civil rights movement issues. He also focused on international issues by lending his iconic status as a nonviolent thinker and activist to the anti-war movement. His opposition to

Profile 8.1 **Martin Luther King, Jr**

Martin Luther King, Jr (15 January 1929 to 4 April 1968) was the leader of the African-American civil rights movement. He was born in Georgia to a family of Baptist pastors. He graduated from high school at 15. Later, he received his BA degree in 1948 from Morehouse College, a distinguished Negro institution of Atlanta. After studying theology at Crozer Theological Seminary in Pennsylvania for three years, he enrolled at Boston University, receiving his degree in 1955. He married Coretta Scott, the younger daughter of Obadiah and Bernice McMurray Scott of Marion, on 18 June 1953. They had two sons and two daughters. In 1954, Martin Luther King was appointed pastor of the Dexter Avenue Baptist Church in Montgomery, Alabama. After Rosa Park's arrest in December 1955 for refusing to give her seat on a bus to a white person, King was elected president of the Montgomery Improvement Association, which led the Montgomery bus boycott, which lasted 382 days. On 21 December 1956, the Supreme Court of the United States declared unconstitutional the laws requiring segregation on buses. King's home was bombed and he was arrested on the charges of conspiracy. But he emerged from this challenge as a great Negro leader and was elected in 1957 as the president of the Southern Christian Leadership Conference (SCLC). He took the ideas and principles for his movement from Gandhi, Thoreau and the New Testament. In 1963, he led a massive protest in Birmingham, Alabama, to protest segregation in restaurants and eating facilities. He was imprisoned and wrote his famous 'Letter from a Birmingham Jail', a manifesto for nonviolent revolution. The same year, on 28 August, King led the march on Washington. The march involved approximately 250,000 demonstrators; King gave his famous 'I Have a Dream' speech at the Lincoln Memorial. King was named *Time* magazine's Man of the Year. On 10 December 1964 he was awarded the Nobel Peace Prize. Between 1965 and 1968, King continued with his struggle for civil rights and against war in Vietnam. In April 1968 he led a protest march in sympathy with striking garbage workers in Memphis, Tennessee. On the evening of 4 April 1968, while speaking from a balcony at the Lorraine Motel in Memphis, Martin Luther King was shot and killed by James Earl Ray. He was buried at what is now the Martin Luther King, Jr National Historic Site in his hometown of Atlanta, Georgia.

142 Introduction to Nonviolence

the Vietnam War, however, was met with criticism by various parties, including President Lyndon B. Johnson. However, as time passed by, people understood that King's critics did not understand the true nature of his opposition to war, since it was merely an extension of his philosophy of nonviolence and his efforts to end poverty in America. King's support of the anti-Vietnam War movement was a great moment for the twentieth-century nonviolent movement. His primary argument against the Vietnam War were civil rights-based, anti-war arguments being secondary. One such argument centred on the discrimination involved with African Americans being sent to fight in Vietnam. According to King (1986, p. 245), 'The rate of infant mortality among Negroes is double that of whites and there are twice as many Negroes dying in Vietnam as whites in proportion to their size in the population.' Furthermore, King denounced the hypocrisy of the American government in asking Black Americans to fight for freedom in Vietnam when they were considered as second-class citizens at home. He viewed the issues surrounding the Vietnam War in the same way as he did the financial drain of government funds on the poverty programmes in America; he wanted, throughout, to increase attention on the civil rights movement and its demands. As an advocate of nonviolence, King refused to cooperate with an evil system, saying:

> Those of us who struggle against racial injustice must come to see that the basic tension is not between races ... The tension is at the bottom between justice and injustice, between the forces of light and the forces of darkness. And if there is victory it will be a victory, not merely for fifty thousand Negroes, but a victory for justice and the forces of life. (*Ibid.*, p. 87)

Both King's Christianity and his belief in nonviolence meant that he had to oppose the Vietnam War:

> I am a clergyman as well as a civil rights leader and the moral roots of our war policy are not unimportant to me. I do not believe our nation can be a moral leader of justice, equality and democracy if it is trapped in the role of a self-appointed world policeman ... I have always insisted on justice for all the world over, because justice is indivisible. And injustice anywhere is a threat to justice everywhere. I will not stand idly by when I see an

unjust war taking place without any way diminishing my activity in civil rights, just as millions of Negro and white people are doing day in and day out. (King 1992, pp. 343–4)

King's enduring legacy, both in American history and the history of nonviolence, reflects the fact that, although he was not the first to promote the idea of nonviolence in twentieth century, he was certainly one of its most important defenders as a strategist and a thinker. King proved to the sceptics that it was possible to bring about change without violence and hatred. For him, however, it was never about the choice between violence and nonviolence, but as he said few days before he was shot in the head by a sniper, 'it is either nonviolence or nonexistence' (King 1986, p. 276).

Desmond Tutu

Upon his death, in April 1968, Martin Luther King was hailed by the entire world as the most influential figure America had produced for generations. King situated Gandhi's ideas of nonviolent action in the larger framework of Christianity and in the context of North American society. In the same way, Desmond Tutu played an important role as a Christian archbishop applying Christian nonviolence in the South Africa context. Archbishop Desmond Tutu remains a much-loved figure across the world, principally for his role in South Africa's Truth and Reconciliation Commission. During the long years that Nelson Mandela (see Profile 8.2) was in prison, Tutu spoke out against the regime. Tutu was already a high-profile Church figure before the 1976 rebellion in black townships, but it was in the months before the Soweto violence that he first became known to white South Africans as a campaigner for reform.

Inevitably, his pleas for justice and reconciliation in South Africa drew him into the political arena – but he always insisted that his motivation was religious, not political. Tutu constantly told the government of the time that its racist approach defied the will of God and for that reason could not succeed. Desmond Tutu was elected Archbishop of Cape Town in 1986. As the first black head of the Anglican Church in South Africa, he continued to campaign actively against apartheid. In November 1995, the then President Mandela asked Archbishop Tutu to head the TRC. Desmond Tutu practised the

Profile 8.2 **Nelson Rolihlahla Mandela**

Nelson Rolihlahla Mandela (18 July 1918) was born to the Themba family in Transkei, South Africa. Mandela's father, destined to be a chief, died of lung disease when Mandela was nine; his life changed dramatically. He was adopted by Chief Jongintaba Dalindyebo, acting regent of the Thembu people. Mandela studied law at university. In Johannesburg, he joined the African National Congress in 1942. He was repeatedly arrested, being prosecuted in the Treason Trial from 1956–61, but found not guilty. Mandela co-founded the militant Umkhonto we Sizwe (with the South African Communist Party), which bombed government targets. Mandela was arrested on 5 August 1962 and sentenced to five years in jail. His trial gained international attention, with global calls for his release by the UN and World Peace Council. In a statement to the court, Mandela underlined: 'During my lifetime I have dedicated myself to this struggle of the African people. I have fought against white domination, and I have fought against black domination. I have cherished the ideal of a democratic and free society in which all persons live together in harmony and with equal opportunities. It is an ideal which I hope to live for and to achieve. But if needs be, it is an ideal for which I am prepared to die.' Mandela spent 27 years in prison. In 1988, Mandela was transferred to 'secure quarters' near Paarl. A year later, Mandela met with F. W. de Klerk, who had replaced P. W. Botha as the President of South Africa. On 11 February 1990, he was finally released. After global efforts to further democratic transition in South Africa, he and De Klerk were jointly awarded the Nobel Peace Prize in December 1993. In April 1994, Mandela was elected as the first black president of South Africa. He formed a government of 'national unity' and established a new constitution. His inaugural presidential speech stated: 'We have at last, achieved our political emancipation. We pledge ourselves to liberate all our people from the continuing bondage of poverty, deprivation, suffering, gender, and other discrimination. Never, never, and never again shall it be that this beautiful land will again experience the oppression of one by another ... Let freedom reign. God Bless Africa!' In 1997 Nelson Mandela stepped down as leader of the ANC in favour of Thabo Mbeki, and in 1999 he retired as president.

Christian philosophy of nonviolence as the main motivation behind the Commission, basing the 'road for reconciliation' on his particular concept of truth:

> The Truth and Reconciliation Commission has only able to make a contribution. Reconciliation is going to have to be the concern of every South African ... To work for reconciliation is to want to realize God's dream for humanity – when we will know that we are indeed members of one family bound together in a delicate network of interdependence. (Tutu 2000, p. 222)

The key concepts of revealing the whole truth as the only way to forgiveness, redemption and amnesty were chosen on this basis. In Christian theology redemption is an element of salvation that broadly means the deliverance from sin. Universal reconciliation (also called universal salvation, Christian universalism) is the doctrine that sinful and alienated human souls – because of divine love and mercy – may ultimately be reconciled to God. As we can see, Tutu's spirituality of fellowship is a meaningful understanding of the Gandhian communitarian ethos of interfaith dialogue and communal harmony. Tutu accepts the Kingian concept of 'love' as a means for spiritual and material transformation of the individual and the community. Tutu further develops his understanding of humans as agents of moral progress in the world, by relating it to a communitarian theology. For him, as the result of a celebration of differences and divergences by the Kingdom of God, the love of God propels the perpetuity of human fellowship. Therefore, as a theologian of solidarity and reconciliation, Tutu provides us with the spiritual resources to further explore the idea of community as a forum of differences and otherness. For him, the motivation behind confronting the apartheid regime was an effort to realize a community of fellowship and solidarity. Hence, seeking to abolish racism and apartheid through nonviolence was a way for him to help restructure justice and peace in South Africa. This approach is made clear when he suggests that:

> The evil of apartheid is perhaps not so much the untold misery and anguish it has caused its victims (great and traumatic as these must be), no, its pernicious nature, indeed its blasphemous character is revealed in its effect on God's children when it makes

them doubt that they are God's children. (Tutu 1982, cited in Hill 2007, p. 107)

It was in his struggles against the apartheid regime that Tutu contextualized the Gandhian–Kingian strategy of nonviolence as a path towards social reconciliation and political transformation in South Africa. Tutu applied principled nonviolence – the concepts of reconciliation, redemption and forgiveness – in order to establish the TRC in South Africa. For many this was key to the TRC's success, which would not have been possible without Mandela's leadership and Tutu's Christian nonviolence. To understand the complex negotiations around the TRC's concept of reconciliation, it is evident that the dominant view in the TRC was created through an amalgam of transnational human rights values and a Christian ethic of forgiveness and redemption. This dominating ethic focused on amnesty rather than punishment and retribution. The 'truth' of the TRC lay mostly in its officially confirming and bringing into the public space what was already known. 'Truth' was conceptualized and operationalized as the degree of individual acceptance of the collective memory promulgated by the TRC. The TRC was, therefore, unique in applying human rights ideas with wider moral and ethical discourses. Tutu's message of nonviolence, though difficult to accept for many, set a compelling frame of reference for moving beyond the atrocities uncovered. As Tutu writes in the TRC Report:

> Having looked the beast of the past in the eye, having asked and received forgiveness and having made amends, let us shut the door on the past – not in order to forget it but in order not to allow it to imprison us. Let us move into the glorious future of a new kind of society where people count, not because of biological irrelevancies or other extraneous attributes, but because they are persons of infinite worth created in the image of God. (1998, p. 25)

Clearly, Archbishop Tutu's communion with the nonviolent message is rooted in his Christianity; what is more astonishing is the political influence he wielded during his lifetime. Regardless of his religious affiliation or status, the most important duty for Desmond Tutu has been to struggle for peace, love and nonviolence.

Mother Teresa

This same message of peace, love and nonviolence has been the pillar of Mother Teresa's teachings. She was a Catholic contemplative nun who spread the message of love in action – that loving others is the only way to love Christ and bring peace. She worked tirelessly to serve the poor – drawing strength from her belief in God – regardless of public acknowledgment, except if that promoted funds rising for her cause. Despite her own Catholicism, her open-mindedness, respect and religious tolerance led her to include everyone, regardless of their creed, in her care, not simply focusing on Christians or Catholics. Mother Teresa's advocacy of nonviolence was as influential as Tutu's, gaining such status as a result of her limitless passion and devotion for its cause and the strength of her message of love. She was respected and admired by the national and international community, supported always by the Church. Mother Teresa's notion of love is profoundly linked to her Christian religion, permeating every word, deed and thought. It is a form of nonviolence full of sacrifice because it makes no distinction as to who it is aimed at, but it starts closest to home. For Mother Teresa, if someone is not loved, he or she cannot love in return, so we are all responsible for the world's hunger for love. At the same time, this love is not only a set of feelings and kind words, it must also be put into practice by means of work. Mother Teresa's concept of love is based on the concept that we are all brothers and sisters, a big 'world family', very similar to the 'beloved community' defended by Martin Luther King. They share a notion of love that includes sacrifice within, although the latter is seen from a different perspective. For Mother Teresa, the sacrifice lies in loving anyone without distinction, particularly the weakest, and working towards the overcoming of such weakness in order to restore the person's situation. For King, the sacrifice lies in loving those who actually cause us real or potential harm (i.e., 'enemies') by means of avoiding revenge when there is the opportunity to take it. Both of them focus on the fact that within every person there is God and love is the main road to reconciliation.

Mother Teresa always viewed her relationship with God as a deeply personal matter, not attempting to convert people to her belief as the only way to practice nonviolence. However, Mother Teresa says in her book that she 'brought the light of Christ to the poorest of the poor, and she also met Christ in each of them' (Kolodiejchuk and Mother

Teresa 2007, p. 43). Mother Teresa used her faith to identify the suffering of Christ and connect it to the suffering of the poor, which obviously contributed to her practice of principled nonviolence and renewed Christ's message in the Sermon on the Mount – 'you shall not kill' and 'you shall love your neighbour'. However, despite the fact that Mother Teresa was a prominent religious figure, she had to be politically active in order to have any influence in the world and promote nonviolence. That is why Mother Teresa appealed to presidents and chiefs of state to bring about peace and nonviolence in the world, rather than to the Catholic priests. She was an independent thinker, not following any precedent offset by a saint or a hero – just that of Jesus.

Her 'love in action' showed how nonviolence can be interpreted and put to the service of humankind, and how all human beings are responsible and can collaborate to this end. Mother Teresa's great sense of responsibility meant that she reveal to the world the doubts, crises of faith and lack of hope that she experienced at different stages of her life. Although, in some sense, real love must empty us of self, the emptiness one can experience can be difficult to cope with. Reasoning and responsibility were all she had left during her 'dark night' period, making her efforts even more human and admirable. A nonviolent activist by her life of sacrifice, Mother Teresa searched the way of love and compassion among men of various religious traditions up to her last breath. For her, any true reconciliation assumed love but also nonviolence. This faith played an important role for Mother Teresa and, later, the Missionaries of Charity, in serving the poor. Her work was testimony to the existence of violence of poverty, demanding a nonviolent solution.

The Dalai Lama

Tenzin Gyatso, His Holiness the Dalai Lama, the 14th in title, who is recognized by his devotees as the current manifestation of Avalokiteshvara, the Buddha of Infinite Compassion, is also a rare thinker and practitioner of nonviolence. As the true heir of Mahatma Gandhi, he purports that nonviolence is contrary to human nature, which, according to him, is on a quest for happiness. The Dalai Lama offers his reasons for not accepting violence: first, that, as a Buddhist monk, he does not consider violence to be ethical and, second, that he believes firmly in the Gandhian satyagraha. Furthermore, he does not consider violence as empowering for the Tibetans in their stance against the Chinese occupation of Tibet. He says: 'Our strength is truth, justice, reason and human understanding' (Shiromany 1998, p. 253). Humility seems an innate virtue with the Dalai Lama, who presents himself, following the example of Gandhi, as a searcher for truth. This truth is not presented as an intellectual or theoretical quest, but as an actual approach to life. For His Holiness, to practice nonviolence is to live in the midst of human beings while sharing their miseries and problems in a quest for truth. But nonviolence is also a cardinal virtue that is exemplified by kindness in the domain of interpersonal relations. For His Holiness the Dalai Lama, Buddhism is a religion of kindness towards others:

> The Dalai Lama's social philosophy, a 'policy of kindness,' may sound simplistic or naive in the face of seemingly intractable global conflicts and the complex demands of social activism. The vitality of his social philosophy is revealed in the connection between personal, socio-moral transformation and the traditional Tibetan Buddhist approach to training the mind and the heart. In this view, the personal, inward effort to change oneself, to become more open to the world with all its limits, becomes a prerequisite for establishing any meaningful social-political change. (Timm 1997, p. 593)

Going further in his tolerance logic, the Dalai Lama describes the essence of religion as compassion. According to him, any religion must prioritize compassion as a sign of love towards others and every religion must develop peace, nonviolence and tolerance. In an essay entitled 'Human Rights, Democracy and Freedom' (2008), His Holiness affirms:

> Responsibility for working for peace lies not only with our leaders, but also with each of us individually. Peace starts within each one of us. When we have inner peace, we can be at peace with those around us. When our community is in a state of peace, it can share that peace with neighboring communities and so on. When we feel love and kindness toward others, it not only makes others feel loved and cared for, but it helps us also to develop inner happiness and peace. We can work consciously to develop feelings of love and kindness. For some of us, the most effective

way to do so is through religious practice. For others it may be non-religious practices. What is important is that we each make a sincere effort to take seriously our responsibility for each other and the world in which we live.

The message of the Dalai Lama is therefore very clear: to encourage others to be nonviolent, it is necessary to be nonviolent oneself. In other words, nonviolence awakens the innate goodness that is within each of us. The basic idea, therefore, is to eliminate any indifference in regard to the 'other' (any sentient being), and to replace it with a positive attitude as the foundation of universal harmony. One can describe this universal harmony as the notion of 'interdependence', such as the sign of the Buddha. Every element, in the universe is linked to another, for nothing has a separated existence. The human being is part of the universe, just like other species, and it must maintain its harmony with the world through nonviolence and compassion. Therefore, to attain our truth, it is necessary to respect the truth of the 'other'; such a quest for truth can be founded only on nonviolence. In fact, one cannot impose one's truth through violence – on this Dalai Lama's position is clear and without ambiguity.

The Dalai Lama does not advocate violence as a means of struggle for the independence of Tibet. Violence, he believes, will eventually destroy oneself. From his point of view, forgiveness is the only way to have hope for true reconciliation. Hence, for His Holiness the Dalai Lama, just as for Gandhi, ahimsa, the absence of harm, is the only way to get China to bend its policies in Tibet. Over the past 55 years the Dalai Lama has continuously urged his people to endure suffering with self-restraint and self-discipline in the face of Chinese injustice and repression. Through his promotion of nonviolence as the first and best method to overcome injustice, the Dalai Lama has made way for the possibility of peace between the Chinese government and the Tibetans. His daily prayers for Tibet are accompanied by prayers for the Chinese people. Despite the death of over a million Tibetans as a result of China's occupation of Tibet, the Dalai Lama talks about peace as something more than the absence of violence. He notes:

> Peace is actually, I believe, an expression of compassion, a sense of caring … On the level of higher consciousness, peace is an inner achievement which is developed through practice, through

meditation, by believing in either a Creator or one's own responsibility. (Dalai Lama, cited in Hunt 2002, p. 70)

Responsibility is, for the Dalai Lama, the other side of the coin. According to him, there can be no nonviolence without responsibility and interconnectedness. He adds:

> And if you see there is violence, some problem existing somewhere, and you remain disconnected from that problem, then that is not nonviolence. If you are seeing that there is a problem, but you fail to get involved, you are just watching the suffering of others, and that is not nonviolence. Nonviolence requires that you are fully engaged in the problem, fully involved, trying to solve the problem. But without adding any harm to the situation. And so, here, I think the main factor is compassion. (*Ibid.*, pp. 70–1)

As such, His Holiness the Dalai Lama suggests that one's enemies can be seen as teachers of spiritual development, testing one's compassion. He proclaims that without enemies, one cannot learn the concepts of acceptance and patience. But he also acknowledges that nonviolence is not an easy task and that it can be a daily struggle to maintaining peace. In this way, he can truly be considered as the inheritor of the will of Gandhi.

Aung San Suu Kyi

In a similar way as for Desmond Tutu, Mother Teresa and the Dalai Lama, Aung San Suu Kyi is a selfless personality who displays caring and fearless qualities. Like the Dalai Lama, Aung San Suu Kyi's spirituality has provided her with direction and strength, enabling her to endure years under house arrest in isolation.

> Thrust into the political arena by her sense of duty to the people of her country, Suu Kyi won the most stunning democratic election in history, overcoming the brute force of the military dictators who used all means at their disposal to thwart the will of the people. Suu Kyi ... {has not been] permitted to take office. (Hunt 2002, p. 4)

Her freedom was severely restricted until a short time ago and she had to make sacrifices for the sake of others in the name of peace and justice. In Suu Kyi's opinion, genuine democratic institutions cannot exist without respect for justice and peace; that is why the practice of nonviolence is essential to Aung San Suu Kyi. She notes:

> Nonviolence means positive action. You have to work for whatever you want. You don't just sit there doing nothing and hope to get what you want. It just means that the methods you use are not violent ones. Some people think that nonviolence is passiveness. It's not so. (1997, p. 25)

Aung San Suu Kyi has a simple and clear message which is that only by resisting violence and overcoming fear one can be free. She writes: 'It is not power that corrupts but fear. Fear of losing power corrupts those who wield it and fear of the scourge of power corrupts those who are subject to it' (Suu Kyi, 1991, p. 181). Fear stifles and slowly destroys all sense of right and wrong. Fear contributes to corruption: 'when fear is rife corruption in all forms becomes entrenched' (*ibid.*). For her, the nonviolent revolution in Burma is an attempt by the Burmese people to act as the Buddha taught. In Buddhism, she argued, 'each man has in him the potential to realize [this]' (*ibid.*, p. 175). But under despotic rule, man is valued least, as a 'faceless, mindless – and helpless – mass to be manipulated at will' (*ibid.*). Therefore, at the centre of Aung San Suu Kyi's movement, the core quality is inner strength. It is the spiritual steadiness that comes from the belief that what you are doing is right, even if does not bring you immediate benefits. From the beginning, Suu Kyi made ordinary people her ultimate priority. For her, good politics are about the people. She genuinely loves people, cares for them and learns from them. That is why she believes in what Václav Havel called 'the power of the powerless'. Suu Kyi affirms:

> I think power comes from within. If you have confidence in what you are doing and you are shored up by the belief that what you are doing is right, that in itself constitutes power and this power is very important when you are trying to achieve something. If you do not believe in what you are doing your actions will lack credibility. (1997, p. 159)

According to Aung San Suu Kyi, the struggle for nonviolence is about democracy. And democracy is about securing sincerity and freedom:

> Basically, sincerity is the desire not to deceive anyone. That's why sincerity is truth, because sincerity means you're not attempting to deceive anybody ... And sincerity doesn't just simply mean not trying to deceive, but it also means trying to reach out to others. (*Ibid*., pp. 197–8)

That is why Suu Kyi believes in the duty to establish confidence in the people and make them realize that the powerless do have power, and that power can be manipulated through nonviolent means and actions in order to obtain the desired goals and outcomes. 'Violence is not the right way,' affirms Suu Kyi (*ibid*., p. 152). Dialogue is not born from violence. Violence creates fear and fear develops into violence. Aung San Suu Kyi has shown the world that the promise of achieving peace remains within our reach. Through her steadfast struggle for democracy in Burma, she has proved to us that the removal of hatred and violence is possible and the quest for peace is essentially a journey in search of compassion within us, leading to kindness to others. Aung San Suu Kyi has become a powerful symbol of peaceful defiance in the face of violence. Suu Kyi has shown us that all serious political struggles that focus on the idea of nonviolence contribute to the progress of democracy. As such, Aung San Suu Kyi finds a place in the pantheon of nonviolence next to leaders like Mohandas Gandhi, Martin Luther King, Jr, the Dalai Lama and Desmond Tutu. Each of these peacemakers exemplifies the tradition of nonviolence that runs through the ages as a constant awareness of the dignity of human beings and a capacity to seek truth and justice without violence.

Further reading

Allen, J. (2007) *Rabble-Rouser for Peace: The Authorised Biography of Desmond Tutu*. A biography of Desmond Tutu recounting his struggle for justice and nonviolence in South Africa.

Frost, B. (1998) *Struggling to Forgive: Nelson Mandela and South Africa's Search for Reconciliation*. An examination of South Africa's past, present and future through the lens of forgiveness and nonviolence.

Hasday, J. L. (2007) *Aung San Suu Kyi (Modern Peacemakers)*. An insightful biography of the Burmese leader, influenced by Gandhi's philosophy of nonviolent protest.

Kirk, J. A. (ed.) (2007) *Martin Luther King, Jr. and the Civil Rights Movement: Controversies and Debates*. An invaluable sourcebook on the American civil rights movement and its most influential leader.

Laird, T. (2006) *The Story of Tibet: Conversations with the Dalai Lama*. A colourful journey through Tibetan thought and nonviolence, expressed in interviews with the Dalai Lama.

Chapter 9

Nonviolence in the Twenty-First Century

Although the twenty-first century is still young, a handful of meaningful political changes have occurred throughout the world as a result of nonviolent uprisings. At the turn of the century it would have been impossible to imagine that some of the last dictatorial regimes to plague Europe, the Maghreb and the Middle East would be seriously threatened or disappear.

The overthrow of Slobodan Milosevic in 2000 was not only an important moment for Serbia, but it also proved to the international community that nonviolent strategies of resistance were once again effective and relevant. As early as 1998 a youth organization by the name of Otpor (Resistance) was formed to protest the fixed election that saw Slobodan Milosevic re-elected as president. Having been influenced by the work of Gene Sharp and Robert Helvey, Otpor's strategy was based heavily on pragmatic nonviolence. As such, the movement employed all three classes of nonviolent protests: nonviolent protest and persuasion, noncooperation and nonviolent intervention.

The success that followed the movement's nonviolent strategies was impressive. Incorporating political protests in acts of street theatre, the group quickly caught the attention of the general populace and most importantly the media. When Milosevic stepped down, the movement saw that their experience and methods could serve to bring down other dictators. As a result, two of Otpor's founders, Srdja Popvic and Slobodan Djinovic, decided to establish the Centre for Applied Nonviolent Action and Strategies (CANVAS). As a non-profit, non-governmental organization, CANVAS offered educational material and workshops related to strategic nonviolent conflict. Since opening its doors in 2004, the organization has provided training for activists from Zimbabwe to Egypt, and has had contact in one way or another with every country involved in the Arab Spring.

Although the term 'Arab Spring' was first used around the time of Ben Ali's fall, when the first demonstrations began appearing in Egypt, the term can be broadened to include the events that shook Iran in 2009. The Iranian civic Movement of June 2009, referred to as the Green Movement, was one of the most significant moments in that country since the revolution that ushered in the Islamic Republic. What initially began as protests surrounding the fraudulent re-election of Mahmoud Ahmadinejad quickly turned into a struggle for civil liberties and an end to the theocratic regime. Like the uprisings that followed it, it would be wrong to consider the Green Movement as a spontaneous action that emerged as a result of Ahmadinejad's re-election. The uprisings that shook Iran that June were the result of two decades of societal evolution that have seen more young people obtain higher levels of education, against a background of social and political repression sponsored by the state. The changes that have taken place since the 1979 revolution have created two cleavages in Iranian society. One of these cleavages is dominated by the older, conservative generation, which holds tightly onto traditional practices and represents the last stronghold of the regime. The other cleavage is that of a liberal reformist youth which has increasingly allied with the country's intellectuals to demand an end to an illegitimate regime.

The movement's power was in its numbers – an important factor for the future development of Iranian democracy – which is why the regime has gone to extraordinary lengths to see it destroyed. The youth that took to the streets made up one-third of those eligible to vote; nearly 70 per cent of the country's population is under the age of 30. This means that 70 per cent of the population does not have first-hand knowledge of the events surrounding the revolution of 1979 and can, therefore, adopt a new intellectual direction in critiquing the regime. As such, this presents an opportunity to move away from the violent tendencies of Marxist-Leninist and radical Islamic critiques that have been dominant. Moreover, the combination of nonviolent techniques and the use of social media to confront the regime has not only magnified the illegitimacy of the regime in the eyes if the Iranian public, but also it has exposed the internal divisions of the regime.

The two-pronged strategy of nonviolent demonstrations and the use of social media was evident in the successful movements of Tunisia and Egypt, which led to the fall of Ben Ali and Mubarak. In Tunisia, the self-immolation of Mohamed Bouazizi was the spark that ignited mass protests around the country. Bouazizi's story was symbolic because it encompassed the major problems affecting Tunisia: increasing poverty, growing corruption and repression. From the beginning of his reign as president, Zine El Abidine Ben Ali counted on the effects of modernization to play down the regime's inability to deliver civil liberties. On the rare occasions that demonstrations did occur, they were quickly and easily put down by the regime's extensive security forces, which were comprised of intelligence units and various police forces.

The protests that erupted on 18 December 2010 were, however, unlike anything else the Maghreb and the Arab world had seen before. For the first time in the region, truly popular nonviolent protests for 'bread and freedom' saw a dictator flee the country. The reason that the Jasmine Revolution was as successful as it was was because it called upon all sections of society to stand up against the brutal regime of Ben Ali. The poorer segments in the countryside were joined by what the regime thought had been its backbone of support, the middle class of Tunis. That Facebook played a crucial organizational role in both Tunisian and Egypt is without a doubt. However, one would do the movement a great disservice to label it a 'Facebook' or 'Twitter' revolution.

Finally, as if the fall of Ben Ali did not surprise enough, when demonstrations throughout Egypt erupted no one foresaw Hosni Mubarak's departure. While it is true that Egypt suffered from far more pressing social and economic issues than Tunisia, Mubarak's grip on the country was seen as so secure that peaceful demonstrations could never force him from power. For nearly 30 years Mubarak was able to outlaw and imprison members of the opposition parties and fix elections. The previous uprisings were easy for the regime to quell because their own violent nature acted to legitimize the brutal response taken by the government. However, when the regime was met with predominantly nonviolent demonstrations it could no longer get away with the use of excessive violence.

The group widely considered responsible for providing the impetus for nonviolent protests was the 6 April Youth Movement. The techniques that the movement developed were largely those theorized by Gene Sharp, but refined by Serbia's Otpor. Travelling to Serbia and taking a course offered by CANVAS, the leaders of the 6 April

Movement learned to pinpoint the weakness in Mubarak's regime (the army), and put together a strategy of captivating the masses and swinging the tide in their favour. The training provided by former members of Otpor led the 6 April Movement to publish a pamphlet on the eve of mass protests (25 January). The pamphlet, titled 'How to Protest Intelligently', called on individuals to occupy government buildings and establish relations with security forces, and advised how to protect protestors.

The Green Movement in Iran

A spectre is haunting the Middle East – the spectre of nonviolence. The powers representing the old ideas and authoritarian Middle East have entered an unholy alliance to exorcize this spectre, but the winds of change are blowing across this region of the world, and it does not seem likely that they will soon dissipate. Never before have people in the region mobilized in such vast numbers to shake off the chains of their autocratic regimes. We can go further and say that we are presently experiencing a paradigm shift in political mentalities and practices in the Middle East, which requires us to abandon the old post-independence assumptions in the Arab world about authoritarian modernization and state-building projects.

For half a century, Arab, Turkish and Iranian populations were accused of being uninterested in seeking democratic freedoms and liberating themselves from their authoritarian rulers. But now millions of Egyptians, Tunisians, Iranians, Yemenites, Syrians and Bahrainis have proved their accusers wrong by mobilizing against their authoritarian rulers. If these uprisings in the Middle East and the Maghreb result in the downfall of the Iranian and Syrian regimes, and result in democratic elections in Tunisia and Yemen, they will have been more effective than the Arab–Israeli wars of the past 60 years. Many commentators in the West have referred to the uprisings sweeping the Middle East and the Maghreb as the 'Arab Spring', the obvious model being the 'Prague Spring' of 1968, when Czechoslovakia enjoyed a brief interval of democratic reform before the Soviet Union invaded. In fact, the protests now blowing through the Middle East have little in common with those of 1968, other than demonstrating once again that civil society can help to provide the independent space that is needed – to use Sir Isaiah Berlin's famous distinction – for 'negative' rather than 'positive' liberty. What united Tunisians, Egyptians and Iranians in their democratic uprisings, as is the case today with the people of Yemen and Syria, was a desire for freedom from interference and a struggle against the concentration of arbitrary power. In each of these upheavals we witnessed the willingness of young people to risk their lives to topple a corrupt government that could or would not generate a free and prosperous future for them. The roots of the Arab Spring can be identified as having a non-Arab beginning in Iran's nonviolent Green Movement, in which young Iranians made extensive use of social media for organizational networking.

Initially, the Iranian uprisings were in response to the rigged presidential elections and the re-election of Mahmoud Ahmadinejad, but they turned into a mass struggle for civil liberties and the removal of the theocratic regime in Iran. The demonstrations were not simply a reaction to the unfair election results but were based on years of built up frustration, dissatisfaction and anger towards the repressive rule of the Islamic Republic. As a nonviolent, young and civil movement desiring change within Iranian society, the Green Movement was a historical struggle to establish an accountable and lawful government. It increasingly became clear that the fraudulent election had given the Iranian people an opportunity not only to defend what little democratic rights they had, but also to attempt to begin to lay new foundations for a true democratic Iran. As the Green Movement grew and gained momentum, the end of the Islamic Republic seemed nigh. As stated above, the Green Movement was not a sudden manifestation within Iranian consciousness, but the result of 20 years of major political and societal evolution leading to the emergence of changing political, social and cultural attitudes among Iran's intellectuals, students, women activists and youth. It highlighted the fact that the Iranian political structure faced a crisis of legitimacy and the current power holders had lost moral credibility by virtue of their cruelty and lies. By asserting the republican principle of popular sovereignty, the Green Movement posed a counter-claim of legitimacy against the political theology of the absolute sovereignty of the Supreme Leader. In addition, most of the demonstrators who questioned the fundamental legitimacy of Iran's electoral process, unlike their parents, belonged to a new generation who did not experience the revolution of 1979 and wanted another Iran. The young Iranians' quest for democracy presented serious challenges not only to the status of the doctrine of the 'Velayat i Faqih' (Guardianship of the Jurist) and questions of its legitimacy, but also to the reform movement and its democratic authenticity. Ironically, 2009's Green Movement parallels two strategies used in the 1979 Islamic revolution: nonviolence and communication technologies. In 1979, Iranian revolutionaries used available technology to circulate Khomeini's speeches clandestinely on cassette tapes. In 2009, Facebook and Twitter became the weapons of choice for young protestors in Iran. Nonviolence was used by protestors to express their concerns and to show the government that they did not want to retaliate to the violence of the paramilitary forces of the Basidj. Many young students and activists believed that nonviolence was the only way to achieve peace and democracy in Iran. The movement, without a doubt, had the capacity to resort to violence in order to counter the brutality of the regime, yet this did not occur. As a result, the demonstrators were determined and encouraged to seek some sort of dialogue with the state rather than plunging the country into another period of bloodshed. The Green Movement's nonviolent nature can be attributed, moreover, to the fact that many Iranians, specifically the younger generation, have moved away from the ideological worldviews of Marxism-Leninism and radical Islamism, which had led to much of the violence that occurred in the first years after the revolution of 1979. The Iranian Revolution of February 1979 was a great socio-political change, with a hybrid synthetic intellectual discourse, but it was undoubtedly not an intellectual change in the direction of a critique of violence in Iran. On the contrary, it was a great political change that heralded the return of massive and long-term violence to the annals of modern Iranian history.

Furthermore, the Green Movement intensified the internal divisions of the regime. It showed the 'deep fissures' of the factional and ideological groups within the Islamic Republic; the Supreme Leader was no longer seen as the 'neutral arbiter' of the state and lost legitimacy in the eyes of many Iranians. It became apparent that the state was not invincible and was internally unstable, since it was dealing with many conflicts regarding the future direction of the Islamic state. As of June 2009, the divide became deeper than ever before between the Iranian state and the Iranian civil society, creating a gap between those who believe that normal economic and political relations with the West are vital to Iran's future and those who disdain such relations as violations of the Islamic revolution's ideals.

Where does Iran's Green Movement stand at the time of writing, over four years later? It is true that it has lost much of its strength and mobilizing capacity inside Iran, while the Arab Spring has toppled regimes across the region. Had the Green Movement's leadership been stronger and more determined, they may have been able to rally oil workers to their cause in order to counter the fact that they were dealing with a rentier state, thus tipping the scales somewhat in their favour. With the hesitation and reluctance of Mousavi and Karroubi, the state slowly rendered them ineffective, using force and threats, and placed them under house arrest. The movement, however, remains a potent agent for civil change, inside and outside Iran; it has moved away from from a central leadership to multi-centred 'executive power base' located among dissidents who are now living in exile. Many believe that the Green Movement lost its unity and its momentum because of the violent crackdown by the Iranian regime. Others would say that the Green Movement had the capacity and potential to accomplish almost anything, yet it was held back and ultimately underperformed due to its biggest weakness: its leadership.

To many observers, the idea of a Gandhian moment in a despotic society like Iran is the stuff of fairy tales. However, Gandhi himself said:

> The nonviolent technique does not depend for its success on the good will of the dictators … Satyagraha is never vindictive. It believes not in destruction but in conversion. Its failures are due to the weaknesses of the satyagrahi, not to any defect in the law itself. (Merton 2007, pp. 38, 47)

In other words, the policy of the weak or the coward is not worthy of the name of nonviolence. This reminds us that Mahatma Gandhi referred to nonviolence not as a mere tactic, but as a spiritual way of life; nonviolence is not just refusal to kill – it is manifestation of love and truth as a force for positive social change. It remains to be seen whether Iranian social movements can commit wholly to brave nonviolence, thereby proving the effectiveness of the Gandhian moment in Iran. It is clear that such a path is a daunting challenge for a society like Iran, living a lifestyle where ends are valued more than the means and social actions have no specific rules, ethos or moral ground. That is why the relevance of Gandhi has been questioned time and again in the Iranian public sphere. Some Iranians tend to think of nonviolence as one of a number of choices available to an oppressed people, as a tactic shrewdly selected when the circumstances are exactly right for it. Others believe that nonviolence only can be effective if the adversary, no matter how wrong-headed, is honourable enough to refrain from crossing the line into mass murder, suggesting that if Gandhi had been born an Iranian citizen, he would probably not have decided on nonviolence as a tactic and that, if he had, he would have been murdered the first day.

This might be true, but over the past half a century the Gandhian moment has provided a seed bed for social ferment and political change across the planet, offering a radical philosophy that has propelled civic movements into nonviolent revolutions. More and more, nonviolent action is taking centre stage in the struggle against tyrannies among peoples across the world. Although public awareness of nonviolent breakthroughs occurring elsewhere is minimal, with the recent rise of civic consciousness among youth and the birth of the Green Movement, individuals and groups have developed nonviolent ways to overcome oppression, establish justice and build democracy in Iran. Perhaps this nonviolent relationship and an unarmed struggle to resolve conflict will eventually build the conditions for nonviolent change, potentially marking the end of a long period of violence and the beginning of a period of new political thought in Iran.

Many would consider this simplistic optimism, which it may be.But if, back in 1980, South African leaders like Mandela had predicted that the apartheid regime would end peacefully and that, in a nonviolent plebiscite, all races of South Africa would elect a black president, no one would have believed it – perhaps not even Mandela –yet it happened, because the time was right for a Gandhian moment of unarmed struggle for justice, peace and freedom. Iran still has a long way to go in terms of the next steps towards fostering the democratic evolution of a society that includes nonviolence, justice and peace. But, as Victor Hugo (2008) wrote, 'An invasion of armies can be resisted, but not an idea whose time has come.' Looking back over the last 100 years in Iranian history, especially since the movements led by civil society, we see the growing influence and impact of nonviolent struggle. Nonviolence is an idea whose time has definitely come in Iran.

The Green Movement used quite limited tactics against the state; street protests were the movement's main weapon. It could have enlisted the support of key segments of the Iranian economy, such as major industries, transportation and worker unions, government employees, bazaar merchants and, most importantly, oil workers. However, although the Green Movement failed to overcome the Islamic Republic politically, it was by no means a philosophical failure. The movement managed to not only impact Iranian politics and political culture, but also further delegitimize the government. The protests and demonstrations also showcased the democratic maturity of the Iranian people, who were willing to risk their lives in order to defend what few rights they had. There is no doubt that the emergence of such a movement indicates that Iran's political future will either bend or break the current system. The genie of nonviolence has been let out of the bottle in the Middle East; neither the old or the new regimes are confident that it can be put back.

Otpor: the fall of Serbia's Slobodan Milosevic

In October 2000 the people of Yugoslavia managed to do something 78 days of NATO bombing failed to do – topple Slobodan Milosevic. Opposition to Milosevic's rule dated back to 1998, when frequent protests were staged on the streets of Belgrade demanding free and fair elections and broad media rights. In 1999, student activists, under the leadership of Otpor (Resistance), organized nonviolent campaigns and protests in an effort to pressure Slobodan Milosevic to resign.

Slobodan Milosevic entered the main stage of politics in 1989 as the President of the Serbia and quickly gained a reputation as a nationalist leader at a time when tensions mired all the republics of Yugoslavia. In this sense, he was no different to any of the other major names in the Yugoslav republics, such as Franjo Tudjman in Croatia and Alija Izetbegovic in Bosnia and Herzegovina. Nevertheless, a product of the communist period, Milosevic gained a reputation for governing Serbia with an iron fist and lacking respect for the rule of law.

Although Slobodan Milosevic and his Socialist Party of Serbia maintained their strong presence at a federal level, by 1997 his power began recede. In that year, he suffered a series of defeats at local elections and accepted the formation of independent municipal governments that were elected on a popular basis, but only after protests gripped Serbia for almost 100 days. The protests over fraudulent election results were initiated in Niš, the third-largest city in Serbia, and were soon joined by the students from the University of Belgrade.

Under the banner of Zajedno (Together), thousands of Serbs took to the streets to demand democratic reforms. Though Milosevic was forced to recognize defeat in the local elections, larger democratic reforms were disregarded and the protests were seen as largely symbolic.

As early as 1998 a group of students formed Otpor, as a result of the previous failed campaigns to oust Milosevic. Learning from their mistakes, the members of Otpor realized that any movement looking to seriously challenge a quasi-dictatorship had to have strong organization that was built around strategy, planning and recruitment (*Bringing Down a Dictator* 2002). Using the symbol of a black clenched fist, Otpor employed techniques of nonviolent resistance to target the very foundations of Milosevic's power. As a post-modern movement, Otpor looked for innovative ways to reach people and often initiated 'cool' protests to appeal to younger people (Rosenberg 2011). The movement shied away from staging classical protest marches because they simply lacked the numbers, but they adopted forms of street theatre and pranks to gain the attention and support of the citizens and opposition media (*ibid.*).

The most famous of these stunts had the group's members flood the major streets of Belgrade with leaflets and stickers with slogans such as *Gotov Je!* (He's Finished!) and *Vreme Je!* (It's Time!). One popular method of raising the consciousness of the public involved pasting Slobodan Milosevic's face on a barrel and asking passers-by to drop a coin in to hit the picture. On Milosevic's birthday, Otpor staged a 'celebration', which included a large cake with crumbling pieces representing his disastrous policies, a birthday card signed with over 2,000 signatures, asking for his resignation, and ironic gifts. Lastly, even when Otpor was not at the helm of protests, its presence and influence was felt through partnerships it formed with individuals and groups throughout the country. Three of these individuals, Dusan Kovacevic, Bojan Boskovic and Ivan Milivojev, were the founders of the 2000 music festival, in Novi Sad, called Exit. One of the largest music festivals in Europe, the inaugural motto was 'Exit the ten years of madness!', referring to Milosevic's regime. By attracting some of the biggest names in the music industry, the organizers of Exit attracted the attention of local citizens and international media.

To take the movement to the next level, Otpor obtained help from the International Republican Institute (IRI) (*Bringing Down a Dictator* 2002). Further to offering money, the institute arranged for one of Gene Sharp's colleagues, Robert Helvey, to give a weekend-long seminar on better organization, using Sharp's book as a foundation for the nonviolent struggle to be employed by Otpor.

Otpor employed all three of Sharp's classes of protest: nonviolent protest and persuasion, noncooperation and nonviolent intervention, the core of the group's objectives being to undermine the loyalty of the traditional pillars of support that the regime enjoyed, including that of the police and military (Binnendijk and Marovic 2006). Maintaining their nonviolent approach, the group members courted arrest by the security forces in the hope of magnifying their cause and gaining support.

As the movement grew in strength, so did the regime's attacks through the media, which painted the group as terrorists, druggies and even agents of the West, and so too did the arrests by the local police forces. By maintaining nonviolent strategies, activists hoped to persuade the police of the deliberate disinformation by the regime. Thus, when the police arrested Otpor members, group sympathizers would stage small protests outside the prisons, while, inside, those arrested used their time in interrogation to talk to their captors and convert them to the cause. By the time of the decisive elections of 24 September 2000, ironically, all but the highest-ranking police officers knew more about Otpor's goals and methods than ordinary citizens (*ibid.*).

The fraudulent elections in September 2000 signalled the end of Milosevic. As a result of growing dissatisfaction and pressure, thanks in large part to the efforts of Otpor, Milosevic resigned on 7 October 2000. With the formation of a democratically elected government it seemed that the organizers of Otpor were ready to return to their normal lives away from the political arena. The organization was largely dissolved, but two of the founding members of the organization, Srdja Popovic and Slobodan Djinovic, continued preaching pragmatic nonviolence and, in 2003, founded the Centre for Applied Nonviolent Actions and Strategies (CANVAS).

CANVAS offers support to other activists engaged in toppling dictatorial regimes through nonviolent strategies. Both founders have lent their expertise to numerous movements in Georgia, Ukraine, South Africa, Zimbabwe, Burma and, recently, Egypt (Rosenberg 2011). Consisting of a small group of employees, CANVAS runs workshops and trains activists, in association with think tanks and NGOs (*ibid.*). The spirit and methods of Otpor have been taken up by organizations such as the Georgian *Kmara!* (Enough!) movement, which ousted

Eduard Shevardnadze, and the Ukrainian *Pora* (It's Time) youth movement participating in the Orange Revolution (Binnendijk and Marovic 2006).

Adopting the strategies used to topple Milosevic, CANVAS has created a manual on the organization of nonviolent struggle. In Popovic, Milivojevic and Djinovic's *Nonviolent Struggle: 50 Crucial Points* (2006, p. 25), the organization presents the key tactics. The first strategy, under the heading of 'Grand Strategy', lays out the methods for securing a victory against dictators. It calls for: (a) the build-up of the movement until elections; (b) the launch of a three-level campaign, which is negative for the opponent, positive for the demonstrators, and one which calls for citizens to get out and vote; (c) the preparation for the possibility of electoral fraud by organizing general strikes and the nonviolent takeover of the government with key allies. The second section, 'Strategy', is concerned with selecting the most important areas of the struggle: (a) the mobilization of youth, mass recruitment and building an alliance with opposition parties and NGOs; (b) communicating with a dominant symbol; and (c) staying on the offensive. The third and final section, 'Tactics', calls on demonstrators to choose battles wisely – those that can be won: (a) low-cost but dramatic public actions like street theatre and (b) the boycott of official media used by the regime as a propaganda tool.

The Jasmine Revolution in Tunisia

The Arab Spring blossomed on 17 December 2010 in Tunisia. It was on this day that the self-immolation of a young man by the name of Mohamed Bouazizi ignited a 28-day protest, known as the Jasmine Revolution, which saw the end of Zine El Abidine Ben Ali's rule.

Ben Ali came to power in 1987, after a constitutional coup had forced the country's first president, Habib Bourguiba, out of office. Prior to his exile in 2011, Ben Ali ruled Tunisia by means of a large and oppressive security apparatus. Early in his leadership, it was believed that democracy and economic development would flourish. However, in common with the other regimes toppled as a result of the Arab Spring, Ben Ali's regime delivered a broad level of modernity and secularity, but at the expense of political and civil liberties. Tunisia's annual Freedom House rating was evidence of deteriorating political conditions. Using a scale of 1 (most free) to 7 (least free) for each of the categories of political rights and civil liberties, Freedom House assigned Tunisia a combined score of 11 out of 14 (Schraeder and Redissi 2011).

The self-immolation of Bouazizi, a young man supporting a family of five by selling produce on the street who was constantly harassed by the local police demanding bribes, sparked protests that could no longer be put down. In December 2010, when Bouazizi refused to pay a bribe, the police physically assaulted him, and his cart and scales were confiscated. Publically humiliated and without any way of retrieving his possessions, Bouazizi resorted to suicidal action. The case symbolized a number of issues that had plagued Ben Ali's regime, such as the lack of development in the rural areas of Tunisia, lack of jobs and rampant corruption of the government.

The defining characteristics of Ben Ali's oppressive regime were the *mukhabarat* (intelligence-based) police state and his neopatrimonial form of government (*ibid.*). Whereas Tunisia's military establishment totalled just 35,000, its security forces numbered an estimated 130,000 – giving the country of 10.5 million a security force to match that of France (*ibid.*). The security forces included the Presidential Guard, National Guard, political police, tourism police and university police. Furthermore, the regime was built around the image of Ben Ali and his extensive family. Not only were the President's portraits on billboards all over the country, but also his family played a leading role in the state's structures. A secret report by the US ambassador, made public by WikiLeaks, reported that, in 2006, more than half of Tunisia's business elite were personally related to Ben Ali through his extended family. The public was well aware of this corruption, and commonly referred to this network as 'the Family' (Anderson 2011).

Although no one could foresee the speed with which the Ben Ali regime would disintegrate, indicators pointed to deteriorating conditions that threatened to erupt into protest. In 2010, unemployment in Tunisia had risen to 14 per cent of the population, with youth unemployment at twice that rate. The fact that university students were heavily involved should come as no surprise; more than 45 per cent of university graduates could not find employment (Schraeder and Redissi 2011).

Another socio-economic factor that fuelled discontent was the rising cost of food. The combination of massive floods in Australia at the end of November in that year and financial speculation on food commodities caused a substantial rise in the price of wheat on the international market. In 2008, the average Tunisian household was spending 36 per cent of its domestic budget on the purchase of basic foodstuffs (*ibid.*).

The force with which the uprisings began shortly after Bouazizi's immolation took people by surprise. Analysts frequently pointed to Tunisia as the poster boy for Arab development. It enjoyed the status of the Arab world's best-educated country, with the largest middle class and strongest organized labour movement (Anderson 2011). Along with the reputation as a developed society, the dominant stereotype of Arab populations as docile made it unthinkable to the mainstream media that any significant political change could occur. Yet, the political uprisings that occurred were significant – this was before Egypt witnessed her own uprisings – because the protestors countered violent oppression with nonviolent civil disobedience.

The first protests took place where Bouazizi had worked and lived, Sidi Bouzid. Here, fellow street vendors, family and friends gathered outside the local government's office, throwing coins at the building's entrance and shouting, 'Here is your bribe' (Raqib 2012). In the following days hundreds of unemployed youth had joined the struggle. Like previous uprisings, the Tunisian government responded to protesters with brutality, in an effort to discourage any further demonstrations. Instead of discouraging demonstrations, however, the brutal responses from the police were captured on mobile phones and uploaded on Facebook, sparking anger in cities all over the country. Al Jazeera became the first news agency to report the story, and it did so with the help of images and videos posted online by the residents of Sidi Bouzid.

Youth, although by no means the main actors, played an important role in publicizing the various uprisings across the country using their mobile phones to upload daily images of protests. Because the internet played such an important role in publicizing the abuses by security forces and mobilizing anti-government protests, the Jasmine Revolution was widely called the first Facebook revolution. According to a survey conducted by Peter Schraeder (Schraeder and Redissi 2011), 91 per cent of university students visited Facebook at least once a day and, on average, spent 105 minutes on the site daily. Furthermore, Schraeder's research found that 64 per cent of student respondents said that Facebook had been their primary source of information regarding the protests. Seeing the potential social networking sites had in promoting unrest, the regime quickly stepped in to censor popular websites such as Facebook, Youtube and Twitter. In response to the government's censorship of the internet, international 'hactivists', such as the group Anonymous, attacked government ministries and the stock exchange to show solidarity.

Just two weeks after Bouazizi's self-immolation, the country was overrun by mainly peaceful protests. On 31 December, lawyers gathered in the country's capital, Tunis, and in the town of Monastir to demand the release of lawyers arrested earlier by the regime. The police responded by beating lawyers and confiscating their mobile phones. On 3 January, hundreds of students marched in the central Tunisian city of Thala. On 7 January, the authorities made a number of arrests, targeting bloggers, journalists and social activists. Over the following days, the security forces responded to protesters using live ammunition, killing eight protesters. In the final days of his rule, Ben Ali had given in to demands by the protestors and promised to lower food prices, the release of political prisoners and to fight corruption. It was evident that Ben Ali had grasped the genuine popularity of events unfolding. On 13 January, for the first time in his 23-year-old rule, Ben Ali addressed the population in the local Tunisian dialect, proclaiming, 'Yes, I have understood you. I have understood all of you: the unemployed, the needy, the politician and those asking for more freedoms' (Raqib 2012). The concessions Ben Ali offered, however, were not enough and, the following day, he abdicated his authority and left for Saudi Arabia.

Aside from toppling the regime, the Jasmine Revolution was significant because it set a precedent for uprisings that followed. First, the Tunisian case exemplified a truly popular movement that drew supporters from all sectors of the political and religious spectrum. Although the uprisings began as a spontaneous movement, Tunisia's largest trade union, the General Union of Tunisian Workers, played a crucial role in organizing the protests. Professional unions, such as the Bar Association representing the country's lawyers, played a leading role in elevating the movement from one dominated by the youth, to one that included all ages (Hanafi 2011).

The Tunisian uprising also destroyed western stereotypes of passive Arab women waiting to be liberated from oppression. Tunisian women not only have a relatively high literacy rate at 71 per cent, but also represent 43 per cent of union members (Cole and Cole 2011). Women were often seen on television protesting side by side with their children and husbands. Women's organizations, such as the Tunisian Association of Democratic Women, encouraged women to show up to rallies and lend their support to democratic transition.

The second, and final, reason the Tunisian uprising proved to be significant was because it demonstrated a link between 'bread and freedom' (Hanafi 2011). Those belonging to the middle class joined with the poor in the rural areas in calling for various reforms. In addition, unemployed individuals considered their livelihoods linked not only to the economy, but also to the freedom of the press and freedom of speech. The population did not stop its protests when Ben Ali proposed to put an end to unemployment; in fact, they came out in even larger numbers when they heard that political reforms were not included in his plans. For decades Arab dictators such as Ben Ali and Mubarak were able to suppress calls for democratization because they were able to provide modernity and surface-level material needs. However, this was clearly no longer the case.

The revolution in Egypt

Within just nine days of Ben Ali's fall, on 25 January, the first protests in Cairo, Egypt, broke out. The international community was quick to proclaim that Egypt was not Tunisia, and that drastic political changes seen in Tunisia were not possible in Egypt. At first glance the two countries do not have very many similarities. Tunisia, a country of only 10.5 million, boasts a well-educated society with fairly good literacy rates and a large and stable middle class. Egypt, on the other hand, has a population of roughly 83 million people, a high rate of illiteracy and widening inequality. Tunisia was an openly repressive police state, which frequently silenced media outlets and severely punished anyone who publicly criticized Ben Ali and his family. In Egypt, it was the military that acted as the main guarantor of stability. However, unlike the Tunisian security forces, the Egyptian military enjoyed a significant amount of popular support from the populace.

Upon deeper analysis, however, it is clear that some similarities between the two nations existed. President Hosni Mubarak's rule had lasted nearly 30 years, like Ben Ali's. Appointed Vice President of Egypt in 1975, Mubarak assumed the presidency in 1981, following the assassination of Anwar Sadat, at which point he also became the chairman of the National Democratic Party (NDP) and quickly gained popularity. Throughout the 1980s Mubarak stressed the importance of the rule of law, pardoning political prisoners and encouraging the development of democratic participation by the Egyptian people. The early years of Mubarak's rule also saw the implementation of popular economic programmes, which focused on improving the quality of life for many Egyptians by building affordable housing and providing better access to medicines.

In his second term in office, starting in 1987, Mubarak refused to reform the constitution, extended the state of emergency, began pushing laws that excluded opposition parties from local councils and consolidated his rule over the NDP. Strengthening the executive branch of government, presidential candidates were selected by the People's Assembly and ratified by a national referendum, where the public was given the choice of 'yes' or 'no' (Lesch 2011, p. 36). Mubarak's powers included the ability to appoint and remove the prime minister and council members, to dissolve the two houses of parliament and to exercise a veto. By extending the state of emergency during the decades he ruled Egypt, the government was able to restrict the movement of individuals, search individuals without warrants, censor publications and forbid meetings – the gathering of five of more individuals was strictly forbidden.

By the 1990s, Mubarak's regime came down with force against Islamists in general, and specifically the political arm of Islam, the Muslim Brotherhood. The regime prosecuted civilians for nonviolent infractions, even after Islamist groups denounced the use of violence. The Mubarak regime's fear of this sector of society was illustrated by fact that the majority of the 17,000 political prisoners detained during his rule identified themselves as Islamists (Shatz 2010). To counter these images of dictatorship, the regime was quick to point to the country's successful economic modernization. The NDP frequently boasted about Egypt's impressive economic record, which saw successive years of growth above 5 per cent, and the important role the country played on the international stage.

The reality of the situation explains why a broad range of the Egyptian populace supported the events that led to Mubarak being ousted. Since the liberalization of the currency in 2003, inflation had soared and, by the end of 2010, the unemployment rate stood at 26.3 per cent. Prior to the uprising, about one in every four Egyptians lived in a shanty town, a third of Cairo's 19 million residents did not have clean drinking water and proper sewage systems. It was becoming increasingly clear that Mubarak's reforms had not transformed Egypt into a 'tiger of the Nile' and that the economy's perceived strength depended on the global price of oil, its tourism industry and American aid, which had accounted for more than $62 billion since 1977 (*ibid.*). Furthermore, like Tunisia, since Egypt imported more than half of the wheat it consumed, its price rise on the global markets further exasperated Egyptian citizens.

Even the country's foreign policy could no longer be used by the regime to gain legitimacy with the populace. Egypt no longer held a dominant role in the Arab world, with Saudi Arabia, Qatar and even non-Arabic nations like Turkey and Iran having a greater say in the region's politics than Egypt. Furthermore, because of Egypt's status as client state of the United States and the close cooperation with Israel regarding Gaza, the regime faced strong feelings of resentment from its own population. The pressure Mubarak's regime maintained on Gaza was certainly an area the Muslim Brotherhood was able to exploit.

The nonviolent protests that erupted against the regime on 25 January were highly symbolic and demonstrated the grievances of the Egyptian people; this was a significant day because it marked the Mubarak-era celebration known as Police Day. The celebration has its roots in the events that transpired on that same day in 1952, when British troops massacred police officers in the town of Ismailiya. While some celebrated the police on this day, those getting ready to join the only political demonstrations they had ever attended used this day to show their displeasure with an increasingly authoritative state that was out of touch with its population. Of particular significance in drawing a large crowd out in the streets was the fact that, since 2009, Police Day had been recognized as a national holiday, which meant people did not attend work.

Pushed to the brink by rising food prices, unemployment, crackdowns on media and academics, years of election fraud and growing discontent at the corruption of elites with ties to the government, Egyptians took to the streets. The estimated 20,000-strong demonstration of 25 January was followed by a 'million-man march' on 1 February. The turning point for the demonstrators occurred only three days into the protests. On 28 January, in what became known as the Battle of Qasr al-Nil Bridge, thousands of protestors were able to push back riot police across the bridge that linked Cairo main square, Tahrir Square, with the affluent district of Zamalek. The media images showing police retreating became symbolic of the tide turning on the regime. Once the bridge was secured, hundreds of thousands of protestors flooded into and occupied Cairo's main square.

The regime replied to the demonstrators by unleashing extreme violence, but at the same time tactically withdrawing their forces from neighbourhoods at night. This latter policy was calculated deliberately by the regime in the hope that the looting that ensued would discredit the legitimate demonstrations. As a result of the lack of police presence, communities stepped up and organized volunteer neighbourhood watch guards to ensure safety.

Like in Tunisia, the protestors in Cairo did not belong to a specific social class, political party, or religious domination. On the contrary, the protests could claim success because they were able to draw a wide range of the populace onto the streets. During the 18-day protests, it was often claimed that one of the potential weaknesses of the demonstrations was that they lacked clear leadership; the popular movement was too fragmented to succeed in providing a viable political alternative. The truly democratic nature of the protests was demonstrated by the fact that they were able to bring together secularists and Salafists, men and women, old and young from across Egypt. Middle-class, middle-aged protestors could be found on the streets of Cairo taking part in their first political demonstrations since the 1970s, carrying the same signs that university students waved around, 'Leave and let's live' (El Amrani 2011). However, throughout the demonstrations, there were moments when established opposition members attempted to claim the demonstrations for themselves and their political ambitions – including political parties such as the Muslim Brotherhood and notable politicians such as Mohammed ElBaradei, both of whom enjoyed some support prior to the uprising, but were unable to claim leadership of the movement.

Perhaps the most important agent in laying the groundwork and organizing the demonstrations was the April 6 Youth Movement. The movement's roots go back to 23 March 2008, when two young activists, Esraa Abdel-Fatah and Ahmed Maher, launched a Facebook page in support of a textile workers' strike in the city of Mahalla al-Kobra to protest deteriorating economic conditions. In an effort to mobilize support, the two invited approximately 300 people to join their Facebook group. Within 24 hours the group received 3,000 members and within a matter of a few weeks 70,000 people joined the cause (PBS Frontline 2011). On 6 April 2008, the textile workers in the city protested and, as a result, four people were killed and 400 were arrested. After the protests, Abdel-Fatah was arrested and, after two weeks in detention, she renounced her role as an activist. Maher and another founder, Mohamed Adel, however, stayed on as leaders of the youth movement and decided to change the direction of the movement.

In the summer of 2009 the movement came to the conclusion that the only way of obtaining serious objectives was through the employment of nonviolent tactics. Studying the nonviolent tactics used by Serbian and Ukrainian youth movements and watching the documentary *Bringing Down a Dictator*, Adel travelled to Serbia to take a course on strategies for nonviolent revolutions offered by Srdja Popovic and Slobodan Djinovic of CANVAS. The training primarily consisted of studying Djinovic's 'power graphs', which were used to spot the potential weakness of the Egyptian government (di Giovanni 2011). Using the power graphs, Adel, along with the staff of four at CANVAS, found the weakness to be Egypt's strongest institution: the military. Once the weak spot of the regime was exposed, the training consisted of learning tactics to target the media and how to employ nonviolent methods.

Returning to Cairo, Adel brought with him copies of *Bringing Down a Dictator* with subtitles in Arabic, and CANVAS textbooks. In addition to distributing the material, Adel organized tiny workshops to disseminate nonviolent methods. Just after the 25 January protests, 6 April published a 26-page pamphlet called 'How to Protest Intelligently'. The pamphlet laid out the goals of the protest: (a) taking over government buildings, (b) establishing close relations with the police and military, (c) protecting fellow protestors (Rosenberg 2011). The tactics that were employed on the streets of Egypt by 6 April and its followers were identical to those used in Serbia. Protestors were instructed to carry flowers, chant positive slogans and persuade the police to change allegiance because their own families could be among the protestors. Signs on the streets soon read, 'Police and People Together Against the Regime' (*ibid.*).

One of the most inspiring aspects of the uprising was the scale to which women were involved. Egyptian women not only organized and strategized, but their personal campaigns were crucial in advocating action and reporting on events (Wolf 2011). Much of this was a result of massive changes that had occurred in education and labour. Two generations ago only a small minority of women had access to higher education, but at the time of the protests they accounted for more than half of university students. Bloggers such as Leila Zahra and Asmaa Mahfouz went online and captured the attention of millions of Egyptians. Such was the impact of female participation that Naomi Wolf has compared it to other major shifts in history. In her conclusion to an article for Al Jazeera, Wolf writes:

> since feminism is simply a logical extension of democracy, the Middle East's despots are facing a situation in which it will be almost impossible to force these awakened women to stop their fight for freedom – their own and that of their communities. (*Ibid.*)

Yet, even after the prominent role women played in the uprising, they continue to be targets of violence. Several months after the events that brought down Mubarak, a women identified as the 'girl in the blue bra' was savagely beaten by the security forces in Tahrir Square. In the wake of the incident, thousands of men and women took to the streets to push for more rights for women in the public sphere. Such is the legacy of the events that unfolded throughout Egypt. Not only have women been empowered by the toppling of Mubarak, but so too has everyone who sees the Egyptian revolution in its beginning stages.

The protests that ensued for 18 days were exemplary of the unity that had been achieved through the common struggle of nonviolent protests. The events in Tahrir Square offered a shining example of the methods preached by nonviolent theoreticians. Protestors regularly fed each other, cleaned the square, detained those who had resorted to violent lootings; the scenes also exemplified religious unity. Coptic Christians protected Muslims while they prayed and when Christians celebrated Mass Muslims formed a human shield around them (Rosenberg 2011).

Under pressure from protestors and the military, Hosni Mubarak stepped down on 11 February and handed power over to the Supreme Council of the Armed Forces while the country took on the task of writing a new constitution. The toppling of Mubarak has not brought an end to demonstrations. Even though Egypt democratically elected President Mohamed Morsi in June 2012, a significant section of the populace is concerned about to the future of Egyptian democracy; the spirit of protest has remained an important tool that citizens have used to maintain a check over the government. Large protests erupted in Cairo on 27 November 2012 to challenge a controversial declaration by Morsi that would have seen his actions safeguarded from the scrutiny of the courts. After days of protests in Tahrir Square and in front of the Presidential Palace, Morsi was forced to scrap his proposal. Actions such as those taken by citizens have shown that the democratic momentum in Egypt is still alive, but it must not stop despite the severe pressure it is coming under.

Speaking about the need for the revolutions to keep momentum, Srdja Popovic, Otpor founder, but a freshwater biologist by training, says: 'A shark moves when it sleeps, if it stops moving, it dies. Sharks only move forward. You have to keep the momentum of revolutions going' (di Giovanni 2011).

Further reading

Affaya, M. N. (2011) 'The "Arab Spring": Breaking the Chains of Authoritarianism and Postponed Democracy', *Contemporary Arab Affairs*. A masterly discussion of the Arab Spring and its anti-authoritarian mechanisms.

Bock, G. (2012) *The Technology of Nonviolence: Social Media and Violence Prevention*. A solid examination of the role of social media in preventing violence before it happens, with case studies of its success in Africa, Asia and the United States.

Kurzman, C. (2012) 'The Arab Spring: Ideals of the Iranian Green Movement, Methods of the Iranian Revolution', *International Journal of Middle East Studies*. An insightful article on understanding the nonviolent nature of the Green Movement in Iran.

Nepstad, S. E. (2011) 'Nonviolent Resistance in the Arab Spring: The Critical Role of Military–Opposition Alliances', *Swiss Political Science Review*. This article examines the nonviolent strategies of the Arab Spring movement.

Octavian, M. and Popovic, S. (2012) 'The Non-Violent Struggle as Asymmetric Warfare: Interview with Srdja Popovic', *Small Wars Journal*. A rare document on one of the founders and key organizers of the Serbian nonviolent resistance group Otpor.

Conclusion

Democracy and nonviolence

The twenty-first century marks a crossroads. The ending of the confrontation between East and West ushered in the possibility of a 'new international order' based on the extension of democracy across the globe, and a new spirit of peace. However, the enthusiasm which accompanied the fall of the Berlin wall and the end of the Cold War seems now far away. The crises and cruelties in Bosnia, Rwanda, Darfur, Afghanistan and Iraq have brought many to the conclusion that the new world order is a new world disorder. However, in a brief note of optimism, the recent revolts in the Middle East demonstrate that democracy is held dear by its citizens, despite the fact that it is a fluid arena which has to deal with unforeseen challenges from both within and outside the society. Spinoza wrote that without passion no human activity, though supported by reason, can prosper. But how can one rekindle in citizens, either spoiled by well-being or resentful because of exclusion from it, the passion for democracy by taking the path of nonviolence?

Democracy has often been limited or destroyed in the name of peace. Tacitus's words, quoted by a Gaelic chieftain on the eve of battle against a Roman legion in the Scottish highlands, stated: 'They make a desert and call it peace,' reminding us that the kind of peace that is delivered by the masters of war is the peace of cemeteries. In other words, peace is something which is produced in common and not fought for. There is no way we can prepare for peace and democracy only by preparing for war. All politics can do is to keep us out of war, but what is needed for the consolidation of democratic institutions is a lasting peace. As Martin Luther King, Jr used to say: 'True peace is not merely the absence of tension: it is the presence of justice.' It would be presumptuous and even dangerous to affirm that the end of an autocracy by war would lead to a democracy. Democracy in a given period is best defined by its political culture rather than only by its peaceful character; an aborted transition to democracy with a weak democratic culture constitutes also a threat to global peace and international stability. We should, thus, perhaps avoid errors committed in the past in the name of a democratization process that believes in the strategy of 'exporting democracy', especially by force. Just because some nations consider themselves as 'democratic' and 'peace loving', that does not give them the right to act in a non-democratic way and impose peace and democracy through war. That is to say, promoting democracy cannot be effective in the absence of a democratic culture and organizing elections is only the starting point of the democratic life of a nation. In fact, the real test of democracy lies not merely in empowering a victorious majority, giving the greatest liberty to the greatest number, but it really consists in a new attitude and approach towards the problem of power and violence. As Claude Lefort (1991) has shown in his book *L'Invention Democratique* (translated into English under the title *Democracy and Political Theory*), democracy is at the origin of a new kind of institution of the social, in which power becomes an 'empty space', dispelling age-old claims to foundation in or legitimation by God made by theocracies. According to Lefort, democracy consists of a particular symbolic regime that, by considering power as a void that cannot be appropriated, forbids a democratic society from seeing itself as an organic unity. The electoral rule of the majority is, therefore, secondary with regard to the major institutive affirmation of the void of power. Democracy is also a political order that does not submit to the theological, though it has deeply religious roots and may be represented by individuals who consider themselves as religious. The fact that democratic thinking was in conflict with religious institutions during its historical formation does not negate the fact that it owes a great deal to the spiritual experience of humanity; furthermore, many religious thinkers have fought against the arbitrary nature of political power and defended the principles of democracy. Among them, Mahatma Gandhi has gained a special place in the hearts and minds of people around the world as a supporter of democracy.

Mahatma Gandhi considered 'Democracy disciplined and enlightened as the finest thing in the world' (1931, p. 199). What he meant was that democratic governance is not power over the society, but power within it. In other words, if democracy equals self-rule and self-control of society, empowerment of civil society and collective ability to rule democratically are essential constituents of democratic governance. Democracy and nonviolence, therefore, are inseparable. Where democracy is practised, the rules of the political game are defined by the absence of violence and a set of institutional guarantees against the domineering logic of the state. Yet, the more we think about it, the more this definition seems unsatisfactory and incomplete. If democracy were no more than a set of institutional guarantees, how could citizens think about politics today and struggle for the emergence of new perspectives of democratic action? And how are we to reconcile the twin convictions that there can be no democracy unless state-centred power is limited and that there can be no democracy without the pursuit of nonviolence? The answer to these two questions resides in the definition of nonviolence as a 'common responsibility' in all spheres of life, including economics and politics.

It goes without saying that politics is the driving force of history, because it is through politics that history is made. Man cannot escape politics without abdicating his humanity as a political animal. But politics is not only the conquest and the preservation of power; it is mainly, as the ancient Greek philosophers thought, the embodiment of the ethical in a historical community. So not all politics is corrupt per se, and not all political powers are evil. But, once established, the political which is conceived in violence necessitates violent action to sustain its own existence. That is to say, there is a paradox between the constitution of the political as an art of governing and the reality of violence. In a statement written in the aftermath of the Russian invasion of Hungary in 1956, Paul Ricoeur (1957) observed: 'The surprise is that, so to speak, power does not have history, that history of power repeats itself, makes no headway: the surprise is that real political surprise does not exist.' There is a problem of political evil, because there is a specific problem of the legitimacy of violence at the heart of politics. The recognition of violence as problematic for politics underscores man's nature as a political animal and the possibility of the degeneration of politics into violence. Violence must consequently be seen as a kind of corrupted politics. Therefore, any attempt to go beyond violence, necessitates the recognition of the paradoxical status of politics. That is why Ricoeur notes that 'if we are to change things we must influence the power of the state. That is politics' (*ibid.*). So we cannot make the mistake of talking about nonviolence as a non-political action or just as the condemnation of one kind of violence, such as punitive violence. We need to accept fully the concept of nonviolent action as a new approach to power, politics and democracy. Gandhi and Martin Luther King, Jr and, more recently, Mandela and Havel, prove that politics as the practice of morality is possible – that nonviolence is not only a political experience, but also an ethical experience, which makes our responsibility towards democratic life more fulfilling. As such, nonviolence is one of the ways in which our human nature – as a social animal – can be truly expressed. In an age when mass communication dominates all the aspects of human life, nonviolence affords people the opportunity to be recognized by others for their humanness, reviving the very face-to- face contact that marked the birth of democracy in ancient Athens.

The spiritualization of politics which comes about with the politics of nonviolence requires that humans deal with each other and resolve their tensions and conflicts through peace and order. In this way, it protects common life against popular tides of passion and demagogic appeals by various ideologies. The more a democratic community develops instruments of nonviolence, the more resistant it is to different political storms. Maybe, this is why the politics of nonviolence is a more valuable safeguard of democracy than the free market. No matter how much we accumulate to provide the necessities of life and to live comfortably, we all know that we need more than material possessions to give meaning to our common life. If we ask the question 'Why do we all live as if democracy matters and is worth our efforts?', the response could be that life is no more than simply the satisfaction of desires. There is an ethical horizon of responsibility without which life has no meaning. This horizon of responsibility is grounded in our everyday social experience, but it does not follow the laws of nature as the rest of the material world does. Responsibility is the key to our identity as moral beings. Responsibility is a reaction to the intolerable in the name of shared human dignity and vulnerability. It is what Jewish philosopher Emmanuel Levinas has championed as the 'humanism of the other man'. The encounter with another is seen by Levinas as the prism through which to grasp the problem of responsibility. Responsiveness to the other reveals, therefore, that which exceeds the realm of the political. The claim of the other person is an opening to a realm of value more extensive than inter-human and intra-human purposes.

We can say of nonviolence that it is a form of humanism that preserves human dignity within the wider realm of life on our planet. More than an attitude or a vision, nonviolence is the last moral stance in life; it faces realistically the pettiness, mediocrity and violence of human beings, but does not regard these qualities as inescapable. If there is to be any chance at all for moral choice to be a middle ground between certainty and doubt, there is only one way to strive for responsibility and civility, and that is nonviolent action. Only by caring about others, not just ourselves, can we be at peace in this world. It is a moral effort which reveals to us the complexity, spontaneity and heterogeneity of life. Therefore, nonviolence as a commitment, more than as a conviction, shows us in our everyday experience that morality is a human possibility and, as Heidegger, says: 'The possible ranks higher than the actual.'

I believe that nonviolence is taking a specific shape in our present situation. Its ethical purpose is to help human beings as social agents in thinking about and responsibly conducting their lives. How one is rightly to value and properly esteem human beings is presently being debated against the backdrop of the horror and intolerable acts of cruelty which have continued with the new millennium. Maybe this is the reason why we can never be fully satisfied with democracy as a philosophical value and as a political reality – to be so would be to forget the essence of democracy as a daily effort of civic responsibility, but also as a continuous struggle against the intolerable. That is why any democracy which turns into a consumer value system and creates no sense of responsibility higher than simple political ideals will end up becoming a community of mediocrity.

Gandhi's analysis and practice of nonviolence was interdependent with his insistence on the idea of responsibility and his belief that democracy comes not as a gift bestowed by the state but from each individual taking responsibility for themself and their society. For Gandhi, tolerating injustice was an irresponsible action; therefore, we should not surrender our autonomy if we want to continue to govern ourselves. He was deeply concerned by the effects of democracy on autonomous judgment and believed that, when moral commitment decays and people become morally unsure of themselves, they look to majoritarian principles to fill the political void. Gandhi, therefore, departed from the Lockean view that we must wait for majorities to decide. For him, there was no suspension of person's moral commitment at any moment in a democracy. Although Gandhi's democracy promises to expose power and make it accountable, he knows that power is about violence – about how power can enable or disable violence.

With this in mind, Gandhi denies the liberal distinction between civil society and the state. According to Gandhi, civil society is capable of promoting a stronger internal democracy. That is why, for him, 'The spirit of democracy cannot be imposed from without. It has to come from within.' Gandhi's view of democracy carries overtones of civic morality prioritizing responsibility over absolute freedom, suggesting that civil society does not represent one modality for democratic practice. Instead, civil society might be seen, in Gandhian terms, as a practice of nonviolent power-sharing among citizens. Civil society is, therefore, an alternative domain of people-centred politics that helps to sustain the process of democracy-building in its long-term societal context. Clearly, more than being mere subjection to a particular legal jurisdiction, civil society is considered by Gandhi as a transparent space of participation predicated on inclusion, a network where nonviolent civility is produced and reproduced. In other words, what was most important to Gandhi, and the nonviolent tradition of democratic thinking, was not the act of participating, but the context in which the participation took place. It is one thing to create good democratic institutions, quite another to educate citizens to think and act democratically. A nonviolent view of democracy, thus, presupposes self-discipline, self-restraint, self-realization and a sense of mutual responsibility. A democratic society could not be sustained in the absence of these and related virtues – without them it would be subject to constant misuse and produce consequences harmful to citizens. According to Gandhi, nonviolent democracy not only should create a collective wisdom, but also it should encourage dialogue and interplay among the citizens, and not allow the political leaders to acquire a hegemonic role and become the arbiter of all others. He believed that a truly democratic and nonviolent society demanded that citizens should be moral agents who govern their affairs themselves and refuse to be helpless playthings of alien and impersonal agencies. Therefore, in a nonviolent view of democracy, political society would be organized in terms of 'expanding circles'. The polity so constructed would not be a collection of passive agents but a 'community of communities'. Gandhi's argument recalls Aristotle's view, that living as part of a community should present both a challenge and an opportunity for human beings. Politics should require citizens to struggle for the moral progress of their community. Interestingly, this is the challenge that has been taken up by most of the thinkers of nonviolence in twentieth century. Martin Luther King, Jr, for example, constantly pointed out to those in the freedom movement that their goal was not only the right to sit at the front of the bus or to vote, but to give birth to a new society based on more human values. In so doing, they would not only empower those on the front lines, but in the process develop a strategy for transforming a struggle for rights into a struggle that brings what King called the 'beloved community' closer to realization. Behind King's conception of the beloved community lay his belief in the 'solidarity of the human family'. 'We are tied together in the single garment of destiny, caught in an inescapable network of mutuality', he said in one of his addresses, affirming that every society is made up of structures that form an interrelated whole – in other words, that human beings are dependent upon each other. It is because of this solidarity that human beings have the right to protest, and for King this was 'the great glory of American democracy'. 'We are here', said King at a speech at Holt Street Baptist Church, Montgomery, on 5 December 1955, 'because of our love for democracy, because of our deep-seated belief that democracy transformed from thin paper to thick action is the greatest, form of government on earth.' For King, as for Gandhi, the promise of democracy was to develop and to strengthen a heightened sense of responsibility among the citizens of a society. That is to say, a democratic society has to resist not only an overpowering state, but also a violent community subject to mob rule. According to Gandhi, 'A democratic organization has to dare to do the right at all cost. He who panders to the weaknesses of a people degrades both himself and the people, and leads them not to democratic but mob rule.' Democracy alone will never be enough; it cannot be established through elections and a constitution. Something more is necessary – an emphasis on democracy as a practice of moral thinking and moral judgment. In other words, we can never build or sustain democratic institutions if they do not have the goal of helping us become more human, offering the Socratic experience of politics as self-examination and dialogical exchange. It is the admission of ignorance in ourselves, and the recognition of ignorance in others, that gives democratic spirit the courage to confront the 'open century' with an awareness both of the complexity of the issues and of the fundamental importance of pursuing solutions. If, through this Socratic experience, every citizen can be drawn out of the simple mechanism of voting and engaged in a more responsive and more responsible process of self-government and self-structuring of the society, we might see the beginnings of a healthy return to democracy. So long as we believe that democracy is only a marketplace depending on fair and voluntary economic and political exchanges with a stable legal system, we cannot build a democracy even though we may defend public liberties. Mahatma Gandhi, who had great faith in nonviolence, was of the opinion that the right approach in this regard was gradually to improve the working of democracy and to make sure that any misuse or centralization of power was eliminated, believing that only then could democracy fully materialize. He saw democracy as the promotion of the principles and practice of nonviolence among the members of a society, with a view to empowering them and increasing their civic participation. Similarly, Václav Havel reminds us that, 'democracy is a system based on trust in the human sense of responsibility, which it ought to awaken and cultivate' (Havel, quoted in Pontuso 2004, p. 131). Perhaps both Havel and Gandhi are too hopeful about the fate of democracy. But miracles do happen. After all, democracy is made by humans and its fate is related to the human condition. Although we can never be certain about the positive results of our actions, we cannot work for a nonviolent democracy if we ignore our responsibilities and deny that, in these strange years after the end of history and on a planet overheated by violence and environmental damage, it is possible to strive for democracy because it is possible to remain true to the ethical.

Further reading

Allsopp, J. (2013) 'Peacebuilding and the Nation-state: Towards a Nonviolent World', *Open Democracy*. A well-written article which tries to answer the question: does the nation-state depend on militarism for its very existence?

Kang, J. M. (2012) 'Martin v. Malcolm: Democracy, Nonviolence, Manhood', *West Virginia Law Review*. A comparative study of two great figures of the African-American movement and their debate over the questions of peaceful resistance and violent struggle as means for political change.

Rummel, R. J. (2002) *Power Kills: Democracy as a Method of Nonviolence*. A comprehensive effort to understand and place in historical perspective the process of democratization of coercive power and force.

Tenembaum, Y. (2011) 'The Success and Failure of Non-Violence', *Philosophy Now*. A critical view on the policy of non-violence in inter-state relations.

Weart, S. (1998) *Never At War: Why Democracies Will Not Fight One Another*. A stimulating approach which offers crucial and practical information about safeguarding peace in democracies.

Bibliography

Abbey, E. (1959) 'Anarchism and the Morality of Violence', MA thesis, University of New Mexico.

Abbott, P. (1985) 'Henry David Thoreau, the State of Nature, and the Redemption of Liberalism', *The Journal of Politics*, 47(1), p. 188.

Abu-Nimer, M. 2003. *Nonviolence and Peacebuilding in Islam: Theory and Practice*. Gainesville: University Press of Florida

Abu Zahra, M. (1961) *Concept of War in Islam*. Trans. Muhammad al-Hady and Tahar Omar. Cairo: Ministry of Waqf.

Ackerman, P. and Duvall, J. 2000. A Force More Powerful. New York: St Martin's Press.

Adam, M. T. (2006) 'Nonviolence and Emptiness: Buddha, Gandhi, and the "Essence of Religion"', *Journal of the Faculty of Religious Studies*, 34(1), pp. 6–7.

Affaya, M. N. 2011. 'The "Arab Spring": Breaking the Chains of Authoritarianism and Postponed Democracy', Contemporary Arab Affairs 4(4), pp. 463–83.

Al-Ghazālī, A. H. (2002) *On the Boundaries of Theological Tolerance in Islam: Abu Hamid al Ghazālī's Faysal al Tafriqa*. Trans. Sherman A. Jackson. Karachi: Oxford University Press.

Allen, J. (2007) *Rabble-Rouser for Peace: The Authorised Biography of Desmond Tutu*. London: Rider.

Allen, R. E. (1980) *Socrates and Legal Obligation*. Minneapolis: University of Minnesota Press.

Allsopp J. (2013) 'Peacebuilding and the Nation-state: Towards a Nonviolent World', *Open Democracy*. Available at: http://www.opendemocracy.net/5050/jennifer-allsopp/peacebuilding-and-nation-state-towards-nonviolent-world.

Alton, C. (2010) 'Tolstoy's Guiding Light', *History Today*, 60(10), pp. 30–6.

Anderson, L. (2011) 'Demystifying the Arab Spring: Parsing the Differences Between Tunisia, Egypt, and Libya', *Foreign Affairs*, 90(3), pp. 2–7.

Arendt, H. (1958) *The Human Condition*. Chicago: University of Chicago Press.

Arendt, H. (1970) *On Violence*. New York: Harcourt, Brace & World.

Avrich, P. (1974) *Bakunin & Nechaev*. London: Freedom.

Azad, A. K. (1995) *Tarjuman-ul-Quran*. New Delhi: Sahitya Akademi.

Ballou, Robert O. (ed.) (1984) *The Portable World Bible*. New York: Viking Press.

Bernstein, R. J. (2013) *Violence: Thinking without Banisters*. Oxford: Wiley-Blackwell.

Bhagavad Gita. Trans. from Hindi by Graham M. Schweig (2007). New York: HarperCollins.

Bharadwaj, L. K. (1998) 'Principled Versus Pragmatic Non-violence', *Peace Review: A Journal of Social Justice*, 10(1).

Bhaskarananda, S. (1994) *The Essentials of Hinduism: A Comprehensive Overview of the World's Oldest Religion*. Seattle, WA: Viveka Press.

Binnendijk, A. L. and Marovic, I. (2006) 'Power and Persuasion: Nonviolent Strategies to Influence State Security Forces in Serbia (2000) and Ukraine (2004)', *Communist and Post-Communist Studies*, 39, pp. 411–29.

Bishop, M. (1974) *Saint Francis of Assisi*. Boston: Little, Brown & Co.

Bock, G. (2012) *The Technology of Nonviolence: Social Media and Violence Prevention*. Cambridge, MA: MIT Press.

Bodewitz, H. W. (1999) 'Hindu Ahimsa and its Roots', in J. E. M. Houben and K. R. Van Koojen (eds), *Violence Denied: Violence, Nonviolence and the Rationalization of Violence in South Asian Cultural History*. Leiden: Brill, chapter 2.

Brickhouse, T. C. and Smith, N. D. (2002) *The Trial and Execution of Socrates: Sources and Controversies*. Oxford: Oxford University Press.

Bringing Down a Dictator (2002) [Film] Directed by Steve York. USA: WETA.

Brock, P. (1992) *A Brief History of Pacifism from Jesus to Tolstoy*. 2nd edn. Syracuse: Syracuse University Press.

Brown, J. M. (2006) *Gandhi: Prisoner of Hope*. New Haven: Yale University Press.

Bunting, M. (2011) 'Aung San Suu Kyi's Idea of Freedom Offers a Radical Message for the West', *Guardian*, 26 June.

Campton, D. and Biggar, N. (2008) *Divided Past Shared Future: Essays on Churches Addressing the Legacy of the Troubles*. Dublin: Centre for Contemporary Christianity.

Carson, C. (ed.) (1998) *The Autobiography of Martin Luther King, Jr*. New York: Intellectual Properties Management/Warner.

Chadha, Y. (1997) *Gandhi: A Life*. New York: John Wiley & Sons.

Chapple, C. K. (1993) 'Nonviolence to Animals, Earth, and Self in Asian Traditions', in H. Coward (ed.), *SUNY Series in Religious Studies*. Albany: State University of New York.

Chapple, C. K. (2002) *Jainism and Ecology: Nonviolence in the Web of Life*. Cambridge: Harvard University Press.

Chesterton, G. K. (1924) *St Francis of Assisi*. New York: George H. Doran.

Cole, J. and Cole, S. (2011) 'An Arab Spring for Women', *The Nation* [online], 26 April. Available at: http://www.thenation.com/article/160179/arab-spring-women#.

Coleman, J. A. (2008) *Christian Political Ethics*. Princeton, NJ: Princeton University Press.

Confino, M., Bakunin, M. A. and Nechaev, S. G. (1973) *Violence dans La Violence*; *Le Débat Bakounine-Nečāev*. Paris: F. Maspero.

Creel, A. B. (1975) 'The Reexamination of "Dharma" in Hindu Ethics', *Philosophy East and West*, 25(2).

Dalai Lama (1984) *Kindness, Clarity and Insight*. Ithaca: Snow Lion.

Dalai Lama (1999) 'Buddhism, Asian Values, and Democracy', *Journal of Democracy*, 10(1), pp. 3–7.

Dalai Lama (2008) 'Human Rights, Democracy and Freedom' [online]. Available at: http://www.dalailama.com/messages/world-peace/human-rights-democracy-and-freedom [accessed 26 December 2012].

Dalton, D. (1993) *Mahatma Gandhi: Nonviolent Power*. New York: Columbia University Press.

Dhawan, G. (1990) *The Political Philosophy of Mahatma Gandhi*. New Delhi: Gandhi Peace Foundation.

di Giovanni, J. (2011) 'Blueprint for a Revolution', *Financial Times* [online], 18 March. Available at: http://www.ft.com/intl/cms/s/2/0ad005b4-5043-11e0-9ad1-00144feab49a.html#axzz1H5THR8GW.

El Amrani, I. (2011) 'Why Tunis, Why Cairo?', *London Review of Books* [online]. Available at: http://www.lrb.co.uk/v33/n04/issandr-elamrani/why-tunis-why-cairo.

Eliot, W. C. (1980) *The Harvard Classics: The Apology: Phaedo and Crito of Olate, the Golden sayings of Epitetus, the Mediations of Marcus Aurelius*. Boston MA: Grolier.

Fanon, F. (1961) *Les damnés de la terre*. Paris: F. Maspero.

Fanon, F. (2004) *The Wretched of the Earth*. New York: Grove.

Finlay, C. J. (2006) 'Violence and Revolutionary Subjectivity: Marx to Žižek', *European Journal of Political Theory* 5(4).

Fisher, M. M. (1935) 'Friends of Humanity: A Quaker Anti-slavery Influence', *Church History*, 4(3).

Francis and Clare (1982) *The Complete Works*. Trans. Regis J. Armstrong and Ignatius Brady. New York: Paulist Press.

Frazer, E. and Hutchings, K. (2009) 'Politics, Violence and Revolutionary Virtue: Reflections on Locke and Sorel', *Thesis Eleven* 97(1).

Frost, B. (1998) *Struggling to Forgive: Nelson Mandela and South Africa's Search for Reconciliation*. London: HarperCollins.

Galtung, J. (1965) 'On the Meaning of Nonviolence', *Journal of Peace Research* 2(3): 228–57.

Gandhi, M. K. (1925) *Young India*. pp. 1078–9, cited in C. S. Mahadevan. 2001. *The Glories of the Gita: Stories from the Padma Purana*. New Delhi: Sterling.

Gandhi, M. K. (1931) *Young India*, 30 July.

Gandhi, M. K. (1938a) *Harijan*, 24 December.

Gandhi, M. K. (1938b) *Satyagraha in South Africa*. Trans. V. G. Desai. Madras: S. Ganesa.

Gandhi, M. K. (1959) *The Message of the Gita*. Ahmedabad: Navajivan Publishing.

Gandhi, M. K. (1960a) *Discourses on the Gita*. Ahmedabad: Navajivan.

Gandhi, M. K. (1960b) *My Nonviolence*. Ahmedabad: Navajivan.

Gandhi, M. K. (1999) *Collected Works of Mahatma Gandhi*. New Delhi: Publications Division.

Gandhi, R. (2006) Mohandas: A True Story of a Man, his People and an Empire, New Delhi, Penguin-Viking,

Ghaffār Khān, A. (ed.) (1995) *Khan Abdul Ghaffār Khān: A Centennial Tribute*. Delhi: Har-Anand.

Gordon, L. R. (1995) *Fanon and the Crisis of European Man: An Essay on Philosophy and the Human Sciences*. New York: Routledge.

Greenwood, E. B. (1975) *Tolstoy: The Comprehensive Vision*. New York: St Martin's Press.

Halverson, J. R. (2012) *Searching for a King: Muslim Nonviolence and the Future of Islam*. Washington, DC: Potomac.

Hanafi, S. (2011) 'Lessons of the Jasmine Revolution', *Al Jazeera* [online]. Available at: http://www.aljazeera.com/indepth/opinion/2011/01/201111 985641326468.html.

Hanigan, J. (1984) *Martin Luther King, Jr and the Foundations of Nonviolence*. Lanham, MD: University Press of America.

Harding, W. (1961) *A Thoreau Handbook*. New York: New York University Press.

Harvey, P. (2000) *Introduction to Buddhist Ethics: Foundations, Values, and Issues*. Cambridge: Cambridge University Press.

Hasday, J. L. (2007) *Aung San Suu Kyi* (Modern Peacemakers). New York: Chelsea House.

Hashmi, H. S. (ed.) (2002) *Islamic Political Ethics: Civil Society, Pluralism and Conflict*. Princeton, NJ: Princeton University Press.

Heiss, R. (1975) *Hegel, Kirkegaard, Marx: Three Great Philosophers Whose Ideas Changed the Course of Civilization*. New York: Delta.

Hill, J. B. (2007) *The Theology of Martin Luther King, Jr and Desmond Mpilo Tutu*. New York: Palgrave.

Holmes, Robert L. (ed.) (1990) Nonviolence in Theory and Practice. Belmont, CA: Wadsworth.

Howe, D. W. (1990) *Henry David Thoreau on the Duty of Civil Disobedience*. Oxford: Clarendon Press.

Hugo, V. (2008) *The History of a Crime*. Gloucester: Dodo Press.

Hunt, S. A. (2002) *The Future of Peace: On the Front Lines With the World's Great Peacemakers*. San Francisco: HarperCollins.

Iyer, R. (1987) *The Moral and Political Writings of Mahatma Gandhi*, Vol. II. Oxford: Clarendon Press.

Jain, S. (1998) *Jain Literature and Philosophy*. Varanasi: Parsvanatha Vidyapitha.

Jain Samaj Europe (2002) *Mahatma Gandhi on Jainism and non-violence* [online]. Available at: http://www.jaincentre.com/jainism.htm.

Johnson, R. L. (ed.) (2006) *Gandhi's Experiments with Truth*. Lanham, MD: Lexington.

Jordens, J. T. F. (1993) *Gandhi's Religion: A Homespun Shawl*. London: Macmillan.

Kang, J. M. (2012) 'Martin v. Malcolm: Democracy, Nonviolence, Manhood', *West Virginia Law Review*, 114.

Khadduri, M. (1984) *The Islamic Conception of Justice*. New York: Johns Hopkins University Press.

King, Jr, Martin Luther (1986, 2nd edn 1992) *I Have a Dream: Writing Speeches That Changed the World*, ed. James M. Washington. San Francisco: Harper.

King, S. B. (1998) 'Transformative Nonviolence: The Social Ethics of George Fox and Thich Nhat Hanh', *Buddhist-Christian Studies*, 18.

Kirk, J. A. (ed.) (2007) *Martin Luther King, Jr, and the Civil Rights Movement: Controversies and Debates*. Basingstoke and New York: Palgrave Macmillan.

Koller, J. M. (1972) 'Dharma: An Expression of Universal Order', *Philosophy East and West*, 22(2).

Kolodiejchuk, B. and Mother Teresa (2007) *Come By My Light: Private Writings of the Saint of Calcutta*. New York: Doubleday.

Kropotkin, P. A. (1970) *Selected Writings on Anarchism and Revolution*. Cambridge, MA: MIT Press.

Kumar, M. (ed.) (1984) *Nonviolence: Contemporary Issues and Challenges*. Delhi: Gandhi Peace Foundation.

Kumar, R. (1991) *Life and Works of Maulana Abul Kalam Aza*. New Delhi: Atlantic.

Kurzman, C. (2012) 'The Arab Spring: Ideals of the Iranian Green Movement, Methods of the Iranian Revolution', *International Journal of Middle East Studies* 44(1), pp. 162–5.

Laidlaw, J. (1995) *Riches and Renunciation: Religion, Economy, and Society Among the Jains*. Oxford: Clarendon Press.

Laird, T. (2006) *The Story of Tibet: Conversations with the Dalai Lama*. New York: Grove Press.

Lecso, P. A. (1988) 'To Do No Harm: A Buddhist View on Animal Use in Research', *Journal of Religion and Health*, 27(4).

Lefort, C. (1991) *Democracy and Political Theory*. Oxford: Wiley.

Leier, M. (2006) *Bakunin: The Creative Passion: A Biography*. New York: Thomas Dunne.

Lesch, A. M. (2011) 'Egypt's Spring: Causes of the Revolution', *Middle East Policy* 28(3), pp. 35–48.

Maccoby, H. (1986) *The Mythmaker: Paul and the Invention of Christianity*. New York: Harper & Row.

Martin R. (1970) 'Socrates on Disobedience to Law', The Review of Metaphysics 24(1), pp. 21–38.

Marx, K. (1994) *Selected Writings*. Indianapolis: Hackett.

Mathai, M. P. (2000) *Mahatma Gandhi's Worldview*. New Delhi: Gandhi Peace Foundation.

Mauser, U. (1992) *The Gospel of Peace*. Westminster: John Knox.

McElrath, J. (2008) *The Everything Martin Luther King Jr Book: The Struggle. The Dream. The Legacy.* Avon: Adams Media.

McKeogh, C. (2009) *Tolstoy's Pacifism*. Amherst: Cambria Press.

Melvin. J. (ed.) (1986) *A Testament of Hope: The Essential Writings and Speeches of Martin Luther King, Jr.* Washington: Harper One.

Merton, T. (ed.) (1965) *Gandhi on Non-Violence*. New York: New Directions.

Merton, T. (1966) Conjectures of a Guilty Bystander. New York: Doubleday.

Merton, T. (1971) Contemplation in a World of Action. New York: Doubleday.

Merton, T. (1997) *Passion for Peace: The Social Essays*. New York: Crossroad.

Merton, T. (ed.) (2007) *Gandhi on Nonviolence*. New York: New Directions.

Minor, R. N. (ed.) (1986) *Modern Indian Interpreters of the Bhagavad Gita*. New York: State University of New York Press.

Morrison, D. R. (2011) *The Cambridge Companion to Socrates*. Cambridge: Cambridge University Press.

Myerson, J. (ed.) (1995) *The Cambridge Companion to Henry David Thoreau*. Cambridge: Cambridge University Press.

Nagley, W. E. (1954) 'Thoreau on Attachment, Detachment, and Non-attachment', *Philosophy East and West*, 3(4).

Nanda, B. R. (1995) *Mahatma Gandhi 125 Years*. New Delhi: Indian Council for Cultural Relations.

Nepstad, S. E. (2011) 'Nonviolent Resistance in the Arab Spring: The Critical Role of Military–Opposition Alliances', *Swiss Political Science Review*, 17(4), pp. 485–91.

New Testament and Psalms: An Inclusive Version (1995) Oxford: Oxford University Press.

Octavian, M. and Popovic, S. (2012) 'The Non-Violent Struggle as Asymmetric Warfare: Interview with Srdja Popovic', *Small Wars Journal*, 26 March. Available at: http://smallwarsjournal.com/jrnl/art/nonviolent-struggle-as-asymmetric-warfare-interview-with-srdja-popovic.

Pal, A. (2011) *Islam Means Peace: Understanding the Muslim Principle of Nonviolence Today*. Santa Barbara, CA: Praeger.

Parel, A. J. (1997) *Hind Swaraj*. Cambridge: Cambridge University Press.

Pauling, C. (1990) *Introducing Buddhism*. Cambridge: Windhorse.

PBS Frontline (2011) *Revolution in Cairo* [online]. Available at: http://www.pbs.org/wgbh/pages/frontline/revolution-in-cairo/inside-april6-movement/.

Pontuso, J. F. (2004) *Václav Havel: Civic Responsibility in the Postmodern Age*. Lanham, MD: Rowman & Littlefield.

Popovic, S., Milivojevic, A. and Djinovic, S. (2006) *Nonviolent Struggle: 50 Crucial Points*. Belgrade: CANVAS.

Puligandla, R. (1975) *Fundamentals of Indian Philosophy*. New York: Abingdon Press.

Qur'an (2007) Trans. Alan Jones. Exeter: Short Run Press.

Radhakrishnan, S. (1927) *The Hindu View of Life*. New York: George Allen & Unwin.

Radhakrishnan, S. (1939) *Eastern Religions and Western Thought*. Oxford: Clarendon Press.

Rahula, W. (1974) *What the Buddha Taught*. New York: Grove Press.

Raqib, J. (2012) 'Case Study: The Tunisian Uprising and Protests, December 2010–January 2011', in G. Sharp (ed.), *Sharp's Dictionary of Power and Struggle*. New York: Oxford University Press.

Richard, A., OFM (1989) 'Concerning Nonviolence and the Franciscan Movement', *The Cord* (republished in the *Pace e Bene* Occasional Paper Series No. 1).

Richardson, R. D. (1986) *Henry Thoreau: A Life of the Mind*. Berkeley and Los Angeles: University of California Press.

Ricoeur, P. (1957) 'The Paradox of Politics', *Esprit*, 250 (May).

Rosenberg, T. (2011) 'Revolution U', *Foreign Policy* [online]. Available at: http://www.foreignpolicy.com/articles/2011/02/16/revolution_u?page=0,1.

Roy, R. (1985) *Self and Society: A Study in Gandhian Thought*. Delhi: Sage.

Rummel, R. J. (2002) *Power Kills: Democracy as a Method of Nonviolence*. New Jersey: Transaction.

Rynne J. T. (2008) *Gandhi and Jesus: The Saving Power of Nonviolence*. New York: Orbis.

Sagarmal, J. (1998) *Jaina Literature and Philosophy*. Varanasi: Parsvanatha Vidyapitha.

Satha-Anand, C. (1991) 'From Violent to Nonviolent Discourse', in E. Boulding (ed.), Peace Culture and Society: Transnational Research and Dialogue. Boulder, San Francisco and Oxford: Westview, pp. 124–32.

Schaff, A. (1973) 'Marxist Theory on Revolution and Violence', *Journal of the History of Ideas* 34(2), p. 265.

Schraeder, P. J. and Redissi, H. (2011) 'Ben Ali's Fall', *Journal of Democracy* 22(3), pp. 5–19.

Schweig, G. (2007) *Bhagavad Gita: The Beloved Lord's Secret Love Story*. New York: Google Books.

Sen, K. M. (1961) *Hinduism*. London: Penguin.

Shannon, W. H. (ed.) (1997) *Passion for Peace: The Social Essays*. New York: Crossroad.

Sharma, I. C. (1965) *Ethical Philosophies of India*. Nebraska: George Allen & Unwin.

Sharp, G. (1973) *Politics of Nonviolent Action* Boston: Porter Sargent.

Sharp, G. (2003) *There are Realistic Alternatives*. Boston: Albert Einstein Institution.

Sharp. G. (2010) *From Dictatorship to Democracy A Conceptual Framework for Liberation*. Boston: Albert Einstein Institution.

Sharp, G. (2012) *Sharp's Dictionary of Power and Struggle: Language of Civil Resistance in Conflicts*. New York: Oxford University Press.

Sharp, G. and Raqib, J. (2009) *Self-Liberation: A Guide to Strategic Planning for Action to End a Dictatorship or Other Oppression*. Boston: Albert Einstein Institution.

Shatz, A. (2010) 'Mubarak's Last Breath', *London Review of Books* [online]. Available at: http://www.lrb.co.uk/v32/n10/adam-shatz/mubaraks-last-breath.

Shiromany, A. A. (1998) *The Political Philosophy of His Holiness the XIV Dalai Lama: Selected Speeches and Writings*. New Delhi: TPPRC and Friedrich-Naumann-Stiftung.

Simmons, E. J. (1973) *Tolstoy*. London: Routledge & Kegan Paul.

Singer, W. (2003) 'The Dalai Lama's Many Tibetan Landscapes', *The Kenyon Review*, 25(3/4).

Singh, R. (1989) 'Status of Violence in Marx's Theory of Revolution', *Economic and Political Weekly* 24(4), pp. 9–20.

Sohoni, S. R. S. (1995) *Badshah Khan: Islam and Non-Violence, Khan Abdul Ghaffār Khān – A Centennial Tribute*, New Delhi: Har-Anand Publications.

Spencer, M. (2012a) 'Principled and Pragmatic Peace', *Peace Magazine*, 28(1).

Spencer, M. (2012b) 'Gene Sharp's Ideas are Breaking Through', *Peace Magazine*, 28.

Stassen, G. H. (1992) *Just Peacemaking: Transforming Initiatives for Justice and Peace*. Westminster: John Knox.

Steger M. B. and Lind N. S. (eds) (1999) *Violence and Its Alternatives: An Interdisciplinary Reader*. New York: St Martin's Press.

Suu Kyi, A. S. (1991) *Freedom From Fear and Other Writings*. London: Penguin.

Suu Kyi, A. S. (1997) *The Voice of Hope: Conversations with Alain Clements*. New York: Seven Stories Press.

Suu Kyi, A. S. (1998) 'The Game Rules in Burma: There are No Rules', *Asahi Evening News*, 25 August.

Tähtinen, U. (1976) *Ahimsa: Non-Violence in Indian Tradition*. London: Rider and Co.

Taylor, C. C. W. (2001) *Socrates: A Very Short Introduction*. Oxford: Oxford University Press.

Tenembaum, Y. (2011) 'The Success and Failure of Non-Violence', *Philosophy Now* 85, July/August, pp. 34–5.

Thoreau, H. D. (1954) *The Journal*. Boston: Houghton Mifflin Co.

Thoreau, H. D. (1960 edn) *Walden and Civil Disobedience*. Boston: Houghton Mifflin Co.

Timm, J. R. (1997) 'Review of Engaged Buddhism: Buddhist Liberation Movements in Asia', *Philosophy East and West*, 47(4).

Tolstoy, L. (1894) *The Kingdom of God is Within You*. Trans. Constance Garnett. Seaside: Watchmaker.

Tolstoy, L. (1904) *My Religion, On Life, Thoughts On God and On the Meaning of Life*. Trans. Leo Wiener. 16 vols. Boston: D. Estes & Co.

Trocmé, A. (2003) *Jesus and the Nonviolent Revolution*. New York: Orbis.

Truth and Reconciliation Commission (1998) Final Report.

Tutu , D. (2000) *No Future Without Forgiveness*. Johannesburg: Rider.

Weart, S. (1998) *Never At War: Why Democracies Will Not Fight One Another*. New Haven: Yale University Press.

Wolf, N. (2011) 'The Middle East Feminist Revoution', *Al Jazeera* [online], 4 May. Available at: http://www.aljazeera.com/indepth/opinion/2011/03/201134111445686926.html.

Zimmer, H. (1969) *Philosophies of India*, 4th edn. Princeton, NJ: Princeton University Press.

Zinn, H. (ed.) (2002) *The Power of Nonviolence: Writings by Advocates of Peace*. Boston: Beacon Press.

Žižek, S. (2002) *Revolution at the Gates: A Selection of Writings from February to October 1917*. London: Verso.

Index